YOU
NEVER
KNOW

TOM SELLECK

WITH ELLIS HENICAN

YOU NEVER KNOW

A Memoir

HarperCollins*Publishers*

HarperCollins*Publishers*
1 London Bridge Street
London SE1 9GF

www.harpercollins.co.uk

HarperCollins*Publishers*
Macken House, 39/40 Mayor Street Upper
Dublin 1, D01 C9W8, Ireland

First published by HarperCollins*Publishers* 2024

1 3 5 7 9 10 8 6 4 2

© Thomas Selleck 2024

Thomas Selleck asserts the moral right to be
identified as the author of this work

Designed by Jennifer Chung

All plate photographs are courtesy of Tom Selleck, except pages 6, 7, 10:
© Emilio Lari; page 12 (*top right*): © AP Images/Reed Saxon;
page 13 (*top left*): courtesy of CBS; page 13 (*bottom left*): © Annie Leibovitz/
Trunk Archive; page 15: © Ron Galella, Ltd./Getty Images;
page 16 (*top right*): © Bettmann/Getty Images

A catalogue record of this book is
available from the British Library

HB ISBN 978-0-00-868569-0
PB ISBN 978-0-00-868570-6

Printed and bound in the UK using 100% renewable
electricity at CPI Group (UK) Ltd

For Jillie and Hannah
Kevin
My mom and dad

CONTENTS

Mulholland Drive

On a sweeping turn, one of the wheels slipped off the pavement onto the soft dirt shoulder. The rear-engine car immediately lost traction, went into an uncontrolled skid and over the edge. Everything after that seemed to slow down. I was in the passenger seat as the car floated in the air, turning over on its axis. We had been bowling, and the two bowling balls flew around the cabin, seeking and all too often *finding* their target. It was a dark night, and I couldn't see where the descent was taking us. Then I felt a painful, overwhelming crunch as the car hit the ground upside down.

Thank God it was over.

But suddenly, we were airborne again. Turning over and over as we fell farther. Then another agonizing crunch, landing on the passenger side.

There was no window by now, and I felt the ground brush my right arm, somehow not crushing it as the car kept rolling. Back into the dark air, turning over once more and landing right side up.

I put my left hand up against the crumpled ceiling, bracing myself for what was sure to come next. But it never came. My mom's red Corvair Monza had landed on a flat spot on the steep slope and rested there. There was an eerie quiet of settling metal.

I *thought* I was thinking clearly. The Showmen were blaring on the radio: "Rock 'n' roll will stand." I turned off the radio. I turned off the headlights. The headlights were gone. I turned off the engine, which was no longer running. I guess I wasn't thinking very clearly.

What about Vicki!?

My girlfriend, Vicki Wheeler, was upside down in the backseat. There were no seatbelts in 1962. She was just starting to wake up. As I helped her onto the seat, I could see her blonde hair was soaked with blood.

"Are you okay, Vic?"

"Yeah. I think so."

It seemed to hit us both at the same time. "Where's Steve?" she said.

I had let my friend Steve Lowe drive my mom's car . . . but he was no longer inside. I jumped out and started to yell, "Steve! Steve!" Finally, up from the dark slope, I heard "I'm up here."

"Steve, are you okay?"

"I think so, but it hurts when I move."

I could see there was a house just below where we had landed. One more rollover and we would have landed on their roof . . . or through it.

Then everything started to speed up. The couple from the house came running. "Are you okay?"

Funny the things that come into your mind. *Does everybody say that?*

"I'm okay, but my friend is up the hill and needs help."

I looked below toward the San Fernando Valley and heard a distant siren. I could see an ambulance winding its way up Beverly Glen to get to Mulholland.

I can't remember much about the ride in the ambulance except thinking how much I had screwed up. My parents were not insured for another driver. Especially another teenager. All I remember after that was sitting in the emergency room with the left side of my face swollen up to, ironically, the size of a bowling ball. And my mom and dad running in.

In all my life, I had never seen an expression like the one on their faces. They had gotten the call in the night that all parents dread. In that moment, I realized how dire the outcome could have been.

"I'm okay," I said. I think I was crying. "I'm sorry, I'm sorry," I repeated over and over.

My mom took my hand, and my dad, interrupting me, said, "Don't worry. Just think about getting better."

Vicki and Steve also ended up at Valley Doctors Hospital in Studio City. Vicki was treated and released. But Steve had a broken pelvis, and we wound up sharing a room. The next morning, I read Steve an article from the *Valley News and Green Sheet,* the paper I used to deliver on my paper route. The headline read "Trio Hurt in Auto's Plunge."

My mom and dad and Steve's parents visited every day. Vicki came with some girlfriends from school. I remember Steve was embarrassed in front of the girls because he was in traction and had a catheter with a urine bag hanging off the side of his bed—you know, teenager stuff.

This being late spring, we both just wanted to get out of there for our graduation from Grant High School. I was out first, but only after they stuck a needle in my left cheek to draw out the swelling that would just not go down. Steve needed to be there for quite a while, but he hobbled through graduation.

There is a point to all this. I had screwed up big-time. And I knew that my parents would take a big financial hit. But even after I recovered, there were no recriminations, no "You're grounded for a year." Nothing like that. They knew they didn't have to push consequences because I would push them on myself. They knew by this time they had succeeded in passing on to me the gift of conscience.

It's kinda hard to explain. But all I know is that when I did screw up, which was a fairly frequent occurrence for a seventeen-year-old, the severest consequence was knowing that I had disappointed my mom and dad.

I don't know how my parents instilled that in me, but they did.

It's not that I was never punished. I got some spankings when I was little, all deserved. But as I got older, I think my parents' discipline started to evolve. My dad took me and my big brother, Bob, down to Van Nuys City Hall for a tour of the police station. I think I was about seven. Bob was nineteen months older. We met some very nice policemen, and we responded to their questions with "Yes, Officer . . . No, Officer." They took us downstairs and showed us some jail cells.

"Is it okay if they go in and see the cell?" my dad said.

The policeman gave my dad a little smile and said, "Sure, Mr. Selleck."

Bob and I anxiously went inside.

"All right, lock 'em up," my dad said.

Without a word, the officer slammed the door shut, locked it, and walked away with my dad, up the stairs and out.

There was a little false bravado between Bob and me, a smug "Yeah, very funny!"

After about ten minutes, it wasn't quite so funny. After twenty minutes, not funny at all. Soon after that, we heard footsteps coming down the stairs. But no one was laughing. The officer unlocked the cell door, and my dad said, "I don't think I need to say anything."

In our little neighborhood on Peach Grove Street, we weren't supposed to play baseball in the street. Don't tell anybody, but all the kids in the neighborhood did anyway. Unfortunately, I got ahold of one and broke a window in our neighbor's house down the block. All of us scattered to our respective little houses.

I asked my mom, "Are you going to tell Dad?"

"No, I'm not going to tell your dad. *You* are going to tell your dad . . . And no TV till he gets home."

Well, when he got home, I told him straight out. He thought for a moment. I had no idea what was coming next. My dad said, "Thank you for telling me. We'll talk in the morning."

Early the next morning, he popped his head into Bob's and my bedroom with his familiar "Up and at 'em!" He walked me down to our neighbor's house and knocked on the door. When Mr. Rockwell answered, my dad said to me, "Tell him."

"Mr. Rockwell, I'm the one who broke your window."

My dad showed me how to measure a broken windowpane. Then he drove me to the hardware store, where we had a piece of glass cut and got all the supplies we needed for the job. And that's how I learned how to replace a window and not play baseball in the street.

These memories are still crystal clear in my mind. And I think that's the point in all this. The lessons you experience, not the ones you are simply told, are the ones you remember most clearly.

Another memory that's crystal clear in my mind is going off Mulholland Drive. It's kind of ironic that, a couple of years later, the Chevy Corvair was discontinued. Consumer advocate groups made sure of that. They said the Corvair had a tendency to roll over. To be honest, I'm actually not sure that's the case. I drove many safe miles in my mom's red Corvair Monza. But I can personally guarantee that it will roll over if you drive it off a 125-foot cliff.

CHAPTER ONE

Just Don't Let 'Em Change You

I knew exactly what the problem was.

I had a lot of distractions.

I was living in the Sigma Chi house my junior year at the University of Southern California. They had a pool table in the rec room and a big couch in front of the TV set. There was always a gin game I could jump into down the hall when I was supposed to be studying. Fraternity life was just too much fun. One last chance to be a kid. Occasionally, we would put towels over the drains in our communal shower, flood the second floor, and play slip-and-slide down the hall. Sometimes we'd go up on the roof with the fire hose and attack any open window in the Sigma Alpha Epsilon house across the street. And I had another distraction. Sleep. I had to take an early class schedule because basketball practice was in the afternoon. After late nights of not studying, I was always sleeping through my early classes. Then I'd walk to campus and go straight to the Trojan Grill and hang out with my friends before practice.

Late one morning, I shuffled down the stairs barefoot in my basketball shorts and T-shirt, rubbing sleep from my eyes after a rough night of playing gin. So I was headed to the kitchen to get some coffee. As I made my way past the common area, I heard it, the hum of active conversation. I stuck my head in and saw a large group of women. In the middle of the group was my mom.

"Oh, hi, Mom."

I had forgotten it was the day of the Sigma Chi Mothers' Club Luncheon.

Now, my mom was very protective of all her kids. "Oh, this is great," she said. "They've canceled your classes. Why don't you join us."

"Uh, okay."

"Go upstairs and change, and you can join us in the dining room."

I got out of there as fast as I could, all the time knowing that I knew that she knew.

My mom would never embarrass me in front of others. But I gotta tell you, and you can ask my brothers, Bob and Dan, and my sister, Marti, and they would all say the very same thing. It was next to impossible to slip anything past my mom.

You'd think I might have learned something from my student-body vice president "scandal" in junior high school when I had to give up my office because of a "U" in work habits. Not easy news to bring home to Mom and Dad. Clearly, work habits were a recurring theme for me. I sure had them in sports, but they were nowhere to be found in my approach to academics.

There was one other thing. Colleges sent your grades wherever you told them to. It wasn't like high school, where you had to get your parents to sign your report card. Skipping that step wasn't good for me. No one in the family knew about my declining course load and horrible GPA. My brother Bob might have had an inkling, but he never said anything. Bob was on track to graduate in June. I kinda wished he had stuck around. He was the one person who could give me a kick in the butt, sit me down, and maybe straighten me out. But Bob would soon be off on his own adventure. A baseball scout named Tommy Lasorda had signed him to a contract with the L.A. Dodgers.

———

I was a senior in name only.

Two and a half years at Los Angeles Valley College, two and a half years at USC, and I still wasn't going to graduate. That was growing clearer by the day.

I'd been on academic probation since the second semester of my junior year, which was what happened at USC when your grade point average slipped below 2.0. Now I was about to get bounced from the basketball team. To remain eligible, I needed to carry a course load of twelve units a semester. I'd been skating by—*barely*. But as the 1966–67 season approached, the thin ice beneath me was starting to crack.

As a business major, I had put off the hard courses as long as I possibly could, so the hard courses were all I had left.

My first semester of "senior year," I had already dropped one class. So I was down to twelve units. Then I took an incomplete in my statistics class, Quantitative Analysis 1, hoping I could use the extra time to catch up. Plus, you had to do your homework for that course. There was a lot of math involved. I had barely cracked the textbook and almost never gone to class. The truth is, there was no way I could pass Quantitative Analysis. I was officially ineligible. Basketball was a real bright spot for me. I was desperate, and I didn't know what to do.

I went to see the professor to plead my case. I really didn't have a leg to stand on, but I had to try.

I didn't know the teacher well, since I'd hardly ever gone to class. He seemed very professorial and somewhat aloof. I explained my situation, what a jam I was in, how much the basketball team meant to me, and how proud I was that I'd earned an athletic scholarship for my last semester. As I told him that I would lose the scholarship, I got embarrassed. I started to cry. I hadn't planned that part. It just happened. I mean, it's not like I was an actor or anything.

Turned out he was a very kind man and gave me a gift D. I was eligible for basketball again.

I was clearly struggling, and the long view wasn't getting any better, despite my momentary reprieve. My spring-semester senior schedule would be even tougher than the fall. After my performance in QA-1, what hope did I have in QA-2? This was not going to end well. I could feel it. Even after five years of college, I wouldn't have enough units to earn my degree.

And with that struggle came a certain amount of guilt. My parents had borrowed the money to send me to college, just as they had for Bob. I certainly wasn't motivated by business school. I'd majored in business because my dad was in business. That's all the thought I ever gave it. I had taken a couple of history electives and really liked those, especially at Valley College. But what are you going to do with a history degree?

I made an appointment to see Dr. William Himstreet, the associate dean of the business school. I had met Dean Himstreet through my parents at football games. His daughter, Sue, was active in one of the campus sororities. He'd always seemed like a friendly guy with a wry sense of humor.

"I need some advice," I said to the dean as I sat down in his office.

I was about to tell him about my academic struggles and my concern about my eligibility and my fear that I would never graduate. But he was way ahead of me.

"You know, Tom," he said. "I pulled your transcript, and I have to say, I was very impressed."

"Oh?"

"Your transcript is one of the most remarkable records of mediocrity I have ever seen. You've never gotten higher than a C in your major, and sometimes worse."

He kinda said it with a glint in his eye. When I asked what I could do about my academic situation, he simply said, "Try harder."

Of course, Dean Himstreet was right, but I must confess that it was not a new problem. Back when I was at Valley College, I had to take an extra semester because USC decided my grades had been "trending downward." So I, of course, found a class that was supposed to be an easy A. The History of the American Theater did, in fact, turn out to be an easy A. At some point, the professor, Robert Rivera, told me I'd be a good type for commercials and that he could recommend an agent if I was interested. Well, I wasn't exactly serious about it, but I'd heard you could make a lot of money doing a commercial. I mean, you never know . . . I went and met the guy. His name was Don Schwartz, and he became my accidental commercial agent.

During my first semester at USC, Don Schwartz called and said he had a job for me. He told me it was an air force training film for their psychiatrists. *Oh-kay.* It was called *The Mental Aspects of Human Reliability.* *Oh-kay.* I was to have three lines as Airman Pickens. *Oh-kay.* The truth is, I never really thought about it as a "job." To me, it meant a paycheck. One day's pay at union scale plus per diem.

In a nice way, it was a happy accident. The training film was shot at Davis-Monthan Air Force Base in Tucson. When I got home from the location, my dad told me that he'd been stationed there as a B-29 mechanic, and at the end of the war, that's the base he was released from. He returned home to Detroit and saw for the first time his second son, two-year-old Thomas William.

———

Word went around the Sigma Chi house that it was easy to get on *The Dating Game.* Someone in the house knew a guy who was in charge of casting the contestants.

"We're going down to be interviewed," one of my buddies said. "You wanna come?"

"Okay," I said, shrugging.

I got chosen. A couple of us did.

Every so often, *The Dating Game* had a segment with a reunion angle. The girl had previously dated one of the three bachelors and then broken up with him. Now she and the ex were on the show together, and the audience was left to wonder: Would she give him another shot?

Students being students, my fraternity brothers had figured out how to rig the game. They'd go on with their real girlfriends and let ABC pick up the tab for an all-expenses-paid date. They'd also have a friend in the studio audience who'd signal the girl in case she needed any help on which chair her boyfriend was in.

The show didn't seem to have a clue, or maybe they did, and it didn't matter to them.

I didn't have a girlfriend. Also, somehow it didn't seem entirely kosher to me.

I was Bachelor Number 2. As showtime neared, I sat on my stool, getting progressively more terrified. The assistant director took one look at my grim expression and suggested helpfully, "When the revolve turns around, be sure to smile."

Be sure to smile. Got it!

I was in the dark with the other two contestants. My heart was pounding so hard I could almost hear it. Then Jim Lange's deep baritone came booming through the studio: "It's time to meet our three eligible bachelors . . . and *heeeere they are!*"

The revolve began to turn. As we came around to where I could see the audience, the lights went up. I remembered what the assistant director had told me: *Smile!*

By then my heart was pounding so ferociously that when I smiled, my upper lip started twitching in perfect sync with my thumping heartbeat. If you look real closely at the old video, you can actually see the twitch. It's not like I had a mustache to cover it up.

The girl asked the risqué questions *The Dating Game* was famous for. I had lame answers, and I lost. I wasn't funny. I didn't enjoy it. I was scared to death every second I was up there.

Over my time at USC, Don would occasionally send me out on interviews for commercials. Not that I was really in danger of getting one; I had no idea what I was doing. So I gotta say, I was somewhat stunned when Don said, "You got the Pepsi commercial."

"I did?"

I kinda knew it couldn't possibly have been my acting ability. Much more likely, it was my *basketball* ability.

In the commercial, my character—excuse me, I didn't think in those terms back then—the guy in the basketball game fakes to the right, shifts the ball to his left hand, leaves his defender with his jockstrap on the floor, drives to the basket, and stuffs the ball with his left hand. That was easy. I was undeniably well qualified. Even after an insane number of takes, I proudly delivered. Our basketball season had just ended, and I was in basketball shape.

The company moved to the set in the locker room. I hadn't considered that this was "the money shot" in the commercial, but it was. In the scene, I am sitting in front of my locker, getting slapped on the back (this was before the high-five cliché) and ecstatically chugalugging a delicious Pepsi. Honestly, I was unprepared for all the repetition. And the director didn't bother to explain why I had to do the scene over and over. In hindsight, I'm sure he thought, *Why bother to explain to this obviously untrained refugee from USC basketball when he won't have a clue anyway?* I did my best to act ecstatically each and every time, consuming a whole lot of Pepsi. Then the director came over to me, and of course I thought I had done something wrong.

He said to me that "the client" thought the color of the real Pepsi was photographing too dark, and we would have to start over. My stomach was more than full. But hey, it wasn't my fault, and I was getting paid. So we began again. Once they'd watered down the Pepsi, it tasted like something that came out of the north end of a southbound cow. The truth is, I had always preferred Pepsi to Coke.

Never again.

For some bizarre reason, they asked me back for the nighttime edition of *The Dating Game,* where the winners got to go on fancier dates.

And for some bizarre reason, I went back. I was still terrified, I still wasn't funny, and I lost again.

At that time of life, some guys will do anything to impress a girl. Any girl. I know I would have. I guess going on *The Dating Game* was a tiny prestige kind of thing, something the girls might notice. Like my doing a commercial. I guess I liked it when someone said, "Oh, he's an actor." I wasn't really an actor. It was just something that made me stand out a little, something girls might notice.

About a week after my second *Dating Game* appearance, I got a call from Don Schwartz, my kinda accidental commercial agent. He said a casting director at 20th Century–Fox named David Graham had seen me on *The Dating Game* and wanted to meet me. Don said the casting director had mentioned the Fox New Talent program and thought I might be a candidate.

"Will you see him?" Don asked.

"I don't know. Why not?"

It wasn't like I was burning to have an acting career. I'd never given that idea any thought at all. My "career" so far consisted of a Pepsi commercial and an air force training film.

Don explained that Fox and Universal both had talent-training programs designed to funnel young actors into the studios' movies and TV shows. "Universal signs people and sticks 'em in a show without any training," Don said. "They just see what happens. If you fail, you're gone. But Fox will actually give you some training, like the old studios used to do. Acting classes, voice classes, dance classes. And the teachers are supposed to be terrific."

A couple of weeks later, Don was back on the phone; I had gotten to know him pretty well by then, and I could hear the excitement in his voice. "Fox wants to see you first thing Monday morning," he said. "I told them that Universal wants to sign you by Tuesday. Then I talked to Universal and told them Fox wants you, and now Universal wants to see you, too. So you have appointments with both of them, but you need to be at Fox."

In Hollywood, there's a technical term for the strategy that Don employed. *Total bullshit,* I believe it's called. It's also called good agenting.

I don't remember much about my interview at Universal. It was just a go-see. I think the head of the talent program, Monique James, might have popped her head in, but that was about it.

When Don called, he didn't reach me at home. I was at the Chapman Park Hotel, just around the corner from the old Ambassador Hotel and Cocoanut Grove nightclub, with the rest of the USC Trojans basketball team. We had Friday-night and Saturday-night home games that weekend, and we were locked in the hotel from Thursday night through Sunday morning. The coaches wanted to make sure the players ate right, not to mention behaved right.

"When you go to Fox on Monday," Don said, "they want you to do a scene for them."

"A scene?"

"A scene from a play."

"Oh."

"I'll bring one of my actresses over. We'll rehearse with you. You can do a scene from *Barefoot in the Park.*"

"Don, I can't do that," I said.

"Don't worry. We'll work with you."

"No! I'm locked in the hotel all weekend. I couldn't meet with her till Sunday afternoon."

Sunday was much too late to get started, Don assured me. "Believe me, I have seen your Pepsi-Cola commercial, and you need more time."

I knew I probably wasn't going to play in either game that weekend. So I sneaked out of the hotel on Saturday afternoon. Not my finest hour.

Don's client knew what she was doing. She had studied acting and had far more experience than I did. She was probably hoping to get discovered. She came back on Sunday and worked with me some more. After we got done rehearsing, I went home and practiced all my lines and all my expressions in the mirror. By the time I finished with all that, I swear I knew the scene better than Neil Simon himself.

When I arrived at the studio lot on Pico Boulevard in the heart of Century City, I met with the head of casting, a guy named Jack Baur. Owen McLean, the studio's VP in charge of talent, was also there. I wasn't nervous when I walked into the room. At least I didn't think so, maybe because I really hadn't made the stakes very high. I was cruising through my lines and my expressions when I reached a spot where my character gets a phone call. Now, most actors in that situation would just make a fist and hold it up to their ear.

That wasn't enough for me. No. I was going to impress the hell out of them. I noticed a real phone on a table next to the couch.

I picked up the receiver.

The dial tone made me freeze.

I was absolutely stunned. "I don't know what I say next."

As head of casting, Jack Baur had probably heard *Barefoot in the Park* auditioned a hundred times. "'For a lawyer, I'm some good kisser,'" he said.

I still had the phone to my ear. "Excuse me?"

"*That's* what you say next."

I fumbled through the rest of the scene, but sadly, my scene partner was dismissed. What a business!

Then Owen said to me, "Since we've gotta make a decision today, we need to talk to our boss."

"Okay."

"Let's go."

I didn't realize I was going with them, but apparently the "we" included me.

So, Jack, Owen, and I walked over to Building 1, the old Fox Executive Building, a grand and very impressive structure that was probably built in the 1930s. They led me down an equally impressive hallway, and we came to a very fancy door. The nameplate read "RICHARD D. ZANUCK."

I knew I was going to see *their* boss. I had no idea I was going to see *the* boss.

The outer office felt like the kind of room where the studio might have hosted elegant cocktail parties or celebrated Academy Award wins. "He's waiting for you," a secretary said with clipped efficiency as the three of us breezed in.

Richard Zanuck was the son of Darryl Zanuck, who cofounded 20th Century–Fox in the 1930s and guided the studio through a couple of its most successful decades. Now his son was in charge. After the formal pleasantries, Jack, Owen, and I sat down in front of the studio president's ornate desk.

"So?" Zanuck asked.

"He did a scene for us, Dick," Owen said, sliding my one-page résumé across the desk. "The kid is pretty green, but that's why we have a talent program. We think he might have potential."

I looked over at Zanuck, who seemed absolutely transfixed by my résumé. Frankly, there wasn't much on it. Certainly, the president of 20th Century–Fox wasn't interested in my Pepsi-Cola commercial and my air force training film.

"You play at USC."

"Yessir."

"I'm a huge UCLA fan."

And there it was: He had invoked what people in L.A. called "the rivalry."

"Well, that's too bad," I answered like a true Trojan.

He came right back at me. "That stall you guys did against us, that was a pretty cheap trick."

The last time USC had faced the undefeated UCLA Bruins, on February 10, our coach, Bob Boyd, had employed a novel strategy. *Stall ball,* it was called, and it was a highly newsworthy event. Passing the ball back and forth, back and forth. Refusing to shoot for two or three minutes at a stretch, just letting the clock run. We slowed the game to a low-scoring crawl. Our maddening strategy came this close to working. We led the national-champion Bruins 17 to 14 at the half and forced the game into overtime before losing 40 to 35.

"Whatever it takes," I said with a shrug. Then I added, "Actually, I ride the pine most of the time. But when we prepare for a game with you guys, the players who aren't gonna see much action run the UCLA offense against the starters. We don't have a tall bench. So, when we're running the UCLA offense, I am Lew Alcindor," the Bruins' seven-feet-two-inch, high-scoring phenom, soon to become Kareem Abdul-Jabbar.

Zanuck looked like a kid staring into a giant bowl of ice cream. "No kidding?" he asked.

"No kidding."

He turned to Owen and Jack and said, "Okay, let's do it."

———

The whole thing is stunning when you think about it.

A kid goes on *The Dating Game* and, through the machinations of a clever agent, two of the biggest studios in Hollywood each think the other is interested in him. This kid, who has no real acting experience and no real desire to become an actor, ends up bullshitting with the president of 20th Century–Fox and is promptly invited into the studio's New Talent program. And what seals the deal is college basketball. Go figure . . . You never know. And all of it happened so quickly, I never once stopped to ask myself, *Why? Why am I doing this?* I'm not sure I can answer that even now. I'd never had the slightest interest in acting. Ever. But in my own unplanned way, I had actually accomplished something. I'd been offered an opportunity that others would kill for. I was developing a healthy respect for serendipity.

Don explained the details. The pay would start at the Screen Actors Guild minimum, slightly over a hundred dollars a week, which sounded astronomical to me. I'd been making no more than expense money at my job as a campus representative for United Airlines. SAG minimum would be enough for me to get my own place after the semester and start to pull my weight financially. And did I mention my semester wasn't going too well?

I went to see my dad at his office to tell him about the offer and get his advice. By then he was managing the Coldwell Banker office for the San Fernando Valley.

"I got this offer to sign a contract with 20th Century–Fox," I told him.

I explained everything. I may have accidentally left out the part about not graduating. He listened intently, probably for anything he could pick up between the lines. When I finished, he sat for a moment. When he spoke, it was forthright, direct, and unwavering. "Well," he said, "I think it's like your brother Bob when he had the offer to sign with the Dodgers. It's one of those opportunities that's considered special. And if you don't go after it, you might get to be thirty-five and have regrets. You might wonder what if . . . ?"

That was all I needed to hear. I wasn't really asking for his advice about what I *could* do. I was asking so I'd know what I *would* do.

It was at that moment that I was reminded of a phrase he used: "Risk is the price you pay for opportunity." You know what? I'm not really sure whether my father actually said that or I just think he did. But either way, he'd lived it, that's for sure.

Then he said, "You're gonna have to tell your boss at United right away."

I knew that, though I was secretly hoping he might say, "Aw, that's okay, son. I'll call 'em for you."

That wasn't my dad.

I said something inadequate, like "Thanks, Dad," and I got up to go.

As I did, my dad spoke, almost to himself but not really. I definitely heard his words.

"Just don't let 'em change you."

Out of the blue: "Just don't let 'em change you."

I didn't say anything else, but I realized how difficult it must have been for my father to give me that advice. Thanks to the management-training program I'd had with United Airlines for my two years at USC, he'd felt I had a leg up in a company whose business he actually understood. Working in L.A. as long as he had, he had to be well aware of the many risks of show business. He'd heard the stories of all the wasted lives. He certainly didn't want his son to get sucked into that swamp. So he knew the perils. But he still gave his advice freely and without hesitation.

———

Many years later, my dad was seriously ill and in the hospital. My mom, my sister, my brothers, and I tried to be there for him. We made sure at least one of us was always by his side. One morning, I was in the hospital room with my brother Dan. My dad had been quiet for a while.

Then he said, "I never played a game of hardball. I never dribbled a basketball until I was well into high school. Don Lund and a lot of my friends always got to play sports."

He was quiet again.

Then, to himself, he said, "It's funny the things you think about."

I looked at Dan. He looked at me. Our father was thinking about what had been and what could have been.

He had grown up in the Depression. His father was a building contractor who needed his youngest son to work with him. My dad's friend Don had been a first-round draft pick by the Chicago Bears as a running back before deciding baseball was a better career choice. Don had played outfield for the Brooklyn Dodgers, St. Louis Browns, and Detroit Tigers. I'd heard a lot of Don stories over the years.

My dad loved sports. He had always taken a keen interest in supporting his children playing sports. If you ever saw my dad, you could see he had an athlete's body.

My dad knew something about regret.

Even with all he had accomplished.

With all he had to be proud of.

What if?

CHAPTER TWO

In the Program

I was really nervous. No, not the kind of nervous where I didn't think I was nervous. I was *really nervous* and I knew it. I was leaving from the valley, having moved back to my parents' house. It was my first day in the 20th Century–Fox New Talent program, and I didn't want to get stuck in freeway traffic. I decided to take one of the canyons.

I headed over the hill, as we called it, up Beverly Glen, and my mind was racing. *What the hell am I doing? I'm just not ready for this. Maybe I could get sick or have car trouble. I could take another day to get my mind right and get off to a better start.*

While I was obsessing, big chunks of road would go by without me noticing. But that was okay. I knew where I was going. I just didn't know where I was . . . *going.*

I reached the top of the hill, the intersection of Mulholland Drive.

About a half mile to my right was the spot on Mulholland where I went off the 125-foot cliff. *Wait, going over a cliff? What's that? Some kind of omen or something? Stop it, Tom! That's really stupid. This is gonna happen. Make the most of it.*

I took a couple of deep breaths and crossed Mulholland and headed down the hill. I remembered what Don had said to me, how lucky I was to be in the Fox talent program, the last of the old studio system.

Really, what's the big deal? The only thing you know for sure is you'll do this for the next six months. And you'll get subsidized to be exposed to something you never knew you wanted to be exposed to. How bad could it be?

Beverly Glen zigzagged across Sunset Boulevard and continued down to Olympic, where I turned left. I knew all these surface streets by heart. Growing up in the valley, I was always going to the movies in Westwood and Beverly Hills. I turned right on a side street. I wanted to be on time.

On my left I saw something I'd never known was there. It was the massive studio backlot. The tops of the movie sets were poking up from the greenery. A row of New York City tenements. A solitary church steeple. A western town.

I couldn't have known it then. But within a very short time, that studio backlot would be gone. Sadly, it would be sold off to developers to create what is now Century City. The 20th Century–Fox backlot had become a remnant of a bygone era.

Once I turned up Pico, the intimidating edifice that is the 20th Century–Fox studio came into view. I had driven by it many times, but somehow it loomed much larger now.

The thought occurred to me that I wasn't exactly driving up in a vintage Duesenberg. I was in my beat-up '64 Volkswagen. But the guard gave me a big smile. Courteously, he asked for my name.

"You have a drive-on, Mr. Selleck," he said. "We've been expecting you. Welcome to Fox."

He was really nice. Nothing like the gate guard at Universal on the go-see Don had arranged, who didn't appear to have ever smiled in his life. The Fox guard handed me a map with a carefully drawn route to my destination. He'd marked Stage 3 with a big X and the number 163. I assumed the number was an address.

As I headed in, I passed the grand Fox admin building, where I'd had my moment of triumph with my new best friend, Richard Zanuck. I saw some modern soundstages on my left, big bare boxes built solely for function. I drove past some rows of charming cottages, the permanent private dressing rooms of the stars, where they could hang out in undisturbed comfort during their downtime.

When I got to the big X on the map, that's when I saw it. Painted on the pavement of an empty parking space. The number 163. How 'bout that? The rookie had his own personal parking place!

Buoyed by my new status, I climbed out of my tiny Volkswagen in a well-rehearsed feat of athleticism and just stood there, looking at the building that was Stage 3. It had an elegant facade in the old art deco style, same as the admin building and the cottages.

I took another deep breath and decided to move out. *Don't know where I'm goin', but there's no use bein' late.*

As I stepped into the lobby, there were two doors on the far wall marked "Stage 3" and "Stage 4." Next to the Stage 3 door was a sign: "PEYTON PLACE. CLOSED SET." All of a sudden, a red light above the door lit up and began to spin, like on a fire engine.

Wow! Mia Farrow or Ryan O'Neal or Barbara Parkins might be in there, actually acting, at this very moment.

I looked around. There was a stairway on the left. The sign above it said "TALENT PROGRAM." When I got to the top of the stairs, I put on my game face and went inside. Two or three nice-looking young people gave me nice smiles as they walked by.

At that point, a woman came out of an office. "Hello, I'm Pamela Danova," she said. "I'm the coordinator of the talent program." Her British accent made the whole enterprise seem even more important. "Please," she said, gesturing me into her office. She offered me a seat on her couch and said, "I know this is your first day, so you're probably nervous."

"No, I'm not nervous—just excited," I said, putting on my best *Dating Game* smile.

"I see," she said. "Let me tell you what we do here. Jon Gregory and his wife, Helene, run the dance classes. A very good teacher, Jack Woodford, is in charge of the voice classes. Of course, most of the time, we have acting classes."

"Of course."

That's when Curt Conway, the acting coach, walked in. Pamela introduced me.

"Welcome," he said warmly. "We're just about ready to start. Come on in."

I followed Curt into a large room with a mini-stage and a wide circle of chairs where eight or ten students were already waiting.

"Class," he said, "this is our newest member, Tom Selleck. And you've already met Linda Peck. Tom, this is Linda's first day too."

I took a chair.

"Linda, Tom," Curt continued, "in this class, we do some exercises and some improvisations, but primarily, we do scene study. I'll assign each of you a scene partner. You will rehearse together, and when you feel ready or I feel you should be ready, you'll put it up onstage."

Then Curt kinda got into the weeds. Weeds I had never walked through before. He talked about the Actors Studio in New York. He talked about Stanislavski and Boleslawski. Several times he mentioned "the Method." This went on for some time. But as he spoke, what came through was his passion for acting and teaching, what he kept referring to as "the work."

When class was over, everybody started trailing out. Linda Peck was right ahead of me.

"Excuse me," I said to her. She turned around.

"I'm Tom."

"Linda."

"So, I guess you've been acting for a while."

"No," she said. "I have never done anything like this in my life."

"Oh . . . okay. Can I ask you something?"

"Sure."

"Did you have any idea what he was talking about?"

"I'm a little rusty on my Stanislavski and Boleslawski," she said. "I didn't have a clue."

"Thank you. I'm right there with you."

Right then one of the regulars said to Linda and me, "We're all about to go to lunch. Come on."

The Fox Studio commissary was a large, bustling room with closely spaced tables, starched white tablecloths, and colorful murals on the walls featuring the abstract likenesses of Shirley Temple, Will Rogers, Janet Gaynor, and other early motion-picture stars. The commissary, I learned later, was built on the site of a French restaurant set.

"Hi, guys," the hostess said brightly as we walked in. Linda and I followed her and the regulars to a great big round table in the middle of an alcove against the far wall. The hostess took the RESERVED sign off the table, and we all sat down. I didn't want to rubberneck on the way in and look like a rookie, though naturally I was curious what famous people might be lunching that day. It could have been anyone. Maybe Charlton Heston, who was wrapping up *Planet of the Apes*. Maybe Barbra Streisand. Maybe even John Wayne.

We had a great lunch. Linda and I sat there and mostly listened while the other students talked about their scenes, rated what they'd seen at the movies, and griped about not getting enough auditions. It was nice for us to start to feel a part of the group, and it was quickly becoming clear that the talent-program schedule didn't exactly operate with commando-like precision.

After lunch, I was sent over to see Sonia Wolfson, a wonderful old-timer in the Fox PR department. She was going to write up a bio on me.

"So, you went to USC on a basketball scholarship," Sonia said as soon as I sat down in her office.

"I didn't really have a scholarship," I corrected her. "I wasn't actually recruited. See, I was a walk-on—"

"And you were discovered on *The Dating Game*."

"Well, it was more like—"

"That's okay, dolly," she said soothingly. "This is what we do."

By the time Sonia was done turning my life into her breathless prose, I was a heavily recruited basketball star at the University of Southern California with a prestigious scholarship who was the new rising star at Fox. That guy—not me, that guy—definitely deserved a feature in *Photoplay* or *Modern Screen*. Which I guess was the point of the exercise.

———

The next day, Pamela stuck her head into the greenroom and said, "Tom, you have a photography shoot this afternoon with Barbara Parkins."

Wow! I hadn't even been at Fox a week, and I already had a job with Barbara Parkins.

"Barbara's running late," a secretary told me when I got to the photography department.

While I waited, the photographer came over and explained to me that they were making a poster to promote the actress's new movie, *Valley of the Dolls*. "Barbara's face will be tilted back in ecstasy," he said, "and she'll have a bedsheet draped strategically over just enough of her breasts. Her costar, Paul Burke, will be embracing her. Except Paul can't be here. That will be you. Of course, you will both have to be naked."

"Can I wear my shorts?"

He rolled his eyes. "If you must."

I'd been sitting for almost an hour when a phone rang and the secretary said to the photographer in a hushed, excited tone, "She's here. She's just pulling up."

Barbara Parkins breezed in. She turned to the photographer and asked impatiently, "So where's the body?"

I really don't think she meant it insultingly. She had no idea I was even in the room. But if show business was shaped like a ladder, I suppose I was learning where to find my rung.

When we started the shoot, Barbara had nothing on except the sheet. I had my shorts. Right away, there was a problem. "Steven," she snapped at the photographer, "I can't hold up the sheet and embrace . . . *Tom*? Is that right?"

"Yes, Tom."

"Tom will have to do it."

Then to me: "Just hold on to the sheet, Tom. They won't see it because it's on your back. So lean in. It's okay, Tom. Nuzzle me."

That's when the photographer weighed in. "Tom, could you give us another inch of right breast, please?"

That was my first job at Fox.

———

The first scene Curt assigned to me was just a goofy exchange from the Charles Strouse musical *It's a Bird . . . It's a Plane . . . It's Superman,* which opened on Broadway that year and totally flopped. No, I didn't have to sing. My scene partner was a seventeen-year-old from Cleveland named Cindy Ferrare. She was very sweet and very pretty. Using her middle name, Cristina, she would become one of the world's top models, costar with David Niven in *The Impossible Years,* be named "the Face of Max Factor," and marry and divorce automaker John DeLorean before marrying Tony Thomopoulos, who would become president of the ABC Broadcast Group. She'd host a talk show, then go on to focus on writing lifestyle and cooking books. But to me, she will always be Cindy.

Each time we finished a run-through, she was very nice, very complimentary. I felt I was awful and that she was just trying to help me calm down. Cindy was definitely the grown-up in the room. For our dress rehearsal, the studio wardrobe department provided me with a Superman costume complete with tights. When she saw me in them, Cindy laughed out loud, caught herself, and said, "Tommy, you look just right."

All my classmates seemed, well, promising. Some had experience. Some had studied drama in college. Some had connections. But anyone could see the potential in all of them. Lyle Waggoner was a big, good-looking, classic-leading-man type. He'd been a finalist for TV's Batman, the role that went to Adam West. But Lyle wasn't at all what he looked like. He had an impish sense of humor. Within a year, he'd be a regular on *The Carol Burnett Show.*

The group also had a real international flair. Corinna Tsopei was a Greek model and actress who'd been Miss Universe 1964. Yutta D'Arcy, who was from Germany, was married to the Egyptian-born leading man Alex D'Arcy, famous for his suave rogues. Cecile Ozorio was an Asian actress who became a good friend and ended up starring in Seymour Robbie's musical-adventure film *Marco* with Desi Arnaz Jr., Jack Weston, and Zero Mostel.

We had Elizabeth Baur, whose father was Fox casting chief Jack Baur. Lizzie didn't need the connection. She was already a trained actress in her own right and would become Officer Fran Belding on *Ironside,* opposite Raymond Burr. We also had a Newman, in this case Melissa, whose uncle was Alfred Newman, Fox's legendary music director; he'd composed more than two hundred film scores and won nine Academy Awards. Missy was an accomplished ballerina whose now voluptuous body had gotten in the way of her dance career. Within a year, she'd have a good part in *The Undefeated* with John Wayne and Rock Hudson. Missy, like Lizzie, had the right last name, but both of them also had tons of talent. Linda Peck had been a very successful model before coming to Fox. And under her married name, Linda Dano, she would go on to a decades-long soap-opera career, playing Felicia Gallant on *Another World* and the character Rae Cummings on several different daytime shows.

Soon after I arrived at the program, a lanky guy with a deep voice joined the group. Sam Elliott was his name. Though he'd grown up in Oregon, his family came from Texas. And from the moment he arrived, I could see he was completely in touch with what Curt would call his "instrument." To me, that meant he knew who he was and what he wanted to do. It's kinda hard to describe. He just seemed more . . . *formed.* I, on the other hand, was a work in progress. Sam and I became fast friends, a friendship that would last a lifetime.

Jack Woodford presented each of us with a little hardcover book of literary passages. He had us sit in a circle and take turns reading selections for vocal training. He actually made the voice classes kinda fun. Dance class required a certain amount of commitment, which I made— even to the uniform of the day, tights. We tried to learn tap, soft-shoe, even modern dance with its strange midbody contractions. Jon Gregory would improvise routines in each discipline, steps I was hopeless at duplicating. And then there was ballet. My body wasn't flexible in a ballet kind of way. So, Helene Gregory, who had become a good friend, would help me hoist my leg up onto the ballet bar to do my warm-ups. But I *was* proud of my leaps, leaping being the closest I was going to get to basketball. I excelled beyond the talent school's wildest expectation, surpassing even the magnificent leaps of the highly focused Sam Elliott.

One day at the start of dance class, a dark-haired vision in a black leotard walked in. She excused herself and found a place to stand right next to me.

"Hi, I'm Linda Harrison," she said.

"I'm Tom."

"I hope you don't mind—dance has always been a part of my life. I've been working here at the studio. I hope it's okay if I join in."

"Please. Ah, welcome."

Helene came up to me after class and said, "What did you think of Linda?"

I said I thought she seemed like a very nice person, very down-to-earth.

"Well, she certainly is," Helene said. "You know, she just finished filming *Planet of the Apes,* starring as Charlton Heston's love interest." Helene started to leave. "Oh, and she's seeing our boss, Richard Zanuck."

"Helene," I replied, "let's get real. Yes, she is charming, and yes, she happens to be very beautiful. But I am well aware that she is light-years ahead of me. And no matter who she's seeing, I would be punching well above my weight. Look, you're my friend, so I hope you will grant me the secret pleasure of having her in the spot next to me for as long as she chooses to join us."

Occasionally, we would have a guest. The one I remember most was Marcel Marceau. No, not because I was an aspiring mime, but because he spent the whole afternoon with us. He talked about the art of mime. He demonstrated his art. He told stories. He was gracious and kind and genuinely interested in our thoughts. And we couldn't get enough of what he was so generous to share.

———

Our talent-program group was very close. We socialized. We became friends. Curt would have us all out for barbecues at his small beach house in Malibu, students, teachers, everyone. If someone had an option picked up, which meant a raise, we all had an excuse to celebrate. I can honestly say I never saw any real jealousy from the group. Look, we were all in the same boat, trying to get jobs but having trouble getting seen. We were sticking together. If someone was lucky enough to actually get a part, even if it was a part we were also right for, we would rather one of us get it than some outsider. Maybe that's a little naive on my part, but that was definitely what all of us, with Curt Conway at the helm, aspired to. If Curt wasn't a father figure, he was at least a favorite uncle.

Whenever we weren't in class, we'd be in the greenroom. We'd all talk and joke and have coffee. Lyle would come in with his portable tape recorder. He and I would act out the different characters in the latest joke we'd heard, complete with homemade sound effects, footsteps, doors closing, and, of course, fart noises. Others would join in, Corinna Tsopei being a valued contributor with her Greek accent, which seemed to give her a unique fart noise. We'd go up the fire-exit stairs to a small platform on the roof and run lines for our scenes or catch some sun or just hang out. Lunch at the commissary was always an event. God, it was all such fun!

But acting class was all business. That, after all, was why we were here. The critique of my scene in *Superman* consisted pretty much of a long, thoughtful pause followed by "It was . . . charming." By then I had heard about teachers who would break you down and basically form you in their image. That wasn't Curt. He was a good man and gentle in his criticisms, always including something positive and fortifying. I think he felt I needed a little time to sit and watch the others.

The next scene he assigned me was Sidney Kingsley's gritty police drama, *Detective Story*. Somehow I had come to think I needed to *become* the character and, in doing so, I would have to have some kind of cosmic experience onstage. I did the scene with my pal Linda Peck. There was a certain kinship there, and Curt had clearly seen that. Linda was as new as I was. But as we rehearsed, I could see she had a natural ability to understand drama.

After we presented our scene, we would pull up two chairs in front of Curt and the class. He was very positive with Linda, but I think it was tempered by the fact that he still had to get to me. Curt complimented me on a couple of moments.

I may have interrupted him when I said, "Yeah, but I didn't really feel it."

He said, "That's okay, Tom."

"You know that moment I had that you mentioned? You know what I was thinking? I was thinking, *What's my next line?*"

"That's okay too."

"I don't like the guy," I said. "I've read Tennessee Williams, and I don't like his guys either. I like his women, but—"

"Tom, it's not your job to *like* the character. It's your job to understand him and portray him."

"Okay. Well, I don't understand him. Can I do a comedy next?"

"I tell you what," Curt said. "Next we'll do *The Rainmaker*. He's a more flamboyant character. I think you'll like him."

He was speaking of N. Richard Nash's bleak depiction of a Depression-era western town. When we pulled up our chairs after *that* scene, I said right off, "I don't like that guy either. Excuse me, I don't *understand* him. He's an asshole."

Curt, realizing this was beginning to waste the class's time, said, "You and I will talk."

I was kinda frustrated. The only thing I had really discovered was that I was—go figure!—a good student. I was prepared. I did my homework. I rehearsed. I learned my lines. But learning your lines is just preparation. I knew what these characters said, but I didn't know why they said it. And I was learning that the *why* of it was what I should be thinking about.

I think Michael Gazzo's *A Hatful of Rain* came next, definitely not a comedy. It was a play about a young married man with a secret morphine addiction, written from improvisations at the Actors Studio. I guess Curt figured it might spark a different kind of perspective in me.

———

When I was a senior in high school, at the start of basketball practice, I was eighth man on the team. I had two things going for me: I wasn't afraid to fail, and I was willing to work. By the beginning of the season, I was a starter and team captain. Same thing at Valley College: I ended up starting. It didn't quite work out that way at USC, but I did earn a scholarship for my last semester. Sports had taught me the value of perseverance, and so it was with Curt and the talent program. I might have been frustrated, but I wasn't bored. By now I was prepared to just put one foot in front of the other and enjoy the ride, wherever it took me. It sure as hell wasn't going to take me to Quantitative Analysis 2.

I decided to step off the grid, so to speak. I loved movies and obviously spent too many nights going to them when I should have been studying. I remembered a movie I saw back at USC, Herb Gardner's *A Thousand Clowns:* I loved it so much I went back and saw it again the next night. It told the story of Murray Burns, an eccentric comedy writer who had to conform to society to retain legal custody of his nephew. Yes, it was a comedy. But it made me laugh *and* cry, often both at the same time.

We were doing scenes from plays in class. I thought, *Maybe* A Thousand Clowns *was a play.* I drove to Samuel French, the source for all plays good and bad. They had it! It *was* a play! I bought two copies. I asked my pal Linda Peck to step off the grid with me. She did and displayed the same natural gifts to suspend disbelief. I may have accidentally forgotten to ask Curt if I could work on two scenes at once. Linda and I put it up as a surprise. Curt was impressed by our initiative. For the first time, I fully enjoyed the ride. And for some reason, I think I understood the *why* of it.

This time Curt started with me. "Tom, that was really very good." Then, in a gentle way, he said, "Why are you doing this? You will never be cast as Murray Burns. Frankly, Tom, you need to understand your instrument." And there it was! "When you walk in the door, here's what you bring: a young, six-feet-four-inch, good-looking leading man. At some level, you have to deliver that."

To which I answered, "I don't want to get you mad at me, boss. But I like this guy."

Everything that Curt said made absolute sense to me. And he was right to assign me scenes that would, as he put it, make me *stretch*. But in doing what was right for those characters, I was doing something that was out of character for me. That was a problem. I was kind of at war with my instrument. I didn't really mind the feeling of failing as long as I learned something, and I had actually learned something from what Curt told me. But I still liked this guy. I liked Murray Burns.

———

Don Schwartz had made sure I could do commercials outside of my Fox contract. Obviously, that was good for him and good for me. I don't really remember my audition, but I got cast in one for a Gallo wine product. They wanted to convince people that Dubonnet aperitif wasn't just for senior citizens.

The set was a western town, and when I arrived, I was introduced to my "leading lady."

It was her! I'd seen the Noxzema commercial, and it was her!

Let me explain. Joe Namath did a shave-cream commercial where he smiles to the camera and says, "I'm about to get creamed." After he finishes shaving, he gets his face caressed and is sung to by a beautiful young woman.

How do I say this? I found her performance very impactful.

And it was *her*.

I tried to have my grown-up-adult-been-there-before face on as she smiled, shook my hand, and said, "Hi, I'm Farrah."

That was a good day. I got paid to flirt with Farrah Fawcett.

"I met him at a party. I was having a Dubonnet on the rocks." Her voice was over images of the two of us, and I was having no trouble with my motivation. Farrah couldn't have been nicer and more fun. It was indeed a good day.

No knock on Joe Namath, but the overwhelming response to that Noxzema commercial was very much "Yeah, but who's that *woman*?" From the impact of her early appearances, she clearly made me and a whole lot of other people want to see more. Yes, she was beautiful. But there was also the force of that persona. I for one—one of many—knew that she was going to stick around.

Over the years, we would bump into each other many times. And I am flattered to say she always remembered that job we had together a long, long time ago.

———

Studio tours had become popular at Universal, and profitable too. A young UCLA grad who'd been a Universal tour guide brought the idea with him to Fox. His name was Michael Ovitz. He would go on to become the most powerful agent in Hollywood and president of the Walt Disney Company. But at the time, he was just a bright young guy at Fox brimming with ideas. The Fox tour started on a much smaller scale, and the talent program was part of it. They'd find a vacant soundstage and put two of us there for a week. We were a regular stop for the twenty or thirty tourists in each group. The tour guide would introduce us as something grand, like "valued members of the Fox family of contract players." Not up to my friend Sonia Wolfson's standards . . . *but still*. We would answer questions, the most prominent being "How did you get started in the business?" Then we would put up a scene. All of us had a couple of scenes in our back pockets, having put them up in class. So, it wasn't a tough gig.

I had gotten to know Mike while a couple of others in the group put up their scenes. That's when he made his request: "Everybody, please. Nothing heavy. Something light and funny."

That was all I had to hear. I mean, no one from the program was going to monitor us or anything. So I pulled out *A Thousand Clowns*.

I'm not sure what my "instrument" said to them. But this brand-new live audience of normal people laughed at the right times. I even got some awwwws. And frankly, with Linda there, "the work" didn't have any *Dating Game* smiles or nerves.

———

Two times we put on a show for the annual Fox motion picture distributors event. Not some of us. All of us. It was mandatory. This was a big deal for the studio. It was also elaborate and expensive. If you wanted to impress the people who were going to put your product into theaters, it was a very big deal.

We had all the wonderful departments at the studio working with us. We had special costumes for the dancing and singing numbers. All the songs were sung to the tune of the musicals Fox had coming out, but they had special lyrics. *Hello, Dolly!* with Barbra Streisand was a priority. We'd all watched as the craft crews had turned almost the entire Fox studio into a set of New York in the 1890s.

Jon Gregory choreographed the dance numbers, always accompanied by his favorite phrase, "Sell it, baby! Sell it!" And Helene helped us through our brain farts. We rehearsed endlessly and even prerecorded our singing, just like in real movie musicals. Several people—no, not me—also put up scenes from upcoming movies. No scenes from television were allowed. I don't really know why, but I still remember a verse in our song, to the tune of "It Only Takes a Moment" from *Hello, Dolly!*:

It only takes a moment
To be starring in the show
With tantrums, star-type tantrums
Telling Richard Z where he can go.
You're up for Tony Rome and
For the part you think you're right,
But they give it to some unknown.
Frank Sinatra! Who is he?

When we put the show up, we were ready. Not so much nervous as excited. No brain farts in the dance numbers. Pretty good lip-synching to the prerecorded lyrics. Missy, of course, was terrific, and Sam and I were, of course, magnificent. After the show, there was a cocktail reception for all the distributors. This was also mandatory.

The distributors were mostly men in those days, so there seemed to be a predominant interest in the female cast. Sam and I, having sung and danced our little brains out, looked at each other and promptly slipped away into a corner and watched the show after the show.

Then we had our own party afterward. Teachers included.

———

By then I had learned so much from Curt. How to prepare. How to build a character. How to see the scene through the eyes of your character. How to respect your obligation to the plot. But I may have learned just as much from being present and watching the other actors and listening to Curt's critiques of them. I got to know each actor's work. When they kept blocking the solution. When they felt they had failed. And when they had a breakthrough, it was so much easier to see when you were watching than when you were the one in that chair, facing Curt and the class.

———

How fortunate it was that serendipity had smiled on me! The program was the perfect place for young actors to nurture their talent. The perfect place to risk, to stretch, to fail, and to grow. Protected from the kinds of mistakes that could have more serious consequences in real jobs. But the business had changed over the years. Producers and directors and even the big stars had become much more independent. They had fought hard to gain that independence. There weren't any more Louis B. Mayers or Samuel Goldwyns or Darryl Zanucks with the clout to demand, "Use my contract players." And the filmmakers weren't about to say, "Yessir."

The studio casting department would submit us; they were mostly turned down. I was one of the newest contract players and had gone on less than a handful of interviews. The first time I realized how fundamental the problem was, I was on an interview for *The Sweet Ride*. The movie starred Jacqueline Bisset and Michael Sarrazin. No, Jacqueline wasn't there. The producer took one look at my slim résumé and said, "You're in the New Talent program?"

"Yes, I am."

"You're one of those people who do the triangle."

"Excuse me?"

"You go from the talent program to the commissary to the pay window."

Yes, it was insulting. And the guy was clearly a little shithead. But if I got the job, I was going to work only two days at most. I'd handled a lot of people like him by now. I chose not to respond to the little shithead.

I didn't get the part.

But I realized something. There was not only resistance to seeing us—there was resentment that they even had to consider us.

Leave it to my friend Sam to find a path through the maze. He figured out that the scripts for all the studio's upcoming movies and TV shows had to go through the legal department. He made friends with some of the secretaries in the department, not hard for someone with Sam's gift of charm. He would make regular visits to legal, take a seat in the corner, and read scripts. He would identify specific parts he knew he was right for and lobby in every way he could to get in the room for an audition. Sam got cast in *The Way West* with Kirk Douglas, Robert Mitchum, and Richard Widmark and won a small role in *Butch Cassidy and the Sundance Kid*.

When I heard about my friend's secret mission, I thought, *Well, that's Sam*. Just to be clear, this wasn't something he could share with me or any of us. Those secretaries had helped Sam and taken a risk in doing so. Sam couldn't, shouldn't, and wouldn't betray that confidence.

The Fox New Talent program was doing its job, and it had produced some promising starts. But the studio had much bigger ambitions. They didn't sign people to become character actors or guest stars. They signed people they thought had the talent to be leading men and leading women. And the gamble would pay off when actors from the program could be loaned out to other studios for starring roles. It would be a home run if the studio received a star's salary at a contract player's rate. That's the way the old studio system had always paid off.

What happened next, no one could have predicted. Yes, the talent program cost money, but it was nothing compared to the rising cost of movies. Maybe it was a board-of-directors thing. No matter what, it was above my pay grade. Out of nowhere, Fox announced it was ending the talent program. Curt, Pam, the Gregorys, and Jack were let go on a Friday night. There was no big going-away party. We were just told our attendance was no longer required. Since we had all signed at different times, our options expired on different dates. All that was left was for us to run out the clock on our contracts.

Then it was gone. Like the old studio backlot, the 20th Century–Fox New Talent program had become a remnant of a bygone era.

CHAPTER THREE

In Uniform

n June 1967, early in my first six-month term at Fox, I got a surprise. It shouldn't have been a surprise, but my mind was focused on my new job. I got my draft-physical notice. Having in effect dropped out of USC, I had lost my student deferment. When you got that notice, it meant if you passed, you had thirty days to either enlist (three years), volunteer for the draft (two years), or join a unit in the reserves (six years, part-time).

Well, I passed my physical. I did have one hitch in the process, taking a long time to pee in front of thirty or forty naked fellow attendees with a lot of other people yelling at us. But eventually, I moved on to the next station, the mass hemorrhoid check. Our group was told to form a circle. In the middle of the circle were a doctor and a guy with a clipboard. The doctor told us to turn away from him.

"Now bend over and spread your cheeks," he said in a loud voice.

He then checked out each of us, occasionally saying to the clipboard guy, in the same loud "command" voice, things like "Hemorrhoid, seven o'clock."

Where was I? Oh, yes. I passed my preinduction physical.

Since World War II, every able male citizen had been subject to the draft. I felt I couldn't consider myself special and shouldn't. It had occurred to me many times that there was nothing fair or equitable in the fact that college kids got a deferment but that a hardworking plumber did not. But I digress. I didn't want to lose the opportunity that had come to me, so the reserves seemed to be the best choice.

This was at the height of Lyndon Johnson's Vietnam War. Most of the reserve units had already filled their quotas. I talked to my dad, who had been drafted after his first year of college, and he said, "I understand. Let me do some checking."

My dad did what any citizen should be able to do. He called his congressman. He was hardly a fat-cat donor, but he had the gift of a salesman and was able to get through the congressman's protective circle.

My dad told me he'd found out there was one reserve unit that had a few openings. He said it was an infantry unit in the California Army National Guard in nearby Glendale. "But you'll have to go down and interview, just like everyone else."

I guess I did okay in my interview with First Sergeant Glenn Wetzel. I was offered a spot and enlisted. Now I was able to keep going at Fox until I got my orders to report for basic training. And legally Fox had to give me my job back at the studio after my six months of training.

On November 2, 1967, I got my orders to report to Fort Ord in Monterey, California, for basic training in the United States Army. I got a nice going-away party from my friends at the talent program, students and teachers alike. I was deeply touched by the affection they showed me. It reassured me that I belonged there and would be welcomed back at the studio when I finished my six months of active duty. And I took pride in knowing that millions of Americans before me probably had their own versions of the ritual of going away to serve.

My going-away party has always brought to mind my friend John Milius's terrific movie *Big Wednesday,* about a group of surfers in the late sixties. William Katt plays the only one of the group who chooses to serve. A decade later, when I saw the movie, his character's going-away party not only brought tears to my eyes but left me sobbing. I don't really know why . . . I *do* know why. I was the only one in my close circle of friends who chose to serve. *Big Wednesday* has, at least for me, an unforgettable sequence where the surfers go to extremes to fail their induction physicals. It's a movie, so it's told in a kind of heightened reality and is very funny—but still. Standing naked in all those lines, I saw the real version of that—more subtle, but behavior I had no respect for. Well, these were the times we were living in.

I was so proud of Billy in that movie. I still call him that because he had always been the kid next door. His mom and dad, actors Barbara Hale and Bill Williams, lived next door to us on Weddington Street in Sherman Oaks. That kid next door had grown into a fine actor and, like all good actors, he's still doing great work.

———

I was to report somewhere in downtown L.A. I was still living at my mom and dad's house at the time, and my dad said, "I'll drive you down there."

"You don't have to, Dad."

He just said, "I know."

I don't remember much being said on the way downtown. I was pre-occupied with the uncertainty of what lay ahead. But then my dad knew that, having probably been just as preoccupied when he left home to serve. And I kinda knew that he knew. So we talked about other things. Small things. Big things. Just not the elephant in the room. Most likely, we spent a lot of time talking about how Bob was doing on the Dodgers' minor league team in single-A baseball. And then we were there. I said something brave, like "See you soon, Dad." There were no hugs—wouldn't look good in front of the army sergeants—but I was sustained by the huge hug I got from my mom when she said goodbye before we left. From then on, it was a bunch of military personnel yelling at us: *"Move! Move! Move! On the bus!"* There was no waving goodbye, but I'm pretty sure I caught a glimpse of my dad standing by his car, watching with pride, thinking, *Been there, done that.*

The eight-hour bus ride up to Northern California was, well, quiet. Actually, I'm not sure we were allowed to talk. So again, much thinking. When we finally climbed off the bus, there were what seemed to be a hundred drill sergeants wearing Smokey Bear hats, yelling in our faces. We stood in line to get our heads shaved. We stood in line to get shots. We stood in line to get our uniforms. We stood in line to get our gear. None of which was ever done fast enough, so more yelling in our faces and a lot of push-ups.

Someday I'll write a book about my time in the military, just not now. But more than in most lines of work, your growth as a person in the acting business has a lot to do with your growth as an actor. You are, after all, the product you're selling. I grew a lot in the crucible of basic training. The honest truth is that I excelled in the military. When I graduated from basic, I was selected as the outstanding trainee. When you graduated, you automatically were given the rank of private. I was promoted to the rank above that, private first class. It was the first such promotion in the history of my basic training company.

Not to brag, but I'm proud of that. I had my shit together.

I did screw up once, and it was a big one. After our first week in AIT, advanced infantry training, we were finally given our first weekend pass. We were allowed to go only thirty miles from Fort Ord. But I was so homesick, I went home to L.A., which was more like three hundred. By the time I got to my parents' house, I had a 104-degree fever, and frankly, stuff was coming out of both ends. There was no way I could make it back.

My dad was not a rescuer. But having served in the army, he understood how serious this could be. He called my company commander and explained my situation. The CO told him that he was looking at my 201 file; he was impressed by my promotion and all the letters of commendation. But if I didn't get to a military hospital right away, it would be out of his hands. My dad drove me down to the army hospital at Fort MacArthur in nearby San Pedro. It turned out that Fort Ord received a lot of soldiers returning from their tours in Vietnam, and I had probably contracted some unknown virus that came from there.

I'd been in the hospital more than a week when I got a big surprise. Five or six of the girls in the talent program, including my friend Linda, paid me a visit. From that moment on until I got out of there, I was the toast of my hospital ward.

———

Six months is a long time. So why not make the most of it? Through the rest of my training, I held leadership positions and, I like to think, responded to every challenge. Late in my tour of duty, I earned the privilege of having my own vehicle. I took a bus down to L.A., legally this time, and drove my beat-up Volkswagen back up to Ord.

And soon it was over. No, not *suddenly* it was over. Nothing happens before you know it when you are counting each day until it's done. As excited as I was to get home, I drove back to L.A. the long way, down the coast on scenic Highway 1. It would give me time to think about my six months on active duty and reflect on all I had accomplished. I decided to wear my uniform. I don't know why. Maybe I had seen too many movies. Well, actually, yes, I do know why. I was proud to wear it. And I wanted to be in uniform when I saw my family.

I remember stopping for gas in Big Sur and not exactly feeling like I was welcome. It served to remind me the zeitgeist had changed. The tone of the times we were living in had become unmistakably different. I chose to pay little attention and got lost in the incredible beauty of the California coast.

After I knocked on the door of my parents' house—no cell phones to say I was almost there—I got a lot of hugs. From my mom. From Marti. I'm not sure about my little brother Danny's welcome; he had an unusual yet appreciated sense of humor. Bob was off playing in the minors, but then my big brother was probably more apt to tease me than to hug me. I'm not really sure when it was that I started hugging my dad and telling him I loved him. That wasn't really the deal when I was growing up. But this might very well have been the moment I started. And, of course, I couldn't wait to see my friends at Fox and get back to work.

Only, after a couple of days, just as I was settling into my life as a civilian, I saw it. There it was in the paper: My National Guard unit had been activated by President Johnson to serve in Vietnam.

Oh-kay . . . change in plans.

In all honesty, I don't remember how I felt. It was, of course, stunning news. But nobody had forced me into this commitment, and I don't want to sound corny, but I did take an oath. Stupid things popped into my head, like *I just unpacked my duffel bag, and now I gotta pack all over again.* Truthfully, I'm not sure what I was thinking in the rush of the moment. But I was going, that was for sure. And I was okay with that. The commitment I had made to becoming an actor would have to wait.

My infantry unit was a big part of what they called the Selected Reserve Force. We were the top priority in the state for fires, floods, earthquakes, and, most importantly, civil disturbances. The unit had been the first ordered into the Watts riots in 1965.

I have no idea what happened after we got the order. Maybe Governor Reagan raised an objection. I just don't know. But within days, President Johnson's order was rescinded, and some lower-priority units went instead. Serendipity was clearly still on my side.

When I drove up to Stage 3 at 20th Century–Fox, *oh my gosh,* they had saved my parking space, number 163. It was kinda like I'd never left. Only one thing had changed. In the trunk of the car were a uniform and my military field gear. And that's where they would reside for the next five years, two weeks, and twenty-five days, along with the requirement to inform my unit of my whereabouts at all times. But I was back in the ball game.

———

As soon as I'd settled back in, my dad chose a moment and made one of his by-now-famous casual suggestions: "You might get more out of your military experience as an officer."

My dad's older brothers, George and Lyle, were both officers during World War II. He had lived the life of an enlisted man. With only one year of college, he didn't have a choice. And there was no escaping that my dad, a man I so respected, had earned the right to be listened to. For me, if I grew up to be exactly like him, that would be just fine. So I listened. I immediately applied for Officer Candidate School. In the Guard, the California Military Academy served that function. You served two weeks in the summer and went one weekend a month for a year and another two weeks the next summer. If you made it through, you graduated with the rank of second lieutenant. After just getting back, I was off to the California Military Academy at Camp San Luis Obispo. Do I need to tell you who drove me up there? Our drive up there is something I cherish. It echoed in so many ways our drive to basic training.

The Guard's officer program, after all, had only the first two weeks to separate the possibles from the never-should-have-been-theres. That process of weeding out had been raised to an art form. We were "greeted" by TAC (Tactical Air Command) officers in Smokey Bear hats, and they were in your face. For two weeks, they were *constantly* in your face, reminding you that they *owned* you. They call it stress training, and it is appropriate and necessary. No sleep, constant harassment, physical training, and endless classes. And the tests were not on paper. They came from the TAC officers yelling in your face and you at attention, eyes front, screaming answers.

The short nights weren't for sleeping. They were filled with personal sessions, trying to help your classmates who were falling behind, endless memorization, polishing your brass, and spit-shining your boots. Your appearance was very much a part of the training. Map reading was probably the most emphasized skill. If you're going to command, you sure as hell have to know where you are on the ground. The consequence of an error in judgment could call in artillery fire on your own troops. There was no dumbing down of the standards just because the military needed officers, nor should there be.

At the end of our first two weeks, I was number one in my class and was very proud to share that with my dad when he picked me up.

———

In the middle of the first week, I think during a brief bathroom break, I asked my TAC officer if I could talk to the CO.

"About what, Cadet Selleck?"

"Sir, personal business, sir."

He gestured to another TAC officer to come over. "Request denied. Stand at ease. Explain."

Under their steely gaze, I explained that I was an actor, and while I could get a regulation haircut for these two weeks, it would limit my ability to make a living for the rest of the year. Long hair was, of course, very much the style at the time. This all sounds pretty silly, but the regulations and conformity to them were a fundamental part of the training, as they should be. I guess by now I was showing some promise as a candidate, because they said, "We'll talk to the CO."

I was taken aside, probably during a "smoke 'em if you've got 'em" break, and they told me that the standards for two-week camps were immutable, but that once our cadet company got back to meetings at the armory in Van Nuys, they could ease the standards a little. Those meetings were largely classroom sessions.

At our first weekend meeting, those of us who had survived showed up ready for pretty much anything. I was acting cadet company commander. I didn't have an acting job, so I had a decent haircut, just not the standard shaved sidewalls. In our first class, a general gave us an inspirational speech, and obviously, my haircut stood out a little. I was noticed and afterward was told that all the general said was "Get him out of here." I had found that the relationship with your TAC officers evolved as you earned their respect. So when they told me, I got a couple of *I'm sorry*s, and that meant a whole lot. And then I resigned. I was done. *Because of a haircut.*

I was reassigned to Charlie Company, 1st Battalion, 160th Infantry, and promoted to the rank of corporal. It was a harsh reminder that, while I may have been a weekend warrior, I was a full-time actor. And the conflict between the two was something I would have to learn to live with.

———

My friend Sam was in the Guard too. I think he was a little ahead of me. As usual. Which meant he would finish his service before I finished mine. Sam, our mutual friend Dennis Durney, and I hung out together in those days. I would kid Sam about being in a "cushy" Air National Guard unit, and he would remind me that I was stupid enough to be a "ground pounder" in an infantry unit.

Look, just because I chose to serve didn't mean that I didn't count the days until my service to my country was completed. The opportunity my Fox contract afforded me was a commitment that was growing with each new day. Part of my responsibility to the Guard was making myself available for emergencies, be they fire, flood, civil disturbance, or whatever. A key element of the Selected Reserve Force was that we were the first to be called. Most times we were called in anticipation of being needed. That meant we would go to the armory in Glendale and wait. All the Guard armories seemed to be about the same in those days, post–Korean War: big gymnasium-like buildings with a cement floor and offices along the walls. Once we were called up, that's where we spent the hours waiting. No, not in the offices. On the cement floor. *Hurry up and wait* was an apt description for the time spent there, and the most efficient way to pass the time was to sleep. There were no cots, nothing so elegant. We all arranged our gear, our packs, our steel pots, and our field jackets on the cement floor in our own individual ways until word came to go or go home.

By 1968, Lyndon Johnson's war wasn't going well at all. I'd been nineteen in 1964 and unable to vote. Johnson was not my guy. But I was enthusiastically supportive of his opponent in the '64 election, Barry Goldwater. My friend Doug Plowden and I volunteered to work for Goldwater. We were alone among our peer group in that support, but at least we had an ally, Hillary Rodham. Yes, Mrs. Clinton was a "Goldwater Girl."

Sometime after the '64 election, I remember hearing William F. Buckley say, "People told me that if I voted for Barry Goldwater in '64, within a year we would be heavily involved in a war in Southeast Asia. I voted for Goldwater in '64 and, sure enough, we were heavily involved in a war in Southeast Asia." I couldn't know it then, but Bill would become a good friend over time.

So where was I? Oh, yes. Things weren't going well in Southeast Asia . . . or at home. It was pretty clear that civil disturbance had become my guard unit's primary mission. On April 4, 1968, Martin Luther King Jr. was murdered. In the wake of that tragedy, we were called in to be held in reserve, if and when we were needed. It wasn't as if we all sat in the armory watching the news on a big flat-screen TV. No cell phones to call home. Just one pay phone, although I'm not sure we were allowed to call out anyway. What stuck in my mind was that we had absolutely no civil-disturbance training. Friday night, on our monthly weekends, we would convoy down to Marine Corps Base Camp Pendleton. We were cramped in the back of our two-and-a-half-ton trucks (we called them "deuce-and-a-halfs") for the long ride. A two-hour drive in a passenger car would be over four hours in the convoy. Once there, we would embark on a Korean War–type military exercise. How this prepared the Selected Reserve Force for riot duty was just one of those questions you learned not to ask in the military. This wasn't really a knock on the Guard. Things changed slowly in the draft military in those days. The fact that we were still issued an M1, a World War II rifle, rather than the M14 we'd trained on in basic, kinda said it all. Our training and equipment simply hadn't caught up with what had become our most important mission.

After a couple of days on the cement floor, we were released. I went home to join a grieving nation. Until June 5 of that same year. I was sitting at home alone watching Bobby Kennedy's victory speech from the Ambassador Hotel. He had won the California presidential primary. After he left the stage, the shocking news came that he had been shot. Then came the news that we had lost him. After some time, I gathered myself. I checked my field gear and packed an extra set of fatigues and a change of underwear and socks. The call came later that night. None of us really knew what to expect as we arrived that next morning. Our orders were just to show up and report for duty. I could see on people's faces the sadness for our loss and the resolve to do what we could if needed.

There were no further orders, just to stand by . . . and wait. Just like after the loss of Dr. King, I think there was a sense in all of us that this kind of limbo was something we would have to get used to. After a day or so, we were released to return home to our families but told to maintain a high state of readiness.

———

In 1969, I was in a walking cast for a broken foot and had been excused from drills while I worked on a movie. But now I had to make up that time, so I worked in the company's supply room. Which was fine by me, as I didn't have a lot of fondness for crawling around Camp Pendleton doing military exercises that had nothing to do with our true mission. I applied myself, worked hard, and even came in on my own to accrue additional time in the somewhat unlikely event that I'd ever get another acting job.

It turned out this was noticed and put me in good stead with First

Sergeant Wetzel. Our supply sergeant, Scotty Boswell, was close to re-
tirement. So I was useful working in supply. By February 1970, my foot
had fully and finally healed. I happily remained in supply while the rest
of the company would go down to Pendleton. That is, until February 25,
when activist attorney William Kunstler spoke at the University of California, Santa Barbara, and student riots subsequently broke out in Isla
Vista, the student neighborhood right next to campus. On the morning
of February 28, the Guard was activated, and I was assigned to a squad
as a rifleman. We convoyed up to the National Guard armory in Santa
Barbara. We were briefed in a cursory way, issued ammunition, and told
to prepare to move in at dusk to enforce curfew. I think it was then that
one of my friends told us a National Guard general had said in the press
something like "Yes, we're going in. But the troops haven't been issued
ammunition."

We sure as hell had ammunition. It would have been, to say the least,
ill advised not to have the means to defend ourselves. We all thought the
general's statement increased the chances of confrontation and the possibility of consequences that nobody wanted. We weren't looking to break
heads. There was more a sense of getting this done with the least damage
to both sides. While this was the job in front of us, it was a job we hadn't
really trained to do. And frankly, we didn't know what to expect, how
hot a situation we were walking into.

We crammed into the back of our deuce-and-a-halfs and rolled into
Isla Vista just as dusk was turning into night. When we came to a stop,
we sat there. We didn't pour out of the trucks and line up in formation,
we just sat there in the back of the truck . . . We sat there for quite some
time. We couldn't see anything from inside the canvas-covered bed of
our truck except out the back. I'm pretty sure I wasn't the only one who
thought we'd make a lovely target for a Molotov cocktail.

There was a certain amount of relief when we were finally ordered
to disembark. Our platoon lined up in formation, the squads were given
their assignments, and we were told not to lock and load until ordered to

do so. The squad I was assigned to was posted at the Bank of America. This was ground zero for the riots. As we marched down the street, there were barricades on our right in front of a large square surrounded by student apartments; to our left were the smoldering embers of what had been the Bank of America. And the students . . . well, there were a lot of them. Not really a mass of them but a lot of them. And they weren't shouting and throwing shit at us, just cruising around, watching. Clearly, the agitators had moved on. To use a term from the era, it was a "happening."

When we reached our post, we lined up and faced the students. Sure, there were some smart-ass remarks and some taunts, but some of the students also offered us cookies, which we politely said no to. After a couple hours of that, the student protestors were suddenly confronted with one of the severest tests of commitment you could imagine . . . *it rained*. And the committed protestors all retreated to their apartments. We could hear the music coming from the parties that ensued while we guarded the smoking embers of a building.

Here's my sense of all this: It must have been fun for a bunch of college kids to burn down a building, kinda like when we blew out the windows of the SAE house with our fraternity's fire hoses. That's what college kids do. That isn't fair . . . but I don't care. Their behavior was a real problem for me and haunts me to this day. I'll tell you why. At about nine p.m. that rainy night, our platoon sergeant, John Lopez, was pulled out of the line, taken aside, and told that three of his children—Frances, five; John, nine; and Juliana, twelve—had been killed in a car crash. His wife, Ramona, was driving the station wagon and was in critical condition along with his other two children, Eddie, seven, and Laura, six. Their friend Damancio and his two daughters, Margie, fifteen, and Celia, thirteen, were also killed in the crash, along with the driver of the van that hit them. That's a pretty heavy price to pay for a *happening* in Isla Vista. If John had been home, the timing and circumstances would have been different. And John Lopez would still have his family.

I never saw Sergeant Lopez after that. I wish I had. I know he was also an LAPD police officer, and my hope is he found comfort from his brothers and sisters there.

When we finally got back to the Glendale Armory, we were packing up when we were told we were being held back on an as-needed status. William Kunstler was speaking at Cal State, Northridge, and there was concern about potential riots. We had one wet uniform in our packs, a deep sense of loss for a fellow soldier, and a knowledge that we shouldn't have been in Isla Vista in the first place. Having seen conduct without conscience or consequence, we were not in the mood for another dose. Someone else should have been held in reserve, but there was no one else to stand that post. We were tired, frustrated, and angry. That was potentially a real problem. But as it turned out, after another night on the cement floor, we went home.

———

On July 1, 1973, I was done. Well, not all of a sudden. Six years is a long time. I don't mean to say I wasn't changed or that I didn't value the time I'd spent serving my country. And the sense of pride that I had earned would increase with each passing year. It was a hard time to be in the military, but nothing I'd been through compared to the experience of so many others who served. And whatever our sacrifice, while not diminished, it is most certainly held in respect and reverence for those who gave the last full measure. I'm no hero, but I served. I was privileged to wear the cloth of our country. I earned the rank of sergeant in the United States Army Infantry. I pulled my weight.

CHAPTER FOUR

Miss West

During my second year at Fox, I had bought a new car, a Fiat 124 Spider (total price, $3,487). My brother Bob and I had rented a funky little two-bedroom cottage on Beverly Glen. After three years in the minors, Bob, with a bad right knee, had decided to hang it up—and not without regret, I might add.

Our place was in an artist community about halfway between Mulholland and Sunset with the tiny Beverly Glen Market in the middle. Bob went into the "family business," becoming director of leasing for Sav-on drugstores. As for me? Now that I'd been fired from Fox, I went down to the unemployment office in Hollywood and put in my application.

It was hard to understand what I can only describe as a real sense of loss. I had felt a yearning for connection with this tribe of actors. We had become a real family and had drawn close. It was like high school graduation—everybody vows to keep in touch, but it doesn't ever work that way. Happily, my friendships with Sam and Linda were built to last.

I was out of the Fox program for less than a month when I got an acting job, and it was for 20th Century–Fox. Apparently, I had to get fired by the studio before I could get hired by the studio. It was a TV western called *Lancer,* in its first season on CBS. The only reason anyone remembers *Lancer* at all is that it's the show Leonardo DiCaprio is doing in *Once Upon a Time in Hollywood,* Quentin Tarantino's gritty look back at the industry circa 1969.

The episode I appeared in was "Death Bait," and I was thrilled to be the star of a network TV show. Actually, that's not true. I was the star of the *teaser,* the scene at the beginning of the show meant to grab viewers' attention. That's not exactly true, either. The real star of the teaser was James Olson, a Chicago-based stage actor who'd already appeared alongside Joanne Woodward in *Rachel, Rachel,* an Academy Award nominee for Best Picture. But being cast in *Lancer* was still a very big deal to me.

Olson plays a big, mean-looking stranger with three guns, a hook for a hand, and a vicious German shepherd. My character is a drunken cowboy who decides to pick a fight with him. Not too smart!

"Hey, mister," I say with an evil laugh. "With a dog like that, I'll bet you don't even take a gun when you go bear hunting." As the man stares down at his drink, I turn to my friend at the bar. "Wish I had me a dog like that," I say, noticeably slurring my words. "I'd put a saddle on him and ride him clean to Kansas City."

With that, the man rattles a chain with his hook, and the growling dog lunges at me, pinning me against the wall of the saloon.

That was the scene. I acted my little brain out, eager to make a good impression. But when I looked over at the director, he was huddled with the dog trainer, and they were both staring at me.

A word about actor paranoia: For a new actor, full of nerves and anticipation, there is almost nothing that can make you feel better about the scene you just did. If the director doesn't say anything, you figure, *He's giving up on me—it's hopeless.* If he says, "That was good—let's try it again," you think, *That was awful. He's just trying to relax me in the hope of getting something out of me that's barely acceptable.* If the director says, "Sorry, we had a problem with the sound—can we do that over?" you're convinced: *The sound was fine. He's just blaming the sound guy so I don't get even more paranoid.*

I tensed up as the dog trainer walked across the set in my direction. He leaned in close and whispered conspiratorially: "The director doesn't think the dog is acting ferocious enough."

It wasn't me! It was the dog's fault! Then the trainer slipped something mushy into my hand. "Here's a piece of steak," he said. "Show the meat to the dog. Then conceal it in your fist. When the dog starts to back you up, hold your fist up to your throat. And the dog will come for you."

A word about a young actor's compulsion to please: Not for one second did I examine the wisdom of doing what the dog trainer asked me to, no matter how dangerous it might be. Plenty of actors—I've known a few—were tragically injured doing something wildly risky in a scene. I was just so glad it wasn't my fault that the words came flying out of my mouth. "Okay, okay. Whatever you say. Sure, I can do that."

We did the scene a second time. I held the meat to my throat, and the dog was appropriately ferocious. Then the director said, "Cut! That was great. Thank you, Tom. Tom, isn't it?"

The episode aired on January 14, 1969, two weeks shy of my twenty-fourth birthday. The truth is, I acted my little brain out. But looking back on my performance, I see *that* was the problem. My drunken cowboy displayed almost every stock-company cliché there is. I was playing a drunk, so I tried to prove I was drunk. A good actor does what drunks do, which is try to prove he's sober. It's the same when good actors play bad guys. Bad guys don't think they're bad. So good actors don't give them evil laughs.

I was sitting with my brother Bob in front of the television, watching my first real job as a professional actor. When the teaser was over, there was a moment of silence, and then Bob said, "That was nice." The phone rang, as it often would in the future at times like this. It was my mom and dad.

"Good job," my father said in the most optimistic tone he could muster, quickly adding, "I'll put your mother on." She said something to me I would hear again and again over the years and would always welcome.

My mom said, "You were great, Tom."

———

What did Owen McLean say in the Fox audition? "The kid is pretty green." Well, I still was. A little more trained but with no idea how to apply it. And whether it's sports or acting, it's hard to keep your eye on the prize when you have no idea what the prize is going to be. I was developing what I would call a bricklayer's mentality about goals. Brick by brick, I would discover the road and learn only later where it might take me. Until the talent program, I had done hardly anything that my big brother, Bob, hadn't done first. And I had followed that road gratefully. The path I was on now wasn't one that Bob or my dad or the rest of my family, for all their wisdom, could understand or help me with. But I realized I had an appetite for my new journey, and my family had given me the tools to take the risk.

When we were packing up at the end of the talent program, my friend Linda had told me that her boyfriend, Sal Dano, was going to teach an acting class, and she invited me to come. At the time, I didn't really know if this was an opportunity or an obligation to a good friend.

I knew I needed to study. I wanted to study. But now it would be on my nickel. Linda's idea was as good a place as any to start.

———

"You have an interview with Mae West at eight p.m. at Fox."

I knew my agent's secretary pretty well, and frankly, I could hear in her tone that she might be sending me up.

"You're kidding me, right?"

"No. You have an interview with Mae West at eight p.m. . . . . *in her dressing room.*"

Oh-kay! "For what?"

"The movie *Myra Breckinridge.*"

"Oh."

That's when I knew this was no send-up, that this was the real deal and a genuine opportunity.

Mae West hadn't made a movie in twenty-seven years, a couple of years longer than I'd been alive. But I was a huge fan of her movies. *She Done Him Wrong* and *I'm No Angel*, both with Cary Grant, were a couple of my favorites. But my absolute number one Mae West movie was *My Little Chickadee* with W. C. Fields. She somehow combined the right blend of sex and humor that let her get away with a whole lot of things no one else could. Every time I watched Mae West in a movie, I gotta say I felt like *I* was getting away with something. She had the heat and the style to pull it off and didn't mind carrying that over to her personal life. Gore Vidal's book *Myra Breckinridge* being made into a movie had generated a ton of publicity, matched only by the idea of Mae West coming back to the screen. It's the story of a man (played by movie critic Rex Reed) who comes out of a sex-change operation looking exactly like Raquel Welch (played, of course, by Raquel Welch). The movie would also feature my Dubonnet commercial partner, Farrah Fawcett.

It was dark when I approached the cottage that was Mae West's dressing room.

I will admit that I thought, *Mae West? At night? In her dressing room? . . . Nah! But still . . .*

When I went in, the front room was full of young actors sitting and waiting. The far door opened, and a well-dressed man approached me. He reached out and shook my hand and said, "Fight on."

"I'm sorry?"

"I'm Stanley Musgrove," he said. "I work with Miss West, but I'm also president of Friends of the USC Libraries."

His greeting was in the language of the loyal USC alumni. I replied in kind: "Great to be a Trojan."

"Oh, you don't have to wait," he said. "Miss West will see you now."

I didn't look around to see the reaction of the actors who had been waiting as he escorted me into the other room.

And there she was.

Mae West.

Sitting in an elegant chair. Dressed elegantly, all in white. Looking ready for a night on the town in the 1930s. Yes, she was older. But still . . .

Stanley introduced me. She held out her hand and said, "How do you do?"

Actually, she didn't say it like her persona on the screen. It was more like Old Brooklyn. I shook her hand. Mae West's hand. And frankly, I don't remember much about the rest of the very brief interview. To be honest, I was a bit starstruck, kinda like if I'd had an interview with John Wayne.

—

"You have an interview with Mae West at eight p.m. . . . . *in her apartment. That's eight—*"

"Yes, I heard you. Where is her apartment?"

The Ravenswood was an elegant old building between Sunset and Wilshire Boulevards that had been built by Paramount Pictures in the early days of the Great Depression. Ava Gardner, Clark Gable, and other stars had lived there during Hollywood's Golden Age.

When I got in the elevator, my mind was racing again. *So I get fired, and now I get my second opportunity in a month at the studio that fired me . . . And, oh yeah, what exactly am I walking into when I get off this elevator? Well, don't know where I'm goin', but there's no use bein' late.*

The door opened, and there was Stanley, who escorted me inside. "It's *Miss West,*" he whispered.

Everything was white. The walls were white. The carpet was white. The furniture was white. Even the grand piano was white. And seated in an elegant white chair was Miss West. She was dressed again for a night on the town, all in white. Miss West said hello and personally handed me some script pages. "I'd like you to read with me," she said.

"Sure," I answered, trying to sound like that happened every day.

She had the first line: "'Oh yeah. Well, I don't care about your credits as long as you're oversexed.'"

Suddenly, Miss West had turned into *Mae West*. She was completely in character. My line was right on the page in front of me. But all that would register in my mind was: *Holy shit! That's Mae West!* And I just laughed.

Finally, I got the line out through my laughter.

That happened a couple more times during the read. When the short scene ended, she didn't say anything. Then she got up and went over and leaned against the white piano. "Come here," she said.

She was still Mae West. I got up slowly, went over, and stood in front of her.

"Put your hands on my waist."

I put my hands on her waist.

"Spread your legs."

Oh-kay! I spread my legs.

But it was Miss West who said, "Well?"

She was looking past me. Stanley, who I had completely forgotten was in the room, answered, "It'll work, Miss West."

It turned out that being only a little over five feet in height, she was concerned that six feet four might not work for what she had in mind. She wanted to create the impression that she was much taller, more statuesque. So spreading my legs was strictly business, and I was learning she was very much a businesswoman. You see, spreading my legs would make me shorter and her taller. When I found out she always wrote her own stuff, I thought maybe my nervous laughter made her think I was enjoying her writing. Which in a way I was, in addition to being starstruck. Or maybe my new friend Stanley had lobbied for me. Or accidentally turning my character into a pubescent sixteen-year-old was what she was looking for. I'm not sure why, but I got the job.

I would be playing Young Stud 4.

When I arrived for my first day on the set, my first part in a big movie, the second assistant director told me, "Relax. There's no way we're getting to you today. But stay close anyway."

All the actors playing young studs just hung out all day. Secretly, I hoped to find my name on the back of one of the chairs, but day players aren't afforded that luxury. The second day, I was told the same thing. But I had kept my eyes and ears open and learned some things. Richard Zanuck had hired a British director named Michael Sarne to do a ninth rewrite and direct the film. Evidently, Sarne was the kind of director who denied himself very little and liked to spend many hours by himself, "thinking." Now, Raquel Welch was writing her own stuff. Mae West was, of course, writing *her* own stuff. And the two of them weren't speaking. We all waited around the rest of the week and part of the second. I didn't mind, since when you are hired at a day rate, each day you go over adds up to much more than had you been hired on at a cheaper weekly rate. I kept hoping that my Dubonnet flirting partner, Farrah Fawcett, would wander through, but no such luck.

The wardrobe department helped me pick one of my favorite suits to wear in the scene. That would make me feel more at home, a good sign. The suit was a tan six-button double-breasted tweed. I must say, I looked pretty good in it. Finally, sometime in the second week, we were told to get dressed. We were going to shoot the scene.

The first part of the scene was in a long hallway. Yes, it was white. Chairs for all the young studs were lined up against both walls. Day players often do their own standing in while the scene is lit. And with the picture so far over budget, no one was about to make an exception and hire stand-ins for us. Lighting took a long time, and the lights were hot. Really hot. My favorite suit was perfect for a brisk fall day in London but not here. And the double-breasted suit jacket had to be buttoned up or it wouldn't look right. Before we were even ready to start, I was sweating.

In the scene, Mae West's Leticia Van Allen, a casting agent with a propensity for seducing young men, is supposed to make a grand entrance. And enter she does, in a floor-length white gown with a long black stole and a furry hat of immense size. "I'll be right with you, boys," she announces. "Get your résumés out."

She stops at the door to her office, looks back, and says to another young stud, "How tall are you?"

"Six feet, seven inches."

"Never mind the six feet. Let's talk about the seven inches."

She goes inside, and her male assistant motions to me. "She'll see you. Yes, you."

We broke to set up the scene in her office. I quickly took off my jacket and realized I had already sweated through my only shirt. I tried to cool down, but by now the whole soundstage was hot.

Her office set had already been prelit. Very soon, the assistant director came and said to me, "We're ready."

A makeup person appeared and blotted me off. "You gotta calm down," she said, "or you're going to have flop sweat," a condition I was about to discover.

A word to new actors: If you are on a hot set and start to sweat, don't say to yourself, *I can't sweat. Don't sweat. Don't sweat.*

I walked over to Mae West, who was looking at my résumé. I had my briefcase in hand, sweating even more and not feeling at all attractive. But Mae West, ever the professional, pressed on. "Oh, yeah," she coos. "Well, I don't care about your credits as long as you're oversexed."

"Oh, that's one of my credits," I assure her. At least I could remember my lines and didn't laugh.

Right then, a curtain falls, revealing . . . "A bed!" I exclaim. "I never did see a bed in an office before!"

"Well, you see, I do a lot of night work sometimes. Come here."

All you see is my briefcase drop and my résumé and her stole float to the floor. Then she says, "You impress me immensely. I'll keep you in mind as a summer replacement."

And then it was done. My time with Mae West was over. And no matter how inescapably unqualified I was, it was so memorable.

Then I got a call from Stanley Musgrove. He said Miss West wanted me to join her for dinner at Chasen's. Since 1936, Chasen's had been a quintessential Hollywood hangout, frequented by luminaries like Frank Sinatra, Alfred Hitchcock, James Stewart, and Groucho Marx. Ronald Reagan proposed to Nancy Davis in a booth at Chasen's. When Elizabeth Taylor was filming *Cleopatra,* she had several orders of Chasen's chili flown to the set in Rome. Chasen's was a place to be seen, I knew that much.

I also realized that Mae West knew how to exploit the Hollywood publicity machine. She knew she had a lot of heat with this movie in the can. My guess was that having a young man on her arm was part of maintaining that heat. I was learning fast that if you're going to stay who you are in my new "town," you need to grow up fast.

It turned out I was right. I had dinner with Miss West and, yes, Stanley. I can't say it was a romantic dinner. But the people gawking at us didn't know that. I valued the time with her, and I didn't care what they thought. And Miss West knew exactly what they thought.

Then I was asked to escort her to a dinner at my alma mater. It was probably for the Friends of the USC Libraries. I sat between Miss West and the great director George Cukor, an old friend of hers. I guess I contributed to the conversation in some small way. Mr. Cukor was very nice and polite. And by now I felt like I knew Miss West a little better and was dying to tell her how much I liked her work. So I took a deep breath and said, "Miss West. I just loved your movie *My Little Chickadee,* with W. C. Fields."

Her smile faded away. "I don't like that man," she said.

She seemed to take a deep breath, and she told me about a scene they had shot where Fields was playing a bartender. She had finished the scene and was leaving the set when the director said to her that the scene continued after her character exited. "And Mr. Fields has a couple of ideas he'd like to work with."

She told the director that was fine.

As she recounted the story, she stopped and took a sip of water. She said that Fields had improvised a very involved sequence that was so good it stayed in the movie. She explained that she had worked long and hard to have her name above the title and to have the writing credit. Now Fields was demanding his name above the title and writing credit.

At this point, I was grateful for one small thing. I hadn't told her that her scene with Fields was my favorite in the movie. Sadly, the two comic geniuses would never work together again.

Miss West could easily have shunned me for the rest of the evening. Instead, she took me in her confidence and cared enough to explain. A very kind gesture. But I still figured this would be our last go-round.

———

During our talent-program days, Sam and I would often hang out with our good friend Dennis Durney. Dennis had grown up in the business. His mom was Dorothy Kingsley, a prolific screenwriter whose films included lavish MGM musicals like *Kiss Me Kate, Seven Brides for Seven Brothers,* and Frank Sinatra's *Pal Joey.* But Dennis was more interested in the production end of the business. There was a regular group of people who would all show up in the same place, usually somewhere at Fox. Dennis, Sam, and I were regulars. And there was Esme Chandlee. Esme came from the world of my pal Sonia Wolfson. There is a famous picture of a luncheon at MGM Studios that seems to have been attended by every actor in the Hollywood film world. That's where and when Esme got her start at MGM.

When Esme called, I figured she'd gotten my number from Dennis.

"Well, did you see it?" she asked.

"I'm sorry, Esme. See what?"

"The profile on Mae West."

I wish I could remember the magazine, but I can tell you it wasn't a short gossip item or a mention in somebody's column. It was a serious in-depth profile about Mae West's return to the screen. In the article, she was talking about discovering Cary Grant. She said a lot about that but finished with the line "Cary Grant had a look."

And then: "Tom Selleck has a look."

"You gotta do something with that," Esme said to me.

"Because she used my name in a sentence?"

"Because she just compared you to Cary Grant."

"Well, that's really very nice," I said. "But *Cary Grant*? That's ridiculous."

"Yes, dolly," Esme said. "You do have a long way to go. But before the movie comes out, nobody knows that."

Esme said she'd get me invited to the *Myra Breckinridge* premiere. I'd have to rent a tuxedo and limo. But I should trust her. It would be worth it. "I'll make sure they take a lot of pictures. And don't worry, you don't have to pay me for anything."

I've never forgotten that gesture. Esme and I would work together for decades to come.

As for Miss West, Esme had me come early to the premiere, when I wouldn't have much competition for pictures. After the red carpet, I was milling around in the crowded theater lobby in my tuxedo, not knowing anyone and wishing I could have some popcorn. Suddenly, it seemed as if lightning had struck. I couldn't really see anything. Miss West wasn't six-four. But from the warm glow of what seemed to be a million flashbulbs, I knew that Mae West was making her entrance.

CHAPTER FIVE

Selling Ecstatically

I t doesn't matter what you think of your performance. It's what the audience thinks. If they think it was good, just say, 'Thank you.'"

From the moment Sal Dano started his class, I could tell this was going to be something more than a favor to my friend Linda. It was a stroke of good fortune. Sal had a certain irreverence about him that was clear as soon as Linda introduced us. And the language he was using about the work of acting carried the same demystifying frankness.

The goal of "becoming the character without distraction" wasn't really going to happen very often, Sal explained. "You have to allow yourself errant thoughts. Otherwise, they will subvert the whole performance. Every actor has moments of thinking, *What's my next line?* or *Why is my fellow actor making such a stupid choice?*"

I had learned so much from Curt. But for me, all that enviable theory was, in practice, inviting a certain self-criticism in the moment. Whatever way my brain is set up, the perfect was often the enemy of the good. And good . . . is pretty good. Giving myself permission to allow errant thoughts could free me up to have fewer of them.

Sal had a gift as a teacher. At least for me he did. I knew I would be back.

—

When I'd moved back home from college and started at Fox, I had insisted on paying my mom and dad rent. I was proud of that because, whether they knew it or not, I had learned from them that I should. Life after Fox had another feature . . . making my nut. There was rent for the place Bob and I shared. Eating. Union dues. Car payments. And now acting classes. I was committed to pulling my own weight, having done it for over two years.

The Hollywood branch of the unemployment office was an interesting experience. You went at a specific time (I think mine was Thursdays at two-twenty p.m.) and waited in a long line. You saw all sorts of actors in the lines. Some successful. Even some you'd worked with. And you made new friends. When you got to the window, you were asked, mostly by nice people, what you'd done to find work that week. Most of the staff knew show business and how hard it was to get a job without an agent and, even if you had an agent, how hard it was to get a job without an interview. I can honestly say most of the staff understood and never gave people a hard time. And for the few who wanted to, the line was too long.

The truth is, I was never really given a hard time. If you didn't come in with a chip on your shoulder and you said please and thank you, that went a long way.

I knew it was going to be tough pulling my weight with acting jobs. When and if they came, they were likely to be one-day bit parts. *Lancer* was one day's work at minimum union scale, less ten percent commission for my agent. My adventure with Miss West paid more, only because of the chaos of the production. I think I got ten days of work on that one but not even enough to pay my half of the rent. Unemployment would help fill the gaps. But it wasn't *in addition to*. It was *instead of*. Getting the government cash simply meant I wasn't working.

All this seemed like a different lifetime from when I did my Pepsi commercial. And with all that had happened since then, it was. I do remember that job cost me more to take than the amount I earned. You had to join the Screen Actors Guild on your second job, and the fee was significantly more than the one-day union scale I got paid.

While it cost me money to do the Pepsi commercial, it was a good investment. No, not in a show-business sense, a career I had never even considered at that point, but because I discovered that I would get a fee each time the commercial ran. It was called a residual. I learned that, if you hit a home run on a network commercial, you might make as much as ten grand. My Pepsi job was more like a single, but it sure helped.

Since I started with the Pepsi commercial, I guess you could say that the advertising world considered me a beverage kind of guy. That myth was dispelled when I got a job for Worldparts. They were an outfit wanting to brag that they had a lot of auto parts. I would be their spokesman, dressed in a French Foreign Legion uniform.

"Worldparts offers quality-made parts for over ninety percent of the import cars on the road today." That's the only line I can remember.

We shot in some sand dunes near San Diego. I was excited about this job because I realized it could recur. My hopes diminished with each take, of which there were many. The director kept coming over to me and saying, "More gruff! . . . More tough! . . . More angry!" I could see the clients conferring behind the camera, and their body language wasn't promising. I tried to give them what they said they wanted. But while I may have looked the part—well, let's just say it wasn't my finest hour. And no, there wasn't a second commercial for Worldparts.

I remembered Curt's words on the importance of delivering what I bring into the room: "Some part of you has to deliver a six-feet-four leading man." That, I'm afraid, was still a work in progress. I guessed I wasn't an auto-parts kind of guy after all. I stored the experience away and did my best to move on.

Something should be said about this kind of work. The premises may have been silly, but the work—or should I say the commitment to the work?—was dead serious. A good job would lead to more jobs. The small community of commercial casting directors would remember who validated their judgment and who did not. And, just as important, commercials were not easy. They had a certain compressed, heightened reality. So the work had to have a reality. But yes, it also had to happen on a dime.

As time went on, I would value any time in front of the camera as an opportunity to learn, if only by failing or succeeding. On my good days, I went home mostly satisfied. On my bad days, the camera became the evil eye that saw through me. On those days, I would act my brains out in the car on the way home, doing the scene over and over. And in that pre–cell phone era, I got some very strange looks from the cars around me.

Even in commercials, you needed to make it look like "here goes nothing" while you committed yourself to the idea that "here goes everything."

Over time, I would learn I wasn't just a beverage kind of guy but also very much a hygiene kind of guy. I got a Safeguard soap commercial. In it, I take a shower (yes, I keep my shorts on) and ecstatically rub Safeguard soap all over my chest. I was discovering that ecstatic behavior was often required when dealing with "the product." Showering with Safeguard soap was kinda like chugalugging the Pepsi. Then I appear in a very nice chalk-striped gray flannel suit and walk through the stages of my workday. I pass by various women who all smell me. I get into a taxi, and the driver, Patti Deutsch, says out loud, "*Mmmm,* he always smells so fresh."

I step into a revolving door with a very attractive woman who wordlessly smells me. Then I walk by Penny Marshall and Teri Garr. Teri says, "He smells just the way a man should smell." Which is fine by me, because I always had a hidden crush on Teri Garr. My reactions in the moment to what they said were not something you could plan, but I knew they were essential to those moments. The clients were happy, and they gave me the suit.

My run as a hygiene guy continued with a Close-Up toothpaste commercial. The script was titled "Fuse Box." In it, the lights have gone out and an "attractive couple" are at, yes, a fuse box. My other half was an actress named Lee Crawford. She had been featured as one of the Golddiggers on *The Dean Martin Show.* But Lee was best known at the time for having the very first spoken words on *The Young and the Restless.*

"Hold the flashlight, will ya, Andy?" she says to me.

I was the hygienically approved Andy. And there was that smelling again. I was sniffing her.

"What are you doing?" she asks playfully.

"You smell good."

"Come on, Andy. The light."

"Your breath! It's so fresh!"

"That's Close-Up," she says.

"Close-Up toothpaste?"

"Why do you think they call it Close-Up? It's the toothpaste with real mouthwash to freshen your breath, and it gets your teeth as white as they can be."

The new fuse is in. The lights come on.

"Dark was fun too," I say with a smile.

Lee gives me a flirtatious smile, a perfect Close-Up smile.

Very early on in the shooting, the director came over. He looked at the clients, who were conferring with each other, and whispered to us, "That was great. We got it. But we're nowhere near overtime. So we're going to have to do versions that will never see the light of day."

When we wrapped, a happy client came over to me. "That was great," he said. He explained that Lee had Close-Up teeth. Then he added, "We think you do too."

That's all he said, and walked away.

It was only then that I realized each competing toothpaste company had their own idea of what their kind of dental work looked like. The concept was validated when I got a second Close-Up job. This time I was a passenger on an airplane who had just finished lunch. The stewardess—yes, that was the correct term in those days—comes up to me and says, "Are you anxious to see your fiancée?"

And I say, "After this flying delicatessen, she may give back the ring." At which point, I blow in my hand and smell my breath. "I better brush my teeth."

I know . . . but this was a job and a good one. So I did my best to create the reality of smelling my breath in the best sense of the actor's ethic. Blowing in your hand and smelling your breath doesn't work, by the way. Then, with a nod of gratitude to my teeth, I got another Close-Up job. A young, eager guy—no, that wasn't me—is trying on a nice suit. He says, "Boy, this new suit is gonna impress my girlfriend." The wise and more sophisticated friend (that was me) says, "Bob, put your money where your mouth is. Whiter teeth and fresh breath will win points with Shelly."

If I'd had a choice, I would have had Lee Crawford around. But I wasn't paying their bills. They got the best I could give them, and I eventually ended up with three well-paying network commercials.

I got to do a commercial with a western theme. I'm not sure if that was because of or in spite of *Lancer* or if *Lancer* had nothing to do with it, but I got to ride a horse. At the time, my only riding experience was the pony rides at Griffith Park in Los Angeles. They would strap me and Bob into saddles, slap the horses, and we would bump up and down for a trip around the ring. I confessed my inexperience, but the director said it didn't matter. "You look right," he told me, "and all we really need is two or three seconds that work. Then you just sit there, look good, and hold our Muriel cigar"—you couldn't smoke on camera—"while Susan sings seductively."

Susan was Susan Anton. Regrettably, I didn't actually work with her. Her scenes were shot separately. My scene partner was the horse. Susan ably and seductively sang, and I sat on my horse well enough to hide my rookie status.

The beverage guy made a comeback in a Schlitz beer commercial. It takes place in a nightclub. An "attractive couple" are enjoying an "attractive blues singer" and ecstatically enjoying a couple of beers. You couldn't drink beer on camera, so the focus was pouring and toasting (ecstatically). I found I had a talent I wasn't really aware of—beer pours. I had a steady hand and was able, under pressure, to get the exact right ratio of beer to foam. Well, at least the right ratio for Schlitz. God knows it was probably unacceptable for Coors or Bud. But then I was exclusive to Schlitz for the run of the commercial. So even though I was confident I could adapt to other ratios, I was ineligible.

My acting partner for Schlitz was an aspiring actress named Sherry Lansing. She knew how to flirt and was great fun, smart, very professional, and, most of all, patient with what was a long day's work. From time to time, I would bump into Sherry on the Paramount lot, where she had become CEO, or on the Fox lot, when she was president of production. She remembers, and I remember. And I think we both enjoy the irony in the journey.

—

After my first basketball season at Valley College, it just naturally followed that I would play baseball next. I loved baseball. I'd played organized baseball since I was nine years old. And for years before that, Bob and I would play catch on the driveway of our house on Peach Grove Street in Sherman Oaks. We always hoped Dad would get home early and join us. I'd played Little League, Babe Ruth League, and high school baseball. But now that I was in junior college, I didn't go out for the baseball team. I think I was a little burned out.

Well, that's the reason I gave myself.

Truth is, I was only six-one my senior year at Grant High. When I graduated, I was just seventeen and a half. Bob had grown early. I had grown late. I don't think my body had caught up to my baseball skills. That's a fancy way to say I wasn't a starter my senior year. At the same time, I was excelling in basketball. I was a starter and team captain. When I got to Valley, I was six-three and still growing and earned the position of starting forward on the basketball team.

For most of my baseball-playing days, I had been one of the best players on my team. Now I wasn't. I had lost confidence and didn't choose to fight through that adversity. I have spoken about regret. That is a big one for me, to this day. And no, it wasn't the injury.

Okay. I think I need to digress.

I was playing in a summer baseball league after I graduated from high school. I was at shortstop. My glove skills hadn't abandoned me. My dad was managing our team, and he put me in as a relief pitcher in the ninth inning. Things didn't go well, and I had a runner on third. I threw a wild pitch, and the ball went to the backstop. The catcher went after the ball. The runner went for home, and I raced in to cover the plate.

The catcher got to the ball and threw it to me at the exact moment the runner crossed home plate standing up and blocked my view. I was waiting for the throw with my glove about chest high. The catcher's throw had some heat on it, and the ball landed squarely in my crotch.

I went down and stayed down for some time. No, I wasn't wearing a cup. Ever the tough guy, I returned for the rest of the inning, which felt like a very, very long time. When I got home . . . how do I say it? Oh well, my left testicle was two and a half times normal size.

Now, this was a tremendously complicated problem. See, I had a date that night. Not just a date but an obsession. I had always put Sydney Epstein on an unreachable pedestal. I was too shy to do anything about it, but now my best friend, Doug Plowden, had fixed me up with her for a double date.

"Ice is your friend." That's what they tell you for an injury with swelling. But even with the significant discomfort it provided, the ice did nothing for me. I was doomed.

Bob and I shared a bedroom in our parents' house. He witnessed this drama. It was getting late in the afternoon when I came to the reality that I had to break the date.

"Bob, I don't know what to say. I'm embarrassed."

"I'll call her," my big brother said to me, as I'd hoped he would. I was listening intently, hoping to somehow glean Sydney's reaction when he called her. He told her that I'd gotten hurt playing baseball and I wouldn't be able to make it that night because "his left testicle is two and a half times normal size."

I mean, why the details?

Well, my big brother, Bob, had always been a big tease, and clearly, this was too good an opportunity to pass up. And no, I never did get to go out with Syd Epstein.

Let's see, where was I . . . ?

So, long story short, I didn't go out for the baseball team at Valley College and chose basketball instead. But it was time to look for a job. My dad had always said that if we were playing sports, he didn't expect us to also have a part-time job. No, he didn't mention that or say anything to me at the time. I just felt the responsibility. I know now he was hoping I would go back to baseball. After all, Bob was now on the USC baseball team. The skills had caught up to the six-feet-six-inch body.

———

Job hunting turned out to be pretty easy, and I had brother Bob to thank for that. There weren't many things I did in my life at that time that he didn't do first. In this case, he had worked part-time in a clothing store called Desmond's when he was at Valley College. After basketball season, he wanted to help out the family so he could move on to USC. Those were the footsteps I was walking in to help out so *I* could move on to USC.

I loved and admired my big brother—so why not?

He had done good work at Desmond's, and it turned out that was the only reference I needed. I was assigned to the boys' department and had a terrific boss. Isabel Lincoln was kind and patient as she showed me the ropes. She was like a grandmother to all of the staff.

The only selling experience I had was a lemonade stand with Bob, our Little League raffle tickets, and homemade candles and mistletoe at Christmastime. The selling part wasn't that easy. Mothers would come into Desmond's with their boys. Most times the boy didn't want to be there. Sometimes Dad did but Mom didn't. Sometimes neither of them did. And if Dad came along, he might not want to be there either. But if he did, he and Mom would disagree. The Catholic-school boys hated trying on trousers, their complaint being "Why can't I wear jeans, like my friends in public school?"

Some moms were openly flirtatious, which to this eighteen-year-old seemed kind of creepy and uncomfortable. I learned my best defense was to not notice and never make eye contact. Sometimes a whole family of boys came in . . . *very complicated*. Often that ended up in a big sale, which I always wrote up in Mrs. Lincoln's book because she was on commission.

When things were slow, I would "straighten the stock," refolding all the shirts that had been tried on and putting them back meticulously with the rest of the shirts in their correct sizes. When I finished, the piles were perfect, the edges and corners perfectly aligned. Then, invariably, a kid would run in and pull a shirt out from the bottom, destroying one of my perfect piles. If he was ahead of his mom, I might catch myself saying in a hushed voice, "Don't touch that!" If Mom was too close, I might suggest, "Let me get that for you."

I'm not sure I always hid my deep-seated resentment. But the truth is, I was there to sell this stuff, and for me to do that, the customers had to mess up my piles. Straightening the stock was part of a cycle, however unwelcome.

When the New Talent program ended, I went to see a friend I had made when I worked at Desmond's. His name was Doug Ruoff, and he managed a men's store in the same mall. Phelps Meager had high-end traditional clothing. At the time, some people referred to the style as Ivy League, but *traditional* was the correct term.

Back when I was at Desmond's, I'd had a discount on clothing and had spent far too much of my paycheck on suits and sport coats that were very much in the traditional style. I would often walk down to Phelps and visit. I couldn't afford their stuff, but I admired it.

I asked Doug if he needed part-time help. He said that at busy times, he absolutely did. He knew the clothes I already had would fit in at his store. I told him I could always make myself available unless I had an acting job. Doug said, "That's fine."

I worked for Doug during his busy times. Thanksgiving to Christmas was when I got in the most hours. I got a discount, which helped me develop an appetite for high-end clothing, and that wasn't necessarily a bad thing except that I was constantly paying off my house account. But I *could* be well dressed and look more successful than I was when I went to publicity events. Yes, Esme Chandlee was still volunteering her PR services. And on many commercials, they asked you to bring your own clothes.

A few times, a director I had worked with said that he told the client to use me on a new job because I had good clothes. I have a lot of memories of those days selling clothes, mostly my friendships with Doug and people I worked with. But my resentment of people messing up my piles, I'm afraid, never left me, being a bricklayer at heart.

I remember Tom Brokaw occasionally came in. Bryant Gumbel came in a lot. They both worked at NBC in Burbank in those days. Years later, when I got to know them, I told them, "I used to sell you clothes at Phelps Meager in the Sherman Oaks Fashion Square."

I was just kidding. Doug Ruoff always handled them. But they both got a big kick out of that. I remember, periodically, a guy came in and talked to Doug. He was repping a line of really nice ties. His name was Ralph Lauren. I told Ralph about that too.

Later, as time went on in my "decade of learning," my salesman days faded away. I wasn't working all the time, but I was slowly becoming a working actor. Not in the things I hoped to do, but enough to where I couldn't commit to the time when Doug needed me. We remained friends, and I am forever grateful to him.

Actors are often students of human behavior. They learn about their craft by observing other people. I learned a whole lot from all those people who messed up my piles.

CHAPTER SIX

Laying Bricks

Nothing in the world can take the place of persistence.

Talent will not; nothing is more common than unsuccessful men with talent.

Genius will not; unrewarded genius is almost a proverb.

Education will not; the world is full of educated derelicts.

Persistence and determination alone are omnipotent.

The slogan "Press On!" has solved and always will solve the problems of the human race.

O ur thirtieth president, Calvin Coolidge, said that.

Well, I was nothing if not persistent through what I now refer to as my "decade of learning." And I was discovering that actors never stop learning, and I loved that idea. But there was another aspect to my education: the business of acting.

The radio personality Fred Allen said, "You can take all the sincerity in Hollywood, place it in the navel of a flea, and still have room left over for three caraway seeds and the heart of an agent." Or, as Alfred Hitchcock put it, "It is no accident that an anagram for *actors* is *scrota*."

I was learning there was *the work* and then there was *the business*—and most importantly, *the business of getting jobs.* I was pretty good with the conversation part of an interview, even in those early days. Then the what-have-you-done question would invariably come up. With nothing of significance to show, I knew what came next: "Have you seen the pages?"

That meant I was about to do what we call a *cold reading*.

When you are reading for a part with two or three lines, it's kinda hard to apply all the theory and practice you got in acting class. To this day, I don't think I am very good at cold readings, and I definitely wasn't back then. The process I am describing was on the occasions when the people in the room were courteous. Many were not. You just did a reading and left.

After I spent some time being trapped in this frustrating cycle, something changed. I got to read for a scene that wasn't three lines but three pages. I thought I understood it and was eager to give it a try. From the moment I went into the room, I could tell there was a problem. The people clearly thought I wasn't right for the part. Or they had already decided they wanted someone else. I got what I would call a polite reading and was dismissed. I was even better in my car after I left. I got mad. I turned around, went back, and demanded a second chance.

And this time, I nailed it!

When I got home, the phone was already ringing. Sure enough, it was my agent. "Tom," he said, "I got a call from casting. They didn't like the reading . . . either one of them."

When tomorrow came, as it always does, I realized I had started to develop an appetite for failure. Cary Grant said, "You have to have the courage to make mistakes, the courage to be bad."

I think from that time on, I granted myself the right to fail. And the more I granted myself the right to fail, the more I risked. And the more I risked, the more I learned. And the more I learned, the more I was willing to deliver myself to the uncertainty of the future.

My dad had always shown respect for the choices I was making as a grown man. Okay, at least I was over twenty-one and could vote. But on occasion, during this post-Fox period, when he thought the time was right, he would suggest, "Maybe you might get your real estate license . . ." The unsaid half of that sentence was ". . . so you'll have something to fall back on."

That was reasonable, sound, and caring advice. And my dad was very good at suggesting. I never felt I was being told what to do. But to me at this time, with miles to go, it seemed like an admission of failure. Maybe I wasn't thinking right, but I know I was dreaming right.

The subject would come up from time to time. But honestly (and stubbornly), I never considered it.

This was the life I had chosen.

———

When I was still in the Fox New Talent program, my good friend Dennis Durney arranged for his mom, Dorothy Kingsley, to sit in on our activities for a while. Turned out she was doing research. Soon after *Myra*, Fox announced a new series called *Bracken's World*, a behind-the-scenes look at the fictitious Century Studios. John Bracken, the studio head, was played by Leslie Nielsen. The series also starred Elizabeth Allen, Peter Haskell, and Linda Harrison, and no, I didn't get to do a scene with Linda. If I had, believe me, I'd remember. I was thrilled to learn that I was to be a regular cast member. Well, I need to be honest about this. I was just part of what was called "the talent school ensemble." As it turned out, I was mostly a background artist, which sounds much better than just an elevated extra. Actually, I hardly ever had even one line. Only one comes to mind: "Are the keys still in the same place?"

I tried to put everything I'd learned into lines like that one, hoping I could be noticed and grow the part. This is just something we actors do, and I find that instinct to be a noble one. In this case, it was also a futile one. But that didn't stop me from trying. It kinda gets in your blood, that instinct. Actually, this might well have been a "who you know" part. But since I had hardly any of those connections, it wasn't going to happen a whole lot for me. I knew I would have to make my own way, and that was fine with me. I was grateful for the experience on *Bracken's World,* not to mention the paychecks for my eight episodes.

That's what you got from those small parts. Experience. A paycheck. And sometimes a lesson. Very early on, I got a small part in the ABC series *Judd, for the Defense.* I was to play a cop at a roadblock. In the script, that was the name of my character, Cop at Roadblock. But I secretly gave him a name, Bob. I was excited because my dialogue was with the series lead, Carl Betz. For those who don't remember, Carl played Donna Reed's husband on *The Donna Reed Show.*

Being one of the last names on the call sheet, I of course came in at the crack of dawn, something I'd grown to expect. I did notice that the call sheet had Carl Betz coming in after lunch. But that was okay with me. I would have the morning to work on my few lines. Then again, maybe I'd also have time to get nervous.

Right after lunch, I was called to the set. I was introduced to Mr. Betz. We shot what they called *the master,* the wide shot. Mr. Betz then did his close-up. Then the assistant director came over and told me they were going to shoot my close-up later.

At least I didn't screw up the scene.

At the end of the day, with the sun going down, I was called back to the set. Without explanation, a camera assistant taped an X on the matte box next to the camera lens.

The director said, "Let's do it."

"Where's Mr. Betz?" I asked.

"He's off the clock. Just look at the X on the matte box."

So the script person sitting nearby read the scene, and I tried to remember what Mr. Betz did in his close-up. You know something? She wasn't as good an actor as Carl Betz.

There was a lesson for me in all this, besides being reminded of my rung on the ladder. I don't mean to single out Carl Betz. He may have had a very good reason for going home that day. It's just the time and place that the practice landed on me.

Over time, I learned that this practice was pretty common in the film business. But it had a lasting effect on me. On those occasions when it did happen, I found myself saying, "If I ever have my own show, I'm not gonna do that."

On my good days, I would remember that promise.

My place should be standing beside the camera when my fellow actors do their close-ups. Any actor you are doing a scene with has the same hope and desire to be good that you do, whether the part is large or small. And I owe every one of them my respect.

———

I once saw a list of my credits somewhere. It had a bunch of shows that I have no recollection of. *Mannix, The Wide World of Mystery,* and *Marcus Welby, M.D.* were all on the list. I guess the parts or my work or both were not memorable enough for even me to remember—*and I was in them!*

Obviously, I didn't work with Robert Young on *Marcus Welby.* I would remember that. And I know I didn't work with Mike Connors on *Mannix* because, years later, we became friends, and I would have remembered. Great guy, by the way. One I do remember was working with George Kennedy on *Sarge.* He played a former marine who was now a priest. It was only one scene where I played a marine. I don't really remember the scene as much as I remember George Kennedy.

From the very first rehearsal, his character and his dialogue seemed effortless and so real. I don't mean to suggest he was "phoning it in." In fact, it was just the opposite. While he made it look easy, it's not.

Sal Dano talked many times about having a critic on your shoulder whispering those errant thoughts that can defeat you. A gifted Academy Award–winning actor, George had an approach to the work that simply commanded you to listen. If you are listening to George, you can't hear the critic on your shoulder, and he goes away. Sometimes the hardest thing for an actor to do is really listen. George Kennedy made it easy.

The lesson I was slowly learning was complicated but really pretty simple. You can go into a room filled with confidence and leave shattered. And you can go into a room nervous and uncertain and leave confident. It isn't the role of the people in the room to nurture your talent, though that wouldn't hurt. The people in the room, in many cases, are as insecure as you are. Often, though not always, they are looking for someone who gives them the confidence to make that leap of faith. Sometimes they know exactly what they want. Either you are it or you have to change their mind. There really are no rules, no absolutes. You either let the process make you crazy or remind yourself that this is the life you have chosen.

I'm not sure I ever got past this roadblock until I started to question the stock company in my head telling me what I *should* do and instead started focusing on what I *could* do. I needed to find a part of myself that could let me do it my own way—and that would be enough.

Sometimes I would literally say it out loud on the way to an interview. "You're enough, Tom." And you know what? It helped me. It honestly did. That critic on your shoulder is a formidable opponent. But if you say it loud enough and mean it, he can be swept away. You need to forget about him. And if you don't commit fully, he will crawl back up and whisper in your ear, "You're not good enough for *this*."

In the era I was "growing up" in, screen tests were fairly common. Most of the big studios carried creative production staffs on their payrolls. So there were elements of cameras, wardrobe, makeup, and crews on salary and available for what in those days was considered an essential studio expense. Much like the doomed Fox New Talent program, these departments would eventually run out their string. But that is another story, a story well above my pay grade.

So, where was I? Okay. Screen tests. They are hard. Actually, they are more than hard. When you did a screen test for a TV series, you had to negotiate and sign a seven-year deal before you even did the test, let alone got the part. Obviously, the studio wanted you at their price, not your price. Fair enough. But for an actor laying bricks, it's pretty much like building a whole new foundation.

It may be easy to blow off a bit part in an episode of *Judd, for the Defense.* There are many face-saving rationalizations you can bravely use, anything from "It's their loss" to "I don't really like that show, anyway." But if you've signed a long-term deal with a major studio, it's almost impossible to ignore the opportunity. And the idea of opportunity can very easily turn into enormous pressure.

I have mentioned that looking at yourself in the bathroom mirror and rehearsing your lines isn't exactly in the actor's handbook. All that amounts to is simply making faces at yourself and judging how you did by the faces you made. The actor's handbook reminds you that you have no idea at the time what the person on the other side of the scene is going to say or do. Actually, I don't really think there is an actor's handbook. But if there were one, it would no doubt maintain that the work is a collaboration and not a competition. You can't know what a given scene is about until you start working with your fellow actors. Be that as it may, the temptation to do what we call "bedroom lines" can prove irresistible and often fatal.

It was a fatality during my first screen test in those early days, with William Shatner for a network pilot. That much I remember. Now, I can usually recall almost everything about an opportunity so promising. But I can't even remember what this pilot was about. I am, however, cursed to remember the bad parts. The awful discomfort of what Curt used to call "actor's hysteria." The flop sweat. Not being able to remember my lines.

It was frustrating, and even in the middle of shooting the scene, I knew I was blowing my chance. The critic on my shoulder certainly agreed. I honestly can't remember anything except that feeling. And I'm not about to go into analysis to find out why I seem to have blocked it out. I'm pretty sure I had done my bedroom lines and was so overprepared that when Bill Shatner opened his mouth, I was stunned into confusion.

On reflection, I do remember the best part, the failure part. And that was the learning part. My scorecard would have a lot more of those failures, and it was best to make friends with them.

———

My second screen test was also daunting. A couple of years out of Fox, I read for a movie of the week/pilot called *The Movie Murderer*. It starred Arthur Kennedy, who'd won a Tony for Arthur Miller's *Death of a Salesman* and was a five-time Academy Award nominee, and Warren Oates, fresh from Sam Peckinpah's *The Wild Bunch*. It was to be directed by the gifted Boris Sagal.

It was a story about two insurance investigators after an arsonist who was destroying prints of movies. I read for the part of Kennedy's cocky young partner. I must have done a serviceable reading because I didn't do any better in the car on the way home. This was a pretty high-end project, and I didn't think I had much of a chance.

Every summer, the Selleck family would drive up to Lake Tahoe. My mom and dad; Bob; my younger sister, Marti; my little brother, Dan; and I would all cram into our parents' small condo in Tahoe City. The first morning after we arrived, just as the sun came up, my dad would wake us up with his famous "Up and at 'em!" Then he'd say, "The lake's smooth as glass. We'll eat later."

The family passion had become waterskiing. And my dad wanted to get on the water before the lake chopped up. Lake Tahoe is big and beautiful but also very deep . . . *and cold*. But we didn't mind. And, of course, the skiing became competitive.

Well, I was showing off, jumping the wake behind our boat, and I had a wreck. Long story short, I broke my foot.

I had missed the traditional "Mom, I'm starved after waterskiing" breakfast when I got back from the doctor. I returned a call from my agent: "They want you to do a screen test for *The Movie Murderer*."

"Oh . . . But I just broke my foot, and it's in a cast."

"You're kidding, right?"

"I wish I was."

My agent said he'd call them and explain.

"They want you to do the test anyway," he said when he called me back later.

"When?" I asked.

"Right away."

I didn't exactly think it through and said, "Okay."

Actually, there was nothing to think through. I had to get back to L.A. as soon as possible. Los Angeles was about an eight-hour drive from Tahoe City. Once on my way, I had plenty of time to think: that it was fortunate I'd broken my left foot so I could still drive; that it was unfortunate I didn't have the pages for the test scene (nobody had a fax in 1969); that I was fortunate to have a walking cast but unfortunate to have that distraction shooting the test. You get the idea. Eight hours gives you too much time to think, and you end up in the weeds.

After I negotiated the extremely hypothetical next seven years of my professional life, including all salary raises, I had only one evening to prepare for the test the next day. I am sure I overprepared like I had the last time, didn't go to bed until the early hours of the morning, and kept waking up thinking I'd overslept. I'm not really sure if I tested with Arthur Kennedy or a substitute. Most likely a substitute. I was thinking of other things. The scene I was doing was a very active one. I didn't get to sit behind a desk and talk. I had to pace around the room in a very agitated state. So I was mostly consumed with minimizing my limping. I didn't have any trouble with my lines. That was not my preoccupation. As in Sal Dano's class, I found it easy to remember my lines unless I was worried about remembering them.

The fact is, serendipity had stepped in. All the traps that the critic on my shoulder could set couldn't compete with the distraction of a broken foot. In that sense, the broken foot was a blessing.

I got the part.

The doctor at the small emergency room in Tahoe had said that the bone in my foot would take four to six weeks to heal. We were to start shooting in a week. The script called for Arthur Kennedy to walk with a cane. If his cocky young partner was hobbling around in a cast—well, you can see the problem. So I implied to the producers in the most artful way I could that the cast was only kind of a temporary thing.

The doctor I went to in West L.A. told me the same thing, that the foot needed to be immobilized for four to six weeks.

"And what if I take the cast off?"

"That would delay healing," the doctor said.

"Okay, take it off."

I explained my situation, and he was kind enough to give in. He said, "I'll write you a prescription for a shoe with a steel shank in it. Wear it when you can."

I told him I had dealt with sports injuries and could deal with the pain.

"I can write you a prescription to deal with the pain," he told me.

"I can't take pain pills and do my work. But again, thanks for understanding."

Once we started shooting, the foot was not a gift but at best a big distraction.

There's nothing quite like first days for an actor, at least this actor. I'd already had many of them, but never in a film with the responsibility to the whole story. That raised the stakes—and the nerves. Our director, Boris Sagal, knew actors, was very encouraging, and made sure I didn't have anything demanding out of the gate. Up till now, the first days had been mostly my only days. Boris had helped me through my screen test, and now he was helping me understand that I was in this for the whole deal, that every actor needs to settle into the character, and this role gave me the time.

I'd never had the responsibility of the arc of a character or that character's responsibility to the story. I think Boris knew what he was getting into when he cast me. If I was handled with kid gloves, I'm grateful.

Arthur Kennedy was everything I'd thought he would be. From the first moment he opened his mouth as the character, what came out was startlingly real. Like Miss West, like George Kennedy, like Bill Shatner—but in Arthur's own way. He was also very kind and supportive to me. I'm pretty sure he and Boris had conferred before they took a risk on the rookie.

Arthur and I would sit around between shots and talk when I could think of something to talk about. I was dying to ask him about being in *Lawrence of Arabia,* but I never did. I wasn't hesitant because I'd brought up W. C. Fields to Miss West. It was something else. If I wanted to be a peer, I didn't want him to feel like he was being interviewed by a fan. I respected him and desperately wanted his respect.

I wanted to ask George Kennedy about *Cool Hand Luke* or Bill Shatner about *Star Trek.* But I didn't. I didn't have a scene with Warren Oates in *The Movie Murderer.* But if I had, I'm sure I would have wanted to ask him about *The Wild Bunch.* To this day, I wish I'd asked. But the instinct not to was so strong, I'm comfortable living with that regret.

And my foot . . . it hurt. I had several walk-and-talks with Arthur, and no, I didn't limp. Actors learn very early on that, whatever is going on with you personally, you should "use it." In this case, I couldn't use it . . . so I didn't. But let me put it this way: When I had a scene sitting down, I was grateful.

As I settled in, I started looking forward to the next day's work. I was gaining confidence and comfort in the idea that any one scene wouldn't make or break my performance. If a scene didn't seem to go as well as I felt it should, I could do better on the next one. And then, all of a sudden, we were done.

I guess I did okay for a rookie. But they're never going to explain that in the credits. You are judged only by your work, and that's how it should be. The project was never going to succeed or fail on the performance of the "cocky young assistant." But if I'd known at the beginning what I knew at the end—I couldn't help saying to myself, "If only I could start over."

The Movie Murderer aired as a movie of the week on NBC on February 2, 1970. It didn't sell as a series, and my foot took three months to heal.

The Movie Murderer did give me a piece of film that I could show to the people who give you jobs and a lead role I could put on my résumé. I knew I shouldn't go back to doing one-day bit parts after this. So much of the acting business is perception, not necessarily reality. It's a small world, and there aren't any secrets about the work you've done. The question to be avoided was "Why would he do such a small part after doing a lead?" Even if the answer was "To make a living."

———

Sometime after my foot healed, I started dating Jacki Ray. I knew Jacki from high school. A better way to put it is I knew *of* her in high school. She went to North Hollywood High, the next-door neighbor to my Grant High. Jacki was already a successful model and, naturally, was talked about. I knew people from North Hollywood. They went to our parties, and we went to their parties. So I never met her, but I saw her a couple of times from a distance. She was very beautiful but also had a very steady boyfriend who, it turned out, would become her husband. Since we were both valley people, I guess I met her somewhere along the line, and I had also heard she had gotten a divorce. So when I bumped into her sitting on a blanket at Will Rogers State Beach, I said hello. Turned out she was also a very nice person, and we ended up talking for quite a while.

We dated for about a year and got married in May 1971. Sal Dano was in our wedding. Bob was my best man. Dan was also up there with us. Jacki's sister, Lynnie, and my sister, Marti, were up there too. And so was Kevin, Jacki's young son. He was three by now, and I had gladly become a part of his life, and Jacki and I both felt it was important that Kevin know I planned to stick around. I still feel that way.

Jacki and I came from such similar backgrounds, and we were the same age. We worked in similar fields. We didn't have to do any groundwork to understand it. Jacki was always supportive and encouraging, and I supported and encouraged her work.

To be completely honest, there are a lot of things I'd like to share about how important our years together were. But I won't. If you will allow me, I need to step out of the cumulative narrative for a bit. A lot has been written about our marriage, and almost none of it is true. Most all of the stuff about me is fabricated, and what's been written about Jacki is downright nasty. She never asked for any of that. And neither did Kevin. So for the people who make shit up, there is nothing here for you. I simply will not feed the machine. For the rest of you, and I know you are legion, I apologize. When I undertook this project, I made a commitment to share my private, personal emotions and feelings . . . *primarily about my work*. And I promise you, the real story of that work is here for the reader, along with the real truth of my emotional journey. Just please know that my journey with Jacki was and remains treasured.

———

Casting, like acting, involves risk. And the people who give the jobs feel much more confident in doing so if you are perceived to be successful and on the rise. Opportunities like pilots don't come along every day. What's left? Feature films and guesting on television.

The feature-film world seemed to operate on a different plain. There was a stratum, an attitude, and, indeed, a structure to the film business in those days. Dare I call it snobbishness? Yes, I will.

There were film actors, and then there were TV actors. That's kinda silly, since the craft's the same. And God forbid you were classified as a male model. That was really a problem. But at this moment in time, that definitely wasn't *my* problem.

My situation put me in the category of a TV actor. So I needed to continue laying bricks by landing guest-starring roles on television. But I was finding out there was some resistance to my getting them. Often my agent would submit me, but I'd be turned down even for an interview. "You'll conflict with the lead" was frequently the official reason that my agent quoted, which translated to "We're just not interested" or "He's too strong and conflicts with our lead." Whatever the reason, I just wasn't getting much of a chance to do what I now felt qualified to do. An exception was ABC's *Owen Marshall, Counselor at Law.* That show starred Arthur Hill and Lee Majors. I read for and got the part of a prosecuting attorney opposite a defense lawyer played by Majors.

The best thing about this opportunity was the plan to bring my character back as an adversary to Lee's. I had learned from some of the scenes I'd done in Sal's class that "attorney dialogue" required a special kind of homework. After all, you weren't the one being asked questions. You were asking them. But I digress. Lee was great and a good guy. And the work was going well. Then our argument was interrupted by the judge: "Will the attorneys approach the bench?"

Lee and I moved toward the bench for what was going to be a waist-up two-shot. After the rehearsal, the director motioned for Lee to come over. I, of course, thought I'd made a mistake. As it turned out, it wasn't about that. Every movie company carries in its inventory what we call an apple box: a sturdy wooden box in the shape of a rectangular apple crate. They also have half-apples and quarter-apples. They are used to support lighting and cameras and such. Apple boxes do have one other use: When the scene was lit and ready, someone brought an apple box, a full apple box, for Lee to stand on so that he and I were the same height.

Lee Majors, I should point out, is not short. It's just that I'm very tall. Lee was good about it. But I could see the writing on the wall. The lead in this series wasn't going to stand on an apple box every time we worked together. No, the part did not recur. Nor should it have. The work on a TV series is demanding enough, and the series lead shouldn't have to mutter to himself, "Oh, the tall guy's working today." I like to think if I had his job, I wouldn't want to be dealing with stuff like that either.

Whatever the reasons, I continued to have trouble guesting on TV shows.

Finally, I landed a lead role in a feature film. It was going to be shot exclusively in the Philippines for United Artists. To be honest, it wasn't really a home run. It was more like a single. Actually, it was more like a sacrifice fly. For those of you who don't have it in your film libraries, the movie was, of course, *Daughters of Satan*.

———

I found out that United Artists had a lot of Philippine pesos left over from another film. They didn't want to take a bath exchanging all those pesos for dollars, so they came up with the idea of spending them in the Philippines on two low-budget films to be shot back-to-back.

Daughters of Satan would be the second film after *Superbeast*. ("Half-man, half-monster, ripping helpless victims to shreds.") I know . . . but that noble instinct we actors have to rise above the material was very much in play here. I fully hoped to come away with a piece of film I could use to get material that was above my current pay grade. So, in March 1972, I flew to the Philippines to star in my first feature film. It would be directed by Hollingsworth Morse. Holly was a terrific guy and had directed episodes of *Lassie, H. R. Pufnstuf,* and the much-acclaimed *Julia,* with Diahann Carroll. I'm sure Holly felt the same way about rising above the material.

My character, James Robinson, is a loving husband to his beautiful wife, Christina, played by Barra Grant. In a shop, he sees a painting of a witch being burned at the stake and is stunned by the resemblance to Christina. He brings the painting home, and for the rest of the movie, his wife keeps trying to kill him. Obviously, James Robinson is not very bright. But he loves his wife deeply, and she finally succeeds in killing him by stabbing him in the back during a passionate embrace. I hope I didn't ruin it for you. While I had no experience in playing death scenes, I'm sure you could see my magic shining through.

Barra was a very good sport and an able scene partner. She was a trained actress and also a writer, and I think she carried the same hope we all had, that our work would rise above the material. In fact, I know she did. These kinds of R-rated movies were often built for drive-in theaters and a quick release. And the audience had come to expect a certain amount of nudity. Nothing enlightened enough to include both genders, for which at the time I was grateful. And *Daughters of Satan* delivered in a kind of minimalist way. At least in that regard.

Jacki came over at the end of filming, and we spent my salary on a wonderful trip to Hong Kong and Taipei, Taiwan, on the way home. Union rules, we flew first class.

When the movie opened, I was surprised to find it was playing at a theater on Hollywood Boulevard. No, not one of the big, exclusive first-run houses. But still. Sure enough, it was a double bill with *Superbeast.* I went with my dear friend Doug Plowden to watch it for the first time. Doug was my best friend from Van Nuys Junior High to Grant High School to Valley College through USC and the Sigma Chi fraternity.

This was my first time sitting with an audience and watching a film I was in. We sneaked in and sat at the back of the theater. Which actually didn't matter, because there was very little audience. But I was excited, and Doug was politely curious. When the movie ended after my shocking death scene, we went out to dinner.

Doug had a terrific sense of humor. His mom, Peggy, was an animator at Disney. Maybe that's where it came from.

"That was awful," he said.

I agreed. Plus, you can't kid a kidder, and Doug was a champion kidder. "I have a serious question," he said. "Why did the movie have an odd number of breasts?"

"I . . . never counted."

"I'm not speaking of a number of odd breasts. I'm speaking of an odd number of breasts. They do come in pairs."

"Well . . . maybe one of the witches got her blouse ripped open while she was being tortured and only one popped out."

Look, we had a lot of laughs that night, as we always did in each other's company. And somehow, I accidentally forgot to add *Daughters of Satan* to my résumé. But the work is never wasted. As in *The Movie Murderer,* I had the experience of being responsible to the character and to the story, not to mention the challenges of shooting out of sequence with no continuity.

———

Head east from Beverly Hills on Wilshire Boulevard. Make a right on Robertson, leaving Beverly Hills and heading toward the Santa Monica Freeway. A few miles down, you will see a Winchell's Donut House on your left and a little hardware store on your right. This isn't the high-rent district, so it's pretty easy to park on the street.

Just left of the hardware is a door. On the door is one word.

DANO.

Go in. Go up a steep, narrow flight of stairs to a landing. Another left, a few more stairs, and another door. Inside, in a converted bedroom, was where you'd find me at least two nights a week. At the far end of that small room was a blacked-out window and a tiny bathroom behind the door on the right. This was our stage, and the stage entrance was from inside the tiny bathroom.

At the other end of the room, there were three rows of folding chairs. The last was elevated so you could see the stage. And in the small space to the left was Sal Dano's director's chair. This cramped little room would be my acting home for most of the decade after Fox. It was cold in the winter and hot and stuffy in the summer, so we usually put on the little window air conditioner when we went downstairs to Winchell's for a break.

My dear friend from Fox, Linda Peck, was a mainstay and, I think, the most gifted member of this acting class. She was my favorite scene partner and, honestly, still is. She was also now Linda Dano. What could have been an obligation to a friend had turned out to be a gift. A gift of clarity to my new chosen craft. And whether he was sitting in his chair or sitting in front of the class giving his critiques, Sal Dano was the gift. He was bright, funny, irreverent, articulate, intuitive, and unconventional. And for a bricklayer like me, he demystified what it took to do good work.

Most of the people in our class were fairly new and inexperienced. Some were completely new. Sal was new in town, and he wasn't one of the big names in the acting-class business. But, boy, was he good! From the first critiques, he gave his new students some simple tools to hold on to. He gave them two words, *FIMP* and *VIPE*. The character's FIMP was the financial, intellectual, moral, and physical attributes. Your VIPE was basically your own instrument: vocal, intellectual, physical, and emotional. Put the two together, and it helped you see the similarities and differences between you and the character you were playing. This was hardly a magic bullet, but it was a good start on the endless journey of learning the craft.

Being an actor himself, Sal was opinionated, didn't suffer fools, and was impatient with skeptics. He was not above saying, "You know what? Why don't you just get out of here?" That was never his finest hour. Sal and I were close friends by then, and I had long ago made peace with this "switch" that he had.

We were a tight-knit band. After a class that could go on for four hours or more, we were all wound up. A lot of us went to the nearby Norm's coffee shop for a snack, and then it was on to Sal and Linda's apartment to play Yahtzee, often until dawn. God, those days were fun!

—

In the future, capital punishment will be outlawed. People convicted of murder will be sentenced to spend their life on an escape-proof island. For Dr. Norman Milford, the mercy killer, his sentence is unjustified.

Tortured by the right or wrong of his acts, he is now hooked on wild mimosa as a substitute for cocaine.

That was the premise and a description of the role I was to play in the movie *Terminal Island*. I know . . . but hey, somebody gives you a donut, you can either see the donut or see the hole. *Terminal Island* was directed by Stephanie Rothman, a product of the prestigious USC film school. It was produced by her husband, Charles Swartz, for Dimension Pictures. They had put together a pretty impressive cast, including an actor named Roger E. Mosley. The whole cast was part of a stratum that I had not attained. They were considered "working actors." But at this moment in time, clearly, they were not working, and neither was I.

In the spirit of full disclosure and to honor my friend Doug, *Terminal Island* had an even number of breasts. I'm pretty sure there were six. No, nothing as ambitious as six pairs. To be honest, by that distinction, there were only three.

Terminal Island came out on June 22, 1973. The poster for the movie stated, "Welcome to Terminal Island, Baby! Where we dump our human garbage!" Enough said. Somehow, this one didn't make the cut for my résumé either.

Terminal Island did provide a memory that to this day is crystal clear. After we finished shooting, I was called in to loop during the post-production period. Looping is simply lip-synching any of your lines that had technical problems, maybe due to an airplane noise or somebody's dog barking in the background, things like that. When I arrived at the looping stage, I was pleased to see Stephanie would be there for the session. Not all directors attended looping sessions. I could tell Stephanie was committed to making the best possible movie, as was I. After saying hello, she immediately gestured that we should move to a spot away from the other people there. She quietly said, "Tom, you're going to have to revoice your entire performance."

That was a tall order, but I said, "Sure. Okay. What happened to the sound?"

She hesitated a moment. It was clear that what she had to say was very difficult for her. Then she said to me, "You're a very nice man, but honestly . . ."

She told me if I didn't change my voice, I was never going to succeed in this business.

She said it with care and concern. Regardless of that, what she said landed pretty hard. The post-sound people were all waiting, thank goodness out of earshot. I put on my game face, and we went to work. All I remember about that long day was that I tried to lower my vocal register a little.

I wasn't about to try and change my voice. I knew quite a bit about acting by then, and I could tell when an actor had a "trained" voice. To me, it seemed like those actors were listening to themselves when they were supposed to be listening to the person they were talking to; that finding each character's "voice" was so much more about who he was, not how he sounded.

Watching TV, Sal and I would have a laugh sometimes at two actors engaging in what he called "the battle of the baritones," each actor going lower in response to the other actor's last line. I know Stephanie wasn't trying to mess with me and meant well. I put her suggestion out of my head and at least tried to move on.

To this day, I can remember the times when I made an error that cost our team a big game. As an athlete, I understood that feeling. But for me as an actor, that lesson would be long in coming.

Many times in interviews over the years, I have joked that when I was twenty-five, I looked thirty-five and sounded fifteen. There was a modicum of truth to that, but where did the voice thing come from? Nowadays, people pay me to do voice-overs, and I'm very proud of the work I do. But when I get in the booth and put on the headset, the critic on my shoulder is still always there. He's saying, "Tom, you're not good enough for this." I have to knock him off. Sometimes figuratively and on many occasions literally. Then I can go to work.

Apologies to Stephanie, because it really isn't her fault. It's just that we actors are a funny lot, and you never know what will stick.

———

I got a one-day gig on the daytime soap opera *The Young and the Restless* in 1974. My agent told me they'd mentioned that the part could recur. By now, I was way past just hopping off the turnip truck, and I knew that the one scene I had was, in effect, an audition. The show had a good producer, John Conboy. I'm sure John wanted to see if I could hold up under the pressure of the real thing.

Very smart.

When I got the pages, I was eager to prepare. I already knew I was supposed to be an old flame of the character played by Jaime Lyn Bauer. Jaime Lyn, a regular, had already generated considerable heat since she'd come on the show. The problem was the scene had no heat. And no matter how I tried to find its core, there was none. What should have been a flirtation scene was all about the exposition, basically telling each other over lunch stuff we both already knew. How we met. What I did for a living. Who I was married to. Stuff like that.

Before this, I had never gone to Sal for help on the things I was doing. For the first time, I did.

Sal read the scene once and immediately said, "You're absolutely right. There is nothing going on here. There is no subtext."

"Thank you, Sal," I said with some relief.

"Tell you what," he said without hesitation. "Play it like you have a secret."

Sal went on to say it didn't matter what the secret was or even that I knew what it was; I should know she'd want to know what it was. "But you're not going to tell her just yet."

What my bright, intuitive friend had done was to give me a subtext. He had given me something to hold on to besides my lines.

So guess what? They asked me back.

My character, Jed Andrews, would appear maybe once a week, and each and every flirtation scene had the same problem as the first one. But I, of course, *had a secret.* The part grew a little, and they brought in my wife, Betty, who was written kinda like a doormat. Of course, Jaime Lyn's character was in charge, a common theme in daytime. I was still having some trouble playing people I didn't like. But I was starting to realize that making those kinds of personal judgments should never be part of the work—and that the characters' flaws were the things that made them interesting.

My success on the show was, well, fortifying. It also provided me with a dilemma. I was offered a regular job playing Jed Andrews. The deal was, I think, for three years.

It would be my first regular job since Fox and would guarantee me an income. No small thing. When the rent comes due, it's due whether you've been working or not. Now I had a wife and son to provide for, not just myself. And there was the satisfaction of growing a character as well as the validation of being asked to stay and be part of an ensemble. When someone is willing to pay you to keep doing what you're doing, that affirmation of your work is hard to say no to.

I said no.

I told them I was flattered by their offer, but I really wanted to stay an independent contractor. I was getting opportunities that I wasn't prepared to lose, and the fact that the business had a kind of unwritten system that put actors into categories played a significant role. Jacki was always supportive when I felt I had to say no, just as I supported her decisions when she felt she had to turn down a job. Sure, we could always use the money, but we respected each other's career choices.

As stupid as it sounds, daytime actors found difficulties being considered for nighttime roles, just as "television actors" found difficulties being considered for film, especially for leading roles. Many actors in daytime television, at the end of their contracts, felt trapped in the medium where they had achieved success. Yes, it was and is ridiculous and absolutely unfair. That rule wasn't written anywhere, but that didn't mean it wasn't a rule. And if you were looking for fairness in this business, you were in the wrong line of work. I didn't consult my dad on the decisions I was making in my chosen field. You kinda had to be in it to understand it. But I know for certain that if I had, he would have reminded me that the opportunity lay in the risk.

I wasn't naive enough to think that once I said no, everything would stay the same as it was before. For the *Y&R* people, to put it bluntly, the guy playing Jed Andrews needed to shit or get off the pot. They had to have a plan for where the show was going. Without a contract, I could go off on another job if it came along. If I'd been in their shoes, I would have had the same concerns, and they were right. I knew that without a commitment, my success in growing my character would be its undoing. Jed Andrews soon disappeared from *The Young and the Restless*.

———

A real opportunity came along while I was doing *The Young and the Restless*. I was cast for an episode of *Lucas Tanner*.

The series starred David Hartman as an ex–baseball player now teaching English in a high school. I was to play a washed-up baseball player who had blown his chance at the big leagues by drinking too much. It was only one scene, but it was with David, a fine actor. And the scene was very well written, with a strong emotional arc and a touching subtext.

When the people who give you jobs want to see a "piece of film," they're not going to sit for two hours of your stuff, looking for a magic moment. This scene was a potentially perfect piece of film. But first I had to deliver. I felt I understood the scene. This time, saying to myself "You're enough" only validated that I was.

The scene was about Lucas counseling a student on whether to sign a big-league contract or go to college first. David's character invites my character to a coffee shop to talk with the kid about his choices. The real reason was to be an example of what not to do, but my character played along anyway, for the kid's sake. After we shot the scene, I felt that I'd delivered. I'm not sure I even acted the scene out in my car on the way home. Maybe a first for me, and I loved that feeling.

The show's casting director, Dorothea Petrie, was on the set watching the scene and introduced herself afterward. Dorothea's husband was Dan Petrie, the director of my friend Sam's breakout movie, *Lifeguard*. Before I knew it, I was reading in Dan Petrie's office for the pilot movie *Returning Home*.

Returning Home was a remake of the classic 1946 movie *The Best Years of Our Lives,* which starred Fredric March, Dana Andrews, and Harold Russell. It earned seven Academy Awards, including Best Picture, Best Director (William Wyler), Best Actor (March), and Best Supporting Actor (Russell). Harold Russell had lost both arms in World War II and also won a special Oscar.

The new film was a pet project of Lorimar Productions head Lee Rich and carried with it a lot of prestige. *Returning Home* starred Dabney Coleman playing the Fredric March part. The Harold Russell part went to James R. Miller, a Vietnam vet who'd lost his arms in the war. The Dana Andrews part was to be played by me.

The Best Years of Our Lives is a favorite for a whole lot of people, including me. I'm not really sure it is ever a good idea to revisit such a classic, but I wasn't thinking of such things in those days, nor should I have been. The movie was sincerely meant as an homage, in no way a rip-off.

Dan Petrie was an enormous help to me during the shooting. He knew actors and how to get them through their inevitable rough spots. I felt that I pulled my weight, as did the rest of the cast. Dabney and I became good friends from that job. I even got some nice reviews. I wasn't exactly sure how long you could "return home." Nevertheless, I was all in.

Returning Home aired April 29, 1975, on ABC. It did not sell as a series.

CHAPTER SEVEN

Nothing's Certain Till It's Certain

L ater in 1975, Quinn Martin Productions announced plans for a new pilot. It seemed like, at any given time in the early 1970s, QM had two or three shows filling the TV airwaves. They had used me in smaller roles on *The FBI* and on *The Streets of San Francisco,* starring Karl Malden and Michael Douglas. They knew who I was. I think that *Streets* episode was also Michael's directing debut. Michael really helped me out in my role as a surveillance technician. I welcomed his encouragement to bring some color to the role and not worry about adding a little humor.

The pilot of *Most Wanted* starred Robert Stack, cherished by the company ever since the phenomenal success of *The Untouchables.* The pilot would also star my friend Shelly Novack. I was offered the part of a computer technician. In truth, the character was a fourth or fifth banana.

When my agent called with the offer, he took full credit (as agents are prone to do) for submitting me. I wasn't sure whether that was the case or QM had thought of me because the role was in the same ballpark as the one I'd played in *The Streets of San Francisco.* But with my previous starring roles in two pilots each airing only once, chances were QM was not even aware of them.

In hindsight, I'm not really sure why I said yes. Sure, I thought I could excel and grow the part. But it was much more likely that my philosophy of having an appetite for failure was under assault and wearing down. I was probably driven by the need to pay the rent, which had turned into a mortgage. Jacki and I were now living on the Westside in a duplex we had invested in with my good friend from the Fox days, Dennis Durney. Dennis lived in the adjoining unit.

While the part was not too challenging, it wasn't in my nature not to commit fully. It was, after all, a real opportunity.

I think it was Dennis who said to me, "Congratulations! *Most Wanted* sold!"

"How do you know?"

"Well, it's in *The Hollywood Reporter.*"

I had been around enough by then not to jump up and down until I got my official notice. I called my agent, who was out of town, as he was too often. He liked three-day weekends. I knew his secretary well, so I asked if she could call and make sure. She called back and passed on the message: "Yes, it sold, and we're very happy for Tom."

I was thrilled by the news, and honestly, all my doubts just disappeared. Jacki was excited and gave me a big hug when I told her. I called my mom and dad, who were thrilled, and I shared the good news with Bob, Marti, and Dan. There followed a couple of celebration dinners where I proudly picked up a tab I couldn't afford, but why not?

A couple of days later, I got a message to call John Wilder. John had written the pilot and was a producer on the show. I called John back and said something like "Congratulations, John. When do we start?"

John said, "Tom, you understand I've got nothing to do with the series, but I felt I had to call you. Nobody wants to tell you, but . . . they're writing you out of the series. I'm sorry, but somebody had to tell you."

John was a good, decent guy and didn't have to make that call. I understood the spot he had put himself in and said something like "I understand, John. Thanks for letting me know."

John tried to put it in a better light and told me at least I wasn't being replaced. The official reason was that there was no room to write for the character every week.

Things got very lonely after that. There was no self-protective "it's their loss." There was a whole lot of "if I were really good, they couldn't have done without me." I was mad at myself for celebrating without the certainty of really knowing I had the part, and honestly, I was pretty embarrassed. Everyone would know. My family. My friends. Certainly, my fellow cast members would know. I couldn't imagine what I would say to my friend Shelly next time we played volleyball at Will Rogers State Beach.

Considering the size of the part, I don't know why this failure landed harder than the others, but it did. Some friends who understood the business tried to help by saying that a mature Robert Stack didn't want competition from someone like me. I don't believe that to this day. And if that had been a factor, Bob wouldn't have had anything to do with it. Bob and I would bump into each other from time to time, and there was no tension on either of our parts. Bob was a world-class skeet shooter. We shot together many times. To me, he was wonderful company, a fine actor, and a great guy.

I fired my agent. No names, but I'm not really sure that wasn't just a face-saving remedy. I guess nothing's certain till it's certain.

I don't know why I let the sense of loss affect my confidence. I should have done what I had done so many times before, just move on. Maybe this was a test. I guess I had never really been fired before. Honestly, it took me too much time to shake out the self-pity and man up to the fact that this was the life I had chosen.

———

With the memory of *Most Wanted* sticking like glue, I went with a new agent. The Jack Fields Agency was definitely a step up. I would describe it as smaller than the big-time agencies but still part of the big time. I had to push myself to get back in the game, and signing there gave me the comfort of knowing that a couple of years ago, there was no way I'd ever even get in the door. I was handled by Mary Oreck, a terrific agent and a very nice person. Immediately, I started to go on a better class of interview. I'm not sure what that means, but I sure felt that was the case.

In early 1977, I got a screen test for a pilot called *Bunco*. It was about two cops who busted con artists. One of the cops had already been cast. Basically, *Bunco* was a buddy-cop show. I don't want to trivialize the show. It put to bed a lot of stuff for me, and I welcomed the opportunity, especially to work with the actor they had already cast. Robert Urich had just come off Aaron Spelling's series *S.W.A.T.*

My screen test offered something new for my screen-test logbook. Both of the actors testing were set to test with Bob on the same day, not unusual. The awkward part was that they would test at the same time. That seemed kind of uncivil, but I guess Lorimar Productions didn't really care about civil. It would save a lot of money not to light the scene twice. I guess I could have refused, but *come on*!

What made it worse was that I knew the other actor testing for the role. John Bennett Perry was a terrific actor, and I would see John on most of the interviews I went on. Whether for commercials or acting jobs, we were frequently up for the same parts. This time, one of us would shoot part of a scene in that lighting setup. Then he would be excused, and the other actor would come in. The only consistent thing was Bob. He was there for both actors. It was, after all, his future too.

I gotta tell you: A screen test is hard enough without this kind of awkward, stupid complication. But stupid is as stupid does. Sorry, I digress.

I found a quiet moment to talk to John. "John, I'm sorry about all this." I mean, I wasn't responsible for it, but *still*.

"Nothing to be sorry about," John said. "If I don't get this, I'd rather have a friend get it than some idiot I don't know."

"Back at you, John."

I got the part. But knowing John's work and, in this case, having seen some of it, I knew he could have been just as good. *I* had come so close so many times, it reminded me of the feeling of just being kind of part of the debris when you didn't get the part. And the bigger the opportunity, the bigger the disappointment.

First days are always hard, but Bob made this one a lot easier. In spite of the awkwardness of my screen test, he and I had already developed a working relationship. For the first time, I was able to just enjoy the work, the process, instead of worrying how somebody thought I was doing. I owe that to Bob. He was a much more seasoned actor than I was but never saw the work as a competition. He couldn't have been more giving, more collaborative, more supportive.

We were directed by Alexander Singer. Alex knew his stuff and wasn't at all as grand as his name implied. He had a great sense of humor. I remember the times Bob and I really nailed a scene and Alex said excitedly, "Bob, Tom, that was almost adequate." That was Alex's highest compliment, and Bob and I kept shooting for that ultimate praise.

There was absolutely no reason why *Bunco* shouldn't sell. But it didn't. I was told that the network's programming guru, Fred Silverman, said that the two of us together couldn't carry a series. Well, I sure felt I had a long-running series in me. And Bob Urich may have done more successful TV series than anybody I'm aware of. We both had a laugh about Mr. Silverman. Bob had already become my good friend, even before we finished shooting. Bob and his wife, Heather, and Jacki and I developed a lasting friendship. Bob left us much too soon. I miss him.

Soon after *Bunco,* Mary left the Jack Fields Agency and helped form McCartt, Oreck & Barrett. Mary brought along some of her clients, including a very satisfied customer. Me.

I already knew Bettye McCartt. She and Mary were good friends, and I would see Bettye from time to time when the two were together. Fact is, Bettye and I went way further back than that—all the way to Fox days and those after-hours group get-togethers. Bettye knew the business well, having worked with producer Al Ruddy on *The Godfather* and *The Longest Yard*. She was smart and a lot of fun, so I always enjoyed her company. In the years after the talent program ended, the core of this group stayed in touch, which wasn't hard. Sam lived a couple of blocks away from our duplex in Brentwood Glen. Esme was doing publicity work for both Sam and me, along with John Cassavetes and his wife, Gena Rowlands. And Bettye McCartt was in that mix too.

At the new agency, Bettye quickly became my main contact. I'm not sure how that happened, but I was happy about it as long as it didn't cause any friction between Mary and Bettye. If there was, I never saw it. Mary had a lot of successful clients, and it wasn't like it would stop our collaboration. But my history with Bettye meant that I was hardly starting from scratch. Bettye also represented a lot of writers, and I thought that was a real positive. I was very excited about this new arrangement, again with a nod to serendipity.

If there was a clock on the business of me getting work, it was speeding up. In late 1977, Bettye called to tell me that Universal wanted to sign me to a series-development deal. I may have said something stupid, like "Why?"

"My guess would be that they saw some of your other pilots, Tommy."

Nobody had called me that since my mom, when I was a kid, except maybe Cindy Ferrare and a couple of basketball and baseball coaches. I think that was the first time Bettye called me that. But it wouldn't be the last. She didn't always call me Tommy, but when she did, it was welcome. My new agent and I were fast developing a lasting friendship.

Bettye said, "I wouldn't recommend the deal, except the guy writing the pilot I know is someone who can and should write for you. His name is Steve Cannell."

"I know who he is. He created *The Rockford Files*."

"That's right."

"I love *The Rockford Files*."

"I know you do."

From that moment on, I was in. Bettye told me the deal was for two pilots. If the first one didn't sell, they would do a second one. She said there was still a lot to negotiate and that, most importantly, she wanted to get my quote up (my price). When I went to meet Steve, I met some of the *Rockford* team—David Chase, Meta Rosenberg, and Charles Johnson. I kept hoping James Garner would walk in, but he didn't.

The first script Steve Cannell ever sold was for Robert Wagner's *It Takes a Thief.* He had written for *Ironside, Columbo,* and *Baa Baa Black Sheep.* He was a Pasadena native who had passed up the family business, Cannell & Chaffin furniture, to be a writer. As we talked, I felt a certain kinship, having also passed up my family business. There was nothing not to like about Steve. He was just a regular guy like me, except he could write. Boy, could he write! And he was fast. Before I knew it, I was reading a script called *Gypsy Warriors.*

If you saw one of those condensed descriptions in *TV Guide,* it would probably call *Gypsy Warriors* "a behind-the-lines World War II buddy story." But in Steve Cannell's hands, with his talent for good stories and interesting characters, it was a different animal altogether. Each character had a unique set of quirks and flaws. I loved Steve's script and was excited to be working with James Whitmore Jr., who had just come off the success of *Baa Baa Black Sheep.* I knew his work from that show. And it was plain to see that his dad, the legendary James Whitmore, had passed on his talent. In this case, the acting gene did not skip a generation.

Our director was Lou Antonio. I was a genuine fan of Lou's work as an actor; he was really good. It turned out he was also a really good director. He wasn't afraid of humor, and I'm certain that came with Steve's blessing. But if we let it get cute, he would put us back on track.

We shot *Gypsy Warriors* up in Northern California. Louie made the work fun, I loved working with Jimmy, and I didn't even obsess about the day's work in the cast van on the way back to the hotel each night. Evidently, Universal loved the show. When CBS penciled us in on the

1977–78 network schedule, the studio ordered three scripts they wanted to be ready when the official commitment came. I know Jimmy and I talked at that point. Jimmy said something like "Looking good, my friend."

I didn't think I should jump on the celebration train just yet. I probably went halfway there with a "So far, so good, Jimmy." Truth was, Steve Cannell had never written a pilot that didn't sell, so why worry?

Well . . . when the network announced the fall schedule, *Gypsy Warriors* was nowhere to be found.

I guess my reaction was *"Oh-kay . . ."*

Actually, it wasn't okay. And Steve's reaction wasn't at all that of a shrinking violet. Almost immediately, Jimmy and I found ourselves in Steve's office. When he told us how sorry he was that the pilot didn't sell, it was pretty clear that he took the rejection personally. Then, with the bit in his teeth, he offered something like "Here's where I think we should go with the second one."

Until that moment, neither of us had known we still figured in his plans. I might have sneaked a sideways look to Jimmy. "So here's my idea," Steve said. The first thing he did was put three ball bearings in his hand and start to pace back and forth like Humphrey Bogart in *The Caine Mutiny*. (Another quick glance between Jimmy and me.) Maybe he was having us on, but whatever it takes. Either way, no one, let alone a Steve Cannell, had ever actually pitched an idea to me before. I was enthralled.

The *TV Guide* description of *Boston and Kilbride* would have been "a buddy show about a couple of freewheeling private eyes in L.A." In an in-your-face gesture to CBS, Steve hired Lou Antonio to direct. I was beginning to understand what made Steve tick. I don't believe I was reading too much into it to think it was important to him that we all knew the first failure was not ours but his. I was touched by that. He had taken it on his shoulders, which wasn't necessary, but I guess he felt it was. What a good man!

Steve even gave our characters our own first names, Tom Boston and Jim Kilbride, which he believed was important in a series (he had done it with Jim Rockford). Two things I think might have come from CBS: We shot some of it in Hawaii; my guess was that Jack Lord's *Hawaii Five-0* was winding down. Also, Jaime Lyn Bauer was cast. My guess: The network was trying to take advantage of our successful coupling in *The Young and the Restless.*

I didn't have a problem with either choice. Going to Hawaii was clearly not an issue. And I enjoyed working with Jaime Lyn, one more positive in the uncertainty of a venture like this. Casting was above my pay grade, anyway.

Louie again made sure the work was fun, which it needed to be. Jimmy and I became fast friends, and Steve loved the work that we were doing.

CBS said no to *Boston and Kilbride.* I don't know, maybe we had too much fun. But the fun we had translated to the screen, and isn't that the point of the work? My opportunity to work with Steve was gone. My chance at Universal was over, and my commitment had ended. But, boy, what a ride we had!

———

Success, whatever that was going to be, wasn't exactly coming quickly; on my good days, I tried to be philosophical about it. Not that I didn't have small successes. I could show the people who give you the jobs my leading roles in six pilots. But since none of them got picked up, they eventually ran as TV movies in dead zones on the schedule, all but guaranteeing that nobody saw them. And on my last one, *Boston and Kilbride,* they even changed the title to *The Chinese Typewriter.* Also, it wasn't always such a good idea to be mentioning pilots that no one would buy.

If I was honest with myself—and I always at least tried to be—at thirty-three, I was still one of the better-kept secrets in town.

To pay our mortgage, there was the occasional commercial, which helped a lot. But I was being more selective, not going out on the really silly ones.

Jacki continued to be very successful in her modeling career, doing print work, and she was now studying acting with Sal. In her modeling book, she had a couple of pictures of us together. Somewhere along the line, somebody asked her, "Who's the guy?" And Jacki said, "That's my husband." And we got hired a couple of times to do ads together. Then her agent, Nina Blanchard, said she'd like to send me out for some things. I said, "Okay, Nina, but you have to know I'm going to be selective in what I say yes to."

This was all in the early days, probably around *Terminal Island* days. I gotta say, the print work sure helped our balance sheet. And I *was* very selective.

I did car ads for brochures where the guy stands behind the star, the car. I did two or three "What Sort of Man Reads *Playboy*?" ads, which obviously portrayed "the man" in a favorable light. I did some jobs where I knew the ad wasn't going to get a lot of exposure.

But one ad had consequences I couldn't possibly see coming. There was a period when several cigarette companies were doing full-page magazine ads of guys holding a pack of the company's brand. All the ads were shot close, from the waist up. They did their best to make each guy look like Vic Virile or Harry Hormone. You get the idea. Anyway, Salem picked me as one of their "guys." The picture they chose was pretty good, except they changed the color of my eyes. Apparently, menthol cigarettes make your eyes blue.

So, where was I? Oh yeah. Consequences. Mine was their most successful ad. Suddenly, I was not just in magazine ads but on billboards as well. Lots of billboards. This hardly paid like a commercial. All I got was five hundred dollars. And apart from a lot of friends thinking I was getting rich, there was one more thing. Kind of a big thing. Anybody who didn't know my work, which was a whole lot of people, thought I was a male model. Even though I had worked as an actor for over ten years.

To this day, it rankles when someone writes that I got started as a male model. Apart from it not being true, there was a deep-seated prejudice in the acting community about male models. I didn't agree with it. It was total bullshit. But I had to be aware of it. I mean, nobody used the term *female models*. See what I mean?

This was well before Steve Cannell entered my life. And there was nothing I could do about it but move on.

———

I checked in with Teddy O'Toole's, who told me, "You have a message from Bettye McCartt." Teddy's was and is a kind of customized answering service for the movie business in L.A. They were the best. They never missed a call, they knew the business, and they wouldn't stop trying to find you if they felt the call was about work. They had a sixth sense about that. It seemed like everybody in town used Teddy's. If someone wanted to know how to reach you, all you had to say was "Just call Teddy's, HO [Hollywood] 2-2301."

"What's going on, Bettye?"

"I had a call from Steve Cannell," she said.

"You did?"

"Yes, I did, Tommy. He gave me the news."

"What news?"

"He said *he* wants to tell you."

What was it that Calvin Coolidge said? "Nothing can take the place of persistence." It turned out that my unrelenting friend had written an episode of *The Rockford Files* just for me.

"I think it's pretty good," Steve said. "Read it and see what you think."

I read it, and it wasn't pretty good. It was *really* good. Fact is, it was perfect.

The episode was called "White on White and Nearly Perfect." Lance White was the perfect detective. He had a history of inserting himself into Jim Rockford's world when even one time would have been too many.

For years, I had walked into interviews and been expected to play a perfect detective perfectly. There were times I guess I did. But the six-feet-four-inch guy who walked in the door was faced with their perception of who they thought a standard leading man should be. I didn't really want to be that. I wasn't that. And my friend Steve had somehow figured that out.

By now, I had been directed to play just about every cliché in the book. So I was elated that Steve's script allowed me (as Lance White) to *spoof* just about every cliché in the book. Steve told me he was going to direct. My guess was that he didn't want to risk an outside director missing the point or, worse, playing it just for laughs.

The Rockford Files always walked that precariously fine line between tragedy and comedy. Steve referred to the territory in between as *humor*. Tricky stuff to get right, but not a problem in Steve's hands. Not to mention the fact that it hit right in James Garner's sweet spot.

I had met James Garner a long time before at Joe Kirkwood's driving range in Studio City. Kirkwood's also had a nine-hole par-3 course, and that's where I bumped into Garner. Actually, I didn't bump into him. And I didn't actually meet him. I almost hit him with a golf ball.

I was playing with a friend on the hole next to Garner's threesome. And I hit what was a frequent occurrence for me, an errant shot. The nine-iron shot floated high in the air toward them, with me desperately trying to will it back. *Don't go there,* I kept saying to myself. I mean, I didn't wanna be the guy who hurt Maverick.

When my golf ball landed next to his feet, he spun around and glared at me.

I think I yelled out something like "I'm sorry."

My new problem was that Garner and his friends had to pass right by me to get to the next hole. As he did, James Garner looked at me and said in that ironic way of his, "I believe the expression is *fore*."

That was the extent of what I now choose to call "my brush with greatness." Of course, he would never remember it, and I would never forget it. And no, I didn't tell him when we were introduced.

From the moment I read "White on White and Nearly Perfect," I was excited about it. Not really nervous, just excited. What a gift I had been given out of nowhere. More than anything I had done, I knew that this was in my wheelhouse. I don't know how Steve knew that, but he sure did. I didn't even have trouble sleeping the night before my first day.

When we were filming one of the pilots, I asked Steve what James Garner was like. All Steve said was "Actors should take 'star' lessons from him."

And I did . . . just in case.

From the moment I stepped on Jim's set, I was made to feel comfortable and, more importantly, respected as an actor. And no mistake, this *was* Jim's set. He seemed to understand that a lead actor also needed to show leadership. The collegial attitude started with him and filtered down to his whole crew.

I knew Jim would be prepared, so I made damn sure I was. Not overprepared, as I had been so many times, just confident about who I was playing. The trap in playing Lance was to try and be funny. Actually, Lance wasn't funny at all. He was just *good*. So good that he must have come from the *good* planet Oz. "The funny" had to come from Steve's words and, especially, from Jim's reaction to Lance's perfectness, if there is such a word. Actually, Lance didn't believe he was perfect, just *good*. But to the realist Jim Rockford, Lance was a nuisance at best and, at worst, a life-threatening liability. Nothing but trouble.

Rockford was always trying to set Lance straight.

"You have to be cynical, Lance. You have to question things. You look for the big lie. Question every—"

Jim is interrupted by Lance's wristwatch alarm, a frequent occurrence.

"You on some kind of medication, Lance? That thing keeps going off."

"That's because I set it at ten-minute intervals."

"Why do you do that?"

"Because time is valuable, Jim. And I don't like to waste it. I like to be aware that it's passing."

"Time is just a measurement, Lance. It doesn't improve because you watch it."

"I'm afraid I don't understand what you're driving at, Jim."

Rockford tries to shift his weight a little. "All right. Let me put it this way. What do you do for fun?"

"I help people."

"What about girls?"

"I like them."

"Do you date them?"

"There's no time, Jim. There never is."

Later on, Lance is checking a bullet wound in his left arm. Rockford notices that Lance has been wounded. "You all right, Lance?"

"It's okay. It's—"

"Don't say it's a flesh wound."

"Just a flesh wound."

What a great time I had! What a great time *we* had! It was nice to feel wanted. And I kinda sensed that Jim was also enjoying the ride. That obviously meant the world to me.

When Jacki and I sat down to watch the broadcast, my big brother, Bob, joined us. I wasn't really anxious. I just kinda knew it was going to be good. And it was. I still remember, when the title "White on White and Nearly Perfect" came up, it was followed by what we call a *separate card.* It said "Starring Tom Selleck."

That wasn't standard billing for a guest actor on a series. I think that was something my dear friend Steve did on his own. I felt so proud.

CHAPTER EIGHT

The Sacketts

I t's a big-time western miniseries about three brothers from Tennessee," Bettye told me. "They are still trying to cast the last of the three. It's called *The Sacketts*."

"It wouldn't be the first time I'm the last guy in town to be seen," I allowed.

"You're gonna know something pretty quick," she said. "They start shooting next week."

Bettye mentioned that my old friend and fellow Fox talent program refugee Sam Elliott had one of the other brother roles and that I'd be seeing the producer, Doug Netter. The director and a couple of people from the network, NBC, might also be there, she said, along with the writer, Jim Byrnes. My audition was set for the next morning.

"Thanks for coming," Doug Netter said cordially when I was shown into the room. "This is Bob Totten, our director."

Totten barely looked up and didn't say anything. The producer asked me what I'd been working on. I told him about the *Rockford* episode.

"Did you get a chance to look at the pages?" Netter asked. As I'd waited to be seen, an assistant had handed me two pages of dialogue, which I had glanced at but not much more. "Would you mind giving us a read?"

When I finished, the producer thanked me without giving any hint of how I thought I had done. Finally, Bob Totten spoke up. "Can you ride a horse?" he asked.

He didn't say it so much as mutter it. Not rudely, just blunt and unengaged. It was only later that I would come to realize how important a question that was, as Totten was being pressed to make one of the biggest decisions of his career. Still, it wasn't quite the question I was hoping for.

A good actor in training, along with doing scenes and working on character, is also constantly building up his skills. But no actor can be an expert at everything, and with so few westerns being made by the late 1970s, horsemanship wasn't at the top of most actors' list. There's a standard tactic a lot of actors fall back on when they're asked about a skill they might not have.

They lie.

"No, I don't ride," I said straight out to Totten. "I'm not afraid of horses. I've been on a horse in a couple of commercials. But no, I'm not an accomplished rider. What I am is a good athlete, and I can learn."

The director seemed to be sizing me up. "At least you're honest." That's all he said.

Totten looked at Doug Netter. Netter looked at me. The producer thanked me for coming. And I was out of there.

Well, this one ain't gonna happen, I said to myself as I headed to the parking lot.

By the time I got home, there was a message from Bettye: "You have a callback for *The Sacketts.*"

———

For the callback, they wanted me to drive out to the Randall Ranch, thirty miles north of the Hollywood sign. "Wear work clothes," Bettye said.

I'd gotten plenty of callbacks over the previous decade. They were usually in studio offices. I'd never had a callback at a ranch before.

Though most moviegoers have never heard of the Randalls, and most people don't even know what a wrangler does, I'm not sure where the American western would be without that family. The Randalls supplied horses, mules, cattle, stagecoaches, and wagons to movie and TV westerns. A native of tiny Melbeta, Nebraska, Glenn Randall Sr. showed up in California in the early 1940s and quickly became one of Hollywood's favorite wranglers, working with Gene Autry, Tex Ritter, Roy Rogers, and the horses they rode in on. He trained and even housebroke Roy's beloved palomino, Trigger, probably the most famous movie horse of all time. Only the Lone Ranger's Silver makes it any kind of race at all. Over the years, Glenn's sons J.R. and Corky joined their dad, looking after the animals on *The Alamo, The Misfits,* and *How the West Was Won.* It was Corky who handled seventy-eight horses for the chariot race scene in *Ben-Hur.* As I headed out to the Randall Ranch for my *Sacketts* callback, Corky was working with Francis Ford Coppola on *The Black Stallion,* which featured some of the most challenging horse scenes ever filmed.

When I got to the ranch, a couple of other actors were already there. The casting director told us to wait until everyone had arrived. I wasn't quite sure who *everyone* was. There was a certain etiquette I had learned to expect as I was being considered for starring roles. This was not normal, not on a project as big as *The Sacketts,* not for one of the leads. Usually, in a callback, people are seen one at a time. This was more like a cattle call. I had been on so many callbacks, I knew the difference. All of us, I had to assume, were here for the same role.

When the group was formed, there were six actors in all. We were told to walk across the riding arena to meet the director.

Okay.

It was a big arena. I could see a small group of people sitting together in an otherwise empty grandstand, two or three rows up. At first I couldn't make out the faces. But as we got closer, I could see Bob Totten, sitting there in grungy boots and a cowboy hat, next to Doug Netter. Behind them was my friend Sam. Next to Sam were Ben Johnson and Glenn Ford. Spotting those two western-movie icons certainly ramped up the pressure another notch or two. Whatever we were here for, I wasn't used to having the primary members of the cast sitting in on my audition.

For a moment, the six of us stood in silence in front of the grandstand, us in the dirt squinting up into the sunshine, them in the bleachers gazing down at us.

Totten took over. "There's a bunch of horses over there," he said, motioning vaguely to the far side of the riding arena, where a couple of wranglers were waiting with a dozen horses. "Go pick one out, put a saddle on it, and ride over here."

Oh-kay!

I took a deep breath or two as we walked across the arena, holding back the small wave of panic that wanted to wash over me.

By the time we got to the horses, one of the actors just kept walking. "This is insulting," he said. That actor (no names, please) was way more established than I was. My first thought was he must have lied about being able to ride. But for all I knew, he could have done westerns before. Either way, he wasn't gonna get this part.

Look, being offended is a choice; you have to make a choice to be offended. I chose not to be offended.

I didn't know what to do. I turned my back to the grandstand and whispered to one of the wranglers, "I have no idea how to do this."

The wrangler looked up at me and paused for longer than was comfortable, kinda like he was trying to decide something. "This one'll do," he said. He handed me the reins of a horse he was holding, and he started talking me through it: Lift that, pull this, buckle that.

I climbed on the best I could and joined the other four as we walked our horses across the arena. As we approached the bleachers, I tried to catch Sam's eye, hoping for some kind of reassurance from my friend. I couldn't get even the hint of a smile.

Totten just stared. Saying nothing. Revealing nothing. Finally, he looked over at Doug Netter. Netter said, "Thank you all." And we were dismissed.

Now, this was not the usual progression of things. I'd never had a callback that was anything like this. Obviously, I didn't get every part I went up for, and this one seemed destined to be in that category.

When I got home, Bettye called me: "You have an offer for *The Sacketts*."

———

A word about my good friend Sam: There was a reason he was sitting in the grandstand that day. Nobody up there knew my work better than Sam did. If he'd had a problem with me playing his brother, he could have very quietly killed it. I've never asked Sam about this. We didn't do such things. But I'm certain that was a big part of why I got to play his brother.

By the time Bettye had worked out my deal, which took a few days, filming had already begun. So I didn't get any read-throughs with the director. No meet-and-greets with the rest of the cast. That stuff is important at the start of any movie. But there was no time for any of that. Skipping it would make everything tougher. I never even got to be properly introduced to Mr. Johnson and Mr. Ford. At least I was given a copy of the script that Jim Byrnes had written from *The Daybreakers* and *Sackett*, two novels by Louis L'Amour. The script was really good. Clearly, there was opportunity here.

Sam's character was the hard and deliberate Tell Sackett, the oldest brother, a Union Army veteran who desperately wanted to be left alone. Sam was coming off of *Lifeguard*, his breakout film with Anne Archer; his career was on a roll. Totten cast a terrific young actor named Jeff Osterhage as Tyrel Sackett, the kid brother who is really the conscience of the movie. Jeff had come from Indiana and, like me, had ties to Detroit. He'd done a TV-movie sequel to John Wayne's *True Grit*, and he actually knew how to ride—at least he thought he did. I was the middle brother, Orrin Sackett, the charming one.

I didn't think I was all that charming, and I knew I didn't get hired for my riding chops. But whatever got me here, I was thrilled to be part of it.

This was no townie western. With Totten in charge, we would film in some spectacular locales. Along the Arkansas River in Cañon City, Colorado. Across the high desert east of Tucson. We fanned out from each of those locations onto the open frontier. In Louis L'Amour's stories and in Bob Totten's hands, the land was every bit as important as any of the actors on the screen.

When I got to Cañon City, our first shooting location, Totten was off filming Sam's gold-prospector scenes before the three brothers got reunited. That gave me a week to settle in and spend time on my riding.

I met up with Totten's chief wrangler, Jay Fishburn, who worked closely with his wife, Donna Hall. Donna took me on as her special project. It was Donna who taught me how to sit a horse. For those of you who aren't familiar with that expression, it is hard to explain but easy to see once you know what it is. Donna started me from the ground up.

"If you are agitated," she said, "you're gonna communicate that through your butt. You need to communicate through quiet hands and legs."

I'd seen enough westerns to know what I wanted to do next. "When do I get to gallop?" I asked.

"You know," Donna said to me, "in a movie, ninety percent of what you're going to do on camera is walking a horse into town, hitting your mark, and getting off—or getting on and leaving. If you're gonna run a horse into town, come to a dead stop on a mark, and expect your horse to sit still while you talk through three pages of dialogue, you sure as hell have better earned that horse's respect."

If I was one thing, it was coachable, from the sports I had played. It was "Yes, ma'am . . . no, ma'am" from then on.

On the third day I was in Cañon City, Donna showed up with a new horse. "This is Utah," she said. "He has a kind eye. He's light in the mouth and has a good mind."

Utah was a leggy sorrel. He looked like a horse from the period more than a modern quarter horse, which is more robust in body.

"Don't ever let anyone put you on a horse that isn't sixteen hands tall," Donna said. A hand is four inches. Her point was that I have very long legs. When I sit down with most people, I'm the same height they are. "In a period western saddle, you sit in a posture that is straight up and down. It doesn't look so good if your legs are dangling on the ground."

Then Donna added, "Utah's no babysitter."

"I appreciate the vote of confidence, Donna."

Somehow, by then, *ma'am* had become *Donna*.

"This horse will do anything you ask of him," she explained, "as long as you make him think it's his idea."

"You'll keep an eye on me?"

"Every day."

With Utah beneath me and Donna's voice in my head, I spent every spare moment on that horse.

———

The *Sacketts* set in Cañon City was totally alive, buzzing with actors, wranglers, crew, techs, horses, and cattle, all God's creatures on two legs and four. And I was in a movie with western legends like Ben Johnson and Glenn Ford.

Glenn Ford had been playing ordinary men in unusual circumstances since the 1940s, bringing that understated authenticity of his to every role. *Cowboy. 3:10 to Yuma. The Rounders.* Ben Johnson had gone from world-champion roper to movie stuntman to John Ford favorite to Academy Award winner as the ex-cowboy theater owner in *The Last*

My mom's ID photo from the General Motors Fisher Body plant in Detroit, where she contributed to the war effort.

Mom visits Dad in Montgomery, Alabama. I think that's where I began.

Mom, "Bobby Dean," and "Tommy."

Little me.

The home of my grandparents Mimi and Hoppy, where I spent my first two years and met my father when he came home to Detroit from the army.

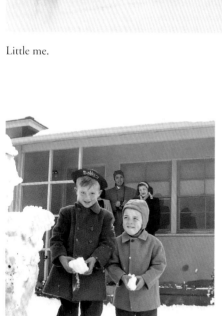

Our first Christmas in sunny California.

Adding Dan to the family with little sister Marti.

At Grant High School.

At Sigma Chi Hell Week with Ron
Montapert. We lost him in Vietnam.

Out on the town with
Miss Mae West.

At Officer Candidate
School.

Jim Garner, Steve Cannell, and Lance White on the set of *The Rockford Files*.

As Orrin Sackett.

With Sam, Jeff, and Uncle Ben on the set of *The Sacketts*.

A moment with Bess Armstrong in *High Road*.
That's cinematographer Ronnie Taylor behind us.

As Patrick O'Malley in
High Road to China.

About to be airborne.

Hanging out with Bettye McCartt.

No, not Brian Hutton, the actor. Brian G. Hutton, the director.

My pal Jack Weston.

With my friend Wilford Brimley.

Two Marines and a Navy SEAL.

Our stunt coordinator, Bob Minor, and
my stunt double, Tom Lupo.

OUTRIGGER CANOE CLUB "CHAMPS"

National champions.

As Nick Lassiter.

Hanging out with Jillie Mack.

With Lon Bentley, *Cats* stage manager
Paul Mills, and Jillie on the *Lassiter* set.

With Dan, Bob, Marti, and my mom and dad.

With Chris Abbott-Fish and Charles
Johnson at Leeds Castle.

With Carol Burnett at the
1983 Academy Awards.

Pals forever.

Carol and me hamming it up in the
vault we were trapped in.

With Jillie and Kevin, across the street from
the number one movie in the world.

Me and the boys with the star of the movie.

Working with the
Great Hildini.

Princess Diana—one of a kind.

The Emmys.

Pualani McGinness and Dave Muntz
today. I couldn't have done it without them.

My friend Nancy.

Dinner with Esme.

Picture Show. They weren't just actors to me. They felt like people I'd always known. And they weren't the only old-timers who showed up for *The Sacketts.* Totten had assembled a regular dream team of western character actors and stars: Jack Elam, who, among other things, did a brilliant job playing villains, and Gene Evans, who once beat John Wayne out of a role (*The Steel Helmet,* 1951). The Mexico-born Gilbert Roland, who'd been holding down romantic leads in English and Spanish since the 1920s. Mercedes McCambridge, who'd been on the radio with Orson Welles and won a Best Supporting Actress Academy Award in *All the King's Men* with Burgess Meredith. Ruth Roman, a Warner Bros. and MGM star from the 1940s and '50s who had the real-life drama of being rescued from the sinking ocean liner *Andrea Doria* with her three-year-old son. Slim Pickens—*Slim Pickens!*—who had started out as a rodeo clown and been in damn near every western ever made, then turned up in *Dr. Strangelove* and *Blazing Saddles.* Pat Buttram, Shug Fisher, Paul Koslo, James Gammon, John Vernon, L. Q. Jones—if you loved classic westerns like I did, this was a gold rush of the people who populated them. They all could have stepped out of the Selleck family television set.

And presiding over it all, with his sandpaper demeanor and unquestioned authority, was the iron-fisted director, Bob Totten.

An L.A. native, he had started young in the business, acting, writing, and directing, becoming one of the youngest people ever to earn a Directors Guild of America union card. It was on *Gunsmoke* where Totten had really made his name, directing twenty-one episodes of the long-running western and guest-starring in eight more. He could see things from the actors' point of view.

Every time a new character arrived on the *Sacketts* set, he was another old pal of Totten's. The actors seemed to have an instant camaraderie with one another and almost a reverence for him. Industry veterans who'd made careers together. Busy actors who kept showing up for smaller roles out of loyalty to Totten. A crew who would do anything for him. He'd probably given work to all of them many times. They had his respect. He had theirs. And I wanted both.

Freed from the TV-budget constraints of *Gunsmoke,* he was on a project for the ages, making a western miniseries on a scale he could only dream of before.

———

I met up with Totten's wardrober, Kent James, whose job was to make sure the actors dressed the way real cowboys did in the years after the Civil War. In most westerns, there was a whole stock-company notion of period attire—jeans, shirt, vest, pointy boots, and stupid hat. That was more realistic than the fringe, sparkles, and other glitzy gear once favored by my idols Roy Rogers and Gene Autry, but it still wasn't right. Kent had studied the era obsessively and channeled insights from the visionary western director John Ford.

"Ford thought you should always start with the hat," Kent said to me. "You gotta get the hat right. Never pick out a hat for your character until you've seen yourself in a full-length mirror. The brim will be too small."

Kent also found a perfect shirt for me. The label inside said "WESTERN COSTUME" and "John Wayne." I guess I was almost his size.

One day—I wasn't on the clock yet—Jeff and I were sitting behind the camera watching Totten film a scene with Sam, Ben, Ruth Roman, and Paul Koslo. I just looked at Jeff and said, "We'd better bring our A game."

Just being on that set was a daily education, and I aimed to make the most of it. Louis L'Amour was around with his wife, Kathy, sharing his exploits as a professional boxer, merchant seaman, mine-assessment worker, and treasured novelist of the West. His dozens of "frontier stories," as he called them, were meticulously researched. To me, they held the heart of our country between their covers.

John Ford's daughter, Barbara Ford, was there, a talented film editor in her own right. Wherever I turned, there was someone to hang out with and, quite frankly, to be awed by. Ben came around and showed Jeff and me roping techniques. I don't want to say we learned to rope. Roping is a mystifying art form that takes a lifetime to conquer. But Totten expected us to carry ropes on our horses, and that meant we had to at least look like we knew what we were doing.

We practiced for hours on a roping-steer dummy. Just about the time we started to get a little cocky, Ben showed up and said, "When you boys get done, maybe you'll try one of these." He flipped the rope into a tight figure eight and landed one side on each of the dummy's horns.

Somehow gravity took a holiday when Ben was around.

———

The first day I was gonna work with Glenn, I showed up early, in costume and with Utah standing by. That gave me time to sit behind the camera and watch the cattle-drive scene that Totten was filming with Glenn, Jeff, and Ben. It was a stifling-hot day in the desert. In the scene, Jeff and Ben are riding alongside a chuck wagon as Glenn's character, Tom Sunday, rides up and out of the blue says:

Fill the can, and fill the cup:
All the windy ways of men
Are but dust that rises up,
And lightly lays again.

"That's Tennyson," Glenn says, and rides off.

The scene throws a big question mark into the character's background, creating a mystery about his past. As far as the audience knew, Tom Sunday was just a guy punching cattle. Not only could he read, he could also recite poetry!

But Glenn kept blowing his lines.

One take and then another.

And Glenn's lines rhymed, which really should have made them easier to remember.

It was a key part of the movie. And Totten being Totten, he wasn't going to shoot a close-up. He was going to shoot big, wide shots with all of us and the herd.

The camera was on a dolly, tracking the action as it moved along at least the length of a football field. Unfortunately, Totten didn't have enough dolly track to get everything he wanted out of the scene. The cattle were being herded a long way. So as the camera passed one section of track, Totten's crew unhooked that section and ran behind the camera, carrying the piece of track all the way to the other end, snapping it in as fast as they could before running back for more. And it was hot! It took superhuman effort to make all that happen, which was the kind of effort that Totten inspired. *And Glenn kept blowing lines!*

It turned out that Glenn had placed cue cards along the dolly track. As the camera dollied along, Glenn was trying to read the lines of the poem off the cue cards. And each time he screwed up, the camera had to return to the starting point. The track had to be taken apart and reassembled. The entire maneuver needed to be executed all over again. And the wranglers had to turn the herd of cattle where they didn't want to go.

I don't suppose I need to tell you, but turning a herd of cattle is a big deal. It's not exactly easy or quick. After each time Glenn stumbled, I could see our director getting more and more frustrated.

After Glenn's third try, Totten blew up.

Did I mention Totten had a temper?

He yanked his cowboy hat off his sweaty head. He threw his hat down and yelled, *"God damn it!"*

Glenn took offense and stormed off to his trailer.

Jeff, along with a couple of wranglers, started to move off toward a shady spot where the chairs were.

"Where you boys goin'?" Ben called out.

Everybody stopped, then started moving back to their marks.

"Where you boys goin'?" That's all I needed to hear. I got on Utah and rode out and joined Ben and Jeff.

And that's where we sat for a good long while.

Ben started telling stories. At that point I didn't even mind the heat.

Doug Netter came over and talked to Totten. When Totten had cooled down, he went to Glenn's trailer. I don't know what was said. It's kinda hard to imagine Bob Totten eating crow. But he wasn't about to lose a day's work. He brought Glenn back, and they finished the scene.

Most of my life, I'd been a Glenn Ford fan. As an actor, he was way ahead of his time. Even in his early movies—film noirs, comedies, and westerns going back to the mid 1940s—he had a naturalistic quality that Hollywood hadn't grown into yet. I'm still a fan. But Glenn was in his sixties by the time of *The Sacketts*. He was clearly wrestling with some problems. I refuse to even try to guess what they were.

"Where you boys goin'?" That was all Ben had to say.

———

Ben was almost done with his part of the movie; we were running out of Ben time. Jeff and I had a night shoot where Glenn's Tom Sunday starts to teach us how to read. But Glenn was nowhere to be found. We got word: "It's gonna be a while. Totten's rewriting the scene, and you boys are gonna have more dialogue."

Jeff and I looked at each other. Sam had finished in the picture. I had only three scenes with my friend—our reunion, his departure, and the shoot-out. And Ben was leaving soon. We realized then and there that we were gonna have to cowboy up and pull our weight.

About that time, Ben and Slim *just happened* to show up.

Neither one was working that night, but Ben had a way of being around just at the right time.

We sat around the campfire, our version of Prairie TV. Ben and Slim started telling stories. Ben got to talking about the towering director John Ford, who'd done more to define the movie western than anyone dead or alive. In many of those old Ford westerns—*Rio Grande, Fort Apache, She Wore a Yellow Ribbon*—Ben was the cowboy riding over impossible terrain. Ford didn't just give Ben his start in the movies. The way Ben told it, the larger-than-life director became like a father to him.

"Now, somebody was always in the box with Ford, especially after he'd had a few," Ben told us. "I guess it was inevitable my time would come."

One day at lunch, Ford was riding Ben pretty hard. That didn't sit well. Ben walked away, and the two men never spoke again.

"So now Ford's dying in Palm Springs," Ben said, picking up the story. "And I get a call from the Duke. And Wayne says to me, 'Pappy's dying. Ben, I can't see him like this.'"

Ben swallowed hard and drove down to the hospital in Palm Springs. This was August 1973. The two men had not exchanged a word since their long-ago bust-up.

"Ford wasn't conscious, so I just sat there," Ben said. "He had that one patch on his eye," the result of ripping a bandage off too soon after cataract surgery.

Ben must have been in the hospital room for a couple of hours when Ford opened his eye. "He looked over and saw me sitting there," Ben said.

With labored breath, Ford said, "Johnson, always stay real."

And John Ford died.

Now, Ben was not a bullshitter, and I don't think he was bullshitting when he shared that story with us. Certainly not with Slim sitting there. To this day, I have no doubt that what Ben told us about Ford on his deathbed was the honest-to-God cowboy truth.

—

Totten was constantly finding ways to capture the grandeur of the land. It seemed like we were always fighting the clock and the light. "Sun's going down," he said to Jeff and me one afternoon, waving his arm into the distance. "Go out there. Just sit and talk."

We didn't know what to do. So we just said, "Yessir."

That silhouette of two riders on horseback. The sun setting behind us. I didn't realize until later what a stunning image that could make. Every detail mattered to Totten.

When it came time to shoot the wild cattle hunt, Ben's last sequence, Totten realized that the shorthorn cattle he'd been sent weren't historically accurate. He used his own money to replace them with longhorns. Everything had to be real. He was also slow to send in stunt doubles. He expected his actors to be capable.

"Just shoot it," he'd order.

Totten did have Walter Scott double me on one scene, and I couldn't argue with that decision. Walter was the perfect double. He looked a lot like me—my build, my height. There wasn't anything he couldn't do from a horse. And this scene was definitely above my pay grade. Jeff and I were whoopin' and hollerin', chasing steers over rough terrain, steers that hadn't read the script. It was what we call a second-unit shoot, one that Walter was directing. Glenn's double was there, but that wasn't for Uncle Ben. He was gonna rope his own steer.

It's one thing to rope a dummy on the ground. But building a loop and throwing it from horseback is kinda like patting your head and rubbing your belly. If that loop gets tangled in your horse's leg, you're in for a hell of a wreck.

Walter got on Utah. No babysitter horse for Walter. Ben's nephew Ben Miller, also a champion roper, was doubling Jeff. It was a thing of beauty what Walter did from horseback, reaching way out and roping the runaway. Boy, he made me look good.

It was in scenes like this one that the land became the character it deserved to be. Big open spaces. Rough terrain. A handful of men driving a herd of cattle where they didn't want to go.

And Totten barking orders at everyone.

He was reaffirming the idea of a West without fences, men making their meager living as cowboys. It was an incredibly difficult life they chose, and it constantly tested them. That was the story that hooked me as a boy. And now that story would never leave me.

————

The truth is, it took a while for me to figure out exactly where I stood with Totten. We didn't have decades of history together, the way he did with the other actors in this tight company. I was just establishing myself with him, and he could be the opposite of reassuring. You did not ever want to get into a position where you had to say, "I'm not sure what happened, Mr. Totten. My horse wouldn't stop on the mark." You'd get a ration of shit, for sure. I'd seen his temper erupt in an instant. It lingered in the background . . . until it didn't anymore.

I'm not saying I didn't have my moments. On my second day at work, we filmed the big shoot-out at the end of the movie. Totten knew exactly how he wanted that scene to go. For my character, a rider would come down the street; I would reveal myself and fire three shots with my 1873 Winchester. Billy Hart, a veteran stuntman, was going to take the fall off the horse. A naked fall.

They'd dug a pit in the street and filled it with soft dirt. That was Billy's target.

Billy came tearing down the street. I fired my first shot. Nothing happened. I worked the lever and fired again. Still nothing.

"*Whoa!*" I yelled.

Billy hesitated a split second and missed the pit entirely, landing with a thud on the hard street. Totten and key members of the crew rushed out to him.

Billy said, "I thought I heard someone say *whoa.*"

"That was me," I said.

"God damn it!" Totten fumed. He yanked his hat off and threw it on the ground.

He didn't say anything else. He just glared at me.

You never know how badly a stuntman is injured. Stuntmen always shake themselves off and say, "I'm all right. I'm all right." But days later, Billy was still hobbling around the set. My guess—it was his ribs. And next he had to do a fall from a roof, which he did perfectly. Sure, the '73 didn't fire, but you don't ever stop a scene. I will never make that mistake again.

———

When the cattle drive ends in Abilene, Tyrel and Orrin are cut loose. The two of us race our horses into town and suddenly come to a full stop. Yes, Utah stood still.

My character has fixated on something: a fetching young woman in a wooden rocker on a gracious porch. She fixates right back, fiddling with the blue scarf in her hands. I dismount and give the reins to my brother. "Do me a favor, Tyrel. Take care of my horse."

As I make my way toward the porch, the young woman rises from the rocker. I say, "Good day to you, miss."

She looks but does not speak.

"Realize I'm being bold as winter coming up on you like this. But I just come off a long trail right into this dusty town. And to see a sight like you, well, it's nice. It's real nice."

She fiddles with her scarf and still says nothing.

"You see, first off, I thought I'd been touched by the sun. But on closer look, it appears it's you that's been touched by the sun, miss. Or rather, blessed by it. Gold hair. And blue eyes. Mercy on me!"

This gets a reaction.

"I knew there was a smile in there someplace. It's just such beauty deserves tribute."

A couple of days later, I got new pages for an added scene. Someone must have found my porch encounter with Laura (Marcy Hanson) "charming."

In the new scene, my character is sitting on a riverbank with a wistful look in his eyes, enjoying the perfume of Laura's blue scarf. The scarf wasn't in the script. That was a piece of Totten business.

As I sit there, basking in the moment, Tyrel rides up. "Orrin, where you been all this time?" he wants to know. "Sweet-talking that yeller-haired gal?"

I correct him. "Gold. Pure gold."

Then Ben rides up and says, "Hey, you boys wanna get paid?"

I climb on Utah, and the three of us are out of there.

"*Cut!*" Totten yelled. He slowly walked over to me. "I can brag on ya on that one."

Totten didn't toss out many compliments. On the Totten flattery curve, I'd say that one was almost like getting a bear hug.

———

Somewhere along the line—not early, thank God—Totten pulled me aside and said, "You know, I didn't want you for this role. I wanted my friend Buck Taylor." That's all he said, and then he walked away.

Oh-kay!

I'd never had a director tell me anything like that before!

Everyone on the set knew Buck. He would have made a terrific Orrin. And he was a part of this western family. But I didn't know the half of it, not even close, until Jeff shared the full truth many years later.

Before I ever had my first read for *The Sacketts,* before I ever set foot on the Randall Ranch, Totten had already chosen Buck for the Orrin Sackett role—at least he thought he had.

A week before I was in the mix at all, there was the same kind of callback at the ranch, and all the same people were sitting in the grandstand. Each time someone was sent home, Jeff and Buck were asked to stay. When everyone else was gone, Totten had Sam, Buck, and Jeff climb on their horses and ride around the giant oval. As they circled back to him, Totten stood and said for everyone to hear, "Ladies and gentlemen, I give you the Sackett brothers."

Buck thought he had the Orrin role. Totten knew Buck had the Orrin role. So did everyone else who was there. And soon the rest of the crew would too. But the network executives had other ideas. It seemed they wanted fresh faces for Tyrel and Orrin, actors who wouldn't be as familiar to western-movie fans. Interviews were hurriedly arranged with a handful of actors, including me. According to Jim Byrnes, the writer, he told the others about my Lance White character in *Rockford,* saying I was someone who should be seen.

I had no idea about any of that while we were making *The Sacketts* or for decades afterward. Not until Jeff filled in the details. But once he did, a lot of things made sense. Why Totten didn't even seem to want to be there for my audition. He already knew the actor he wanted for Orrin.

For his part, Buck didn't slink away, as some actors might have in his position. He took another role on *The Sacketts.* A good role but not the lead.

Everyone on the set had to know that I'd ended up with what had started out as Buck's role. Once the director made his grand announcement, believe me, word got around to the cast, the crew, the wranglers, everyone. Not one of them breathed a word to me, and I would always be grateful that they didn't.

And what about Buck? He never let on either. Learning the rest of the story gave me even more respect for him. What a load he carried through *The Sacketts*! What a stand-up guy he turned out to be! Buck wasn't only Totten's friend. He was everyone's friend. Yet Buck didn't try to sabotage me. He didn't trash me with the other actors or the crew. He was just as gracious and welcoming and collaborative as could be. Thanks to him and Totten and the rest of his company, I got nothing but help and support. Everyone made sure I had no idea what I was walking into.

And Buck Taylor was and still is as solid as you get.

Since I learned the whole *Sacketts* backstory, I've thought a lot about what made Totten tick. "I didn't want you . . ." It's a strange thing to say to an actor.

But you know what? That was pure Totten. I didn't take it in a hostile way. I don't think he was trying to manipulate me or get under my skin or anything like that. At the same time, he didn't seem to care whether I was intimidated by the comment or shattered by it or anything else. It was just something he said, and again I chose not to be offended. I took the comment as a sign of acceptance. I figured it was Totten's way of saying that, despite his early misgivings, I was doing okay.

Totten was never going to tell me that directly. He wasn't wired that way. The fragile feelings of his actors were never his top priority. Just ask Glenn Ford. If Totten had a sentimental bone in his body, he hid it pretty well. Only with a guy like him could a comment like that be considered a gesture of welcome. And that's how I took it.

—

We had a long shoot on *The Sacketts*. Jeff, Glenn, and I had to carry the second half of the picture. We all got to know each other very well. Over the course of a production like this one, a movie takes on a life of its own. The actors, the wranglers, the stuntmen, and the crew. Even Doug Netter, Jim Byrnes, Bob Totten, and my friend Louis L'Amour—this company really was a family, and now it included Jeff and me. The time did come when I could say to myself, *You know what? I'm doing pretty well here.* I hadn't yet had that feeling often in my work, but I had it on *The Sacketts*. And I liked the way it felt.

I even started calling Totten "T." That's what all the rest of the family called him. His wife, Maxine, who was often on the set trying to keep her husband in line, she was "M."

Being on a western in a company like this one—well, it's kinda hard to explain. It was just a different way of working. Maybe I could have experienced something similar on a contemporary movie, but I don't think so. Westerns had meant so much to me, going back to my earliest memories, and now I knew why.

I was certain I would keep that feeling with me for the rest of my life. In the decades to come, I would build my own version of a stock company, assembling a steady group of people I liked, admired, and trusted, giving them all the free rein they needed to do their thing. I'd go back to them year after year, for project after project, in the same and different roles, kinda like Totten did. And just maybe John Ford did too.

We had a big wrap party in Old Tucson when all the filming was done. The great western company had come together, and now they were dispersing again. Sam and Ben came back, probably on their own nickel. Louis and Kathy L'Amour came too.

It wasn't formal, just a group of like-minded people drinking beer and Jack Daniel's. At one point, I noticed T was headed my way with what looked to me like a group of coconspirators. He gave me one of those looks of his and removed one of the grungy boots he'd worn for the whole movie. Then he lifted a bottle of Jack Daniel's and gave it a heavy pour into the boot.

With a bit of ceremony, he handed the boot to me. "Tradition," he said.

Oh-kay!

This was my last challenge as the rookie and, just maybe, T's own unique way of saying *thank you.*

I took the boot and downed the whiskey and whatever else came with it. To some applause, I might add.

That was T. He was that guy. I'd like to think I passed the test.

The Sacketts was a high-profile miniseries, and I was a key part of the cast. There would be industry screenings with people who mattered. My work would get seen, even before the first installment aired on NBC on May 15, 1979.

It's no exaggeration to say that *The Sacketts* changed me. I had done a solid piece of work, and people would actually see it. I had found a genre where I was sure I belonged. I had been exposed to a lifestyle that I had never really considered but I wouldn't soon forget. That job changed my professional opportunities and my whole outlook on what my appetites might be—and not only as an actor. In all of my life. This life should be a part of my life.

I don't think I was really intimidated by T. I had worked with a lot of directors by then and played for some very tough coaches. For some, you just nodded so they didn't know your head was asleep. Some you listened to and still did it your way. And some would say things you would remember for the rest of your life.

I will always remember Bob Totten.

CHAPTER NINE

Don't Know Where I'm Goin', but There's No Use Bein' Late

G reat news!

They wanted me to bring back Lance White for another *Rockford* episode.

I had just finished up a movie of the week for CBS. *Concrete Cowboys* was an adventure-comedy, and it paired me with Jerry Reed. It wasn't a pilot, just a movie of the week. We played modern-day cowboy drifters who hop a freight to Nashville and end up pretending to be private investigators in search of Morgan Fairchild.

The director was the supremely professional Burt Kennedy, who had directed John Wayne, Kirk Douglas, Robert Mitchum, Glenn Ford, Henry Fonda, and just about anyone else who had ever been in a western. That included my new friend James Garner in *Support Your Local Sheriff* and its sequel, *Support Your Local Gunfighter.*

Jerry had done *Smokey and the Bandit* and a couple of other movies with Burt Reynolds. He was a bundle of energy and had a talent that was hard to match. How do I put this? He was funny. He was one of a kind. He could sing. And he had great acting instincts. I mean, he never did anything even close to what he had just done, even in the same scene. For a film editor concerned with continuity and putting two pieces of film together, he was *very* hard to match.

Morgan was a highly trained and, yes, very beautiful actress. She was a terrific balance for me and my energetic friend Jerry. Morgan's career was on the ascent, and we were lucky to have her. She and I became friends, and I knew we would probably work together again.

I guess the thing I remember most about working on *Concrete Cowboys* was not what happened on any given day but what happened on a day that none of us could have anticipated and certainly didn't welcome. We were going to shoot the big bar fight, and it was going to take the entire day. On a TV budget, that's a big deal. It was the day John Wayne died.

All of us knew on the long drive to location. It was kinda like the elephant in the room when we got to the set. Burt looked beat up. Nobody wants to waste time on a TV schedule, but this wasn't a waste of time. Burt talked to us. I guess I said something. I have no idea what I said. There was a sense of kinship in the room. We were talking to our tribe.

The company had brought in a bunch of stuntmen from L.A. for the fight scene. Many had worked with the Duke. Some of them even had the honor to double him once or twice. The scene we were doing was not a dark, fight-for-your-life kind of fight. It was more like what the Duke did in some of his later movies like *McLintock!* or *Donovan's Reef.* In the best sense, it was like a Daffy Duck cartoon, real consequences for an explosion but then Daffy comes out just fine.

This was a talented group of professionals who performed the *dance* that was the essence of a movie fight scene. They knew how to throw a punch. They knew how to take one. Wayne knew how to do both, but it was his reaction to a punch that would set the tone of a fight. This required walking a fine line, and nobody did it better than the Duke.

Some days are hard. Some are easy. This one was hard because of a very real sense of loss. But it was also easy because of whom we honored, and maybe John Wayne just might have been a little bit touched by what went on in that room on that day.

It was well known that the Duke liked tequila. Back at the hotel bar, quite a few of us had a shot (or two) in his honor. And for the lifers—

and I was happy to say I was starting to feel like a lifer—this moment in time felt essential.

Burt always wore a hat just like Wayne wore in the trilogy of John Ford films, *Fort Apache, Rio Grande,* and *She Wore a Yellow Ribbon.*

"Where'd you get that hat?" I asked Burt.

"I'll get Luster Bayless to make you one," he said.

Luster Bayless was one of the most famous western costumers around. And Burt did what he said he'd do. He gave me a hat just like John Wayne's. I have it to this day.

——

I was thrilled to have another chance to play Lance White. It was also liberating. This had to come right from Steve Cannell—and certainly Jim Garner would know about that. The new *Rockford* episode, "Nice Guys Finish Dead," would take place at a private-detectives convention and bring back some of the show's favorite characters, including Jimmy Whitmore and an actor named Larry Manetti. If I had any doubts—and yes, I still had them—about whether Steve was sold on my work, this offer wiped them away. It may sound silly that I needed the added validation, but I guess I did. Actors, at least this actor at this point in time, can be prone to putting too much responsibility on their own shoulders for the success or failure of a project. I suppose that thinking began to creep in when I started doing leading roles.

I had been laying bricks for over a decade and had never really stopped and reflected on the journey. It had been a long road, so the progress was hard to quantify. But the time had served me well. I was twelve years older and was growing into—Curt Conway's favorite term—my *instrument.*

That's a highfalutin way of saying I was growing up. Not just in age but in my work. I was now getting offers instead of readings and screen tests. I was accepted in westerns, and with *Rockford,* my appetite for finding humor in drama had been rewarded. I began to realize that I had served those six pilots pretty well, and doing them had served me well. I had studied all this time, and the work had helped me learn how to apply my craft.

Being a well-kept secret wasn't really such a bad thing. Now that my work was starting to be recognized, I was much more—how did I put it about my friend Sam?—*formed.*

It was hard to imagine being in a better place as far as my job prospects were concerned. Being a bricklayer at heart, I refused to refer to my work as a career. While I knew actors never stopped learning, I could handle lots of roles that fit in my expanding wheelhouse, and I was free from any contractual obligations that could get in the way. So I could maximize any offers that came to me. I was about to do Lance White again and was prepared to deliver myself to the uncertainty of the future.

———

Bettye said she was sending me a script for a pilot at Universal.

"What's the offer?" I asked.

"You wanna hear the rest, Tom?"

"The rest?"

"It's not an offer," she said. "They are assigning it to you under your last pilot deal."

"That's over," I said.

"I know that, Tom."

"They can't do that," I said. "That's just not right."

"I know that too. *So . . . ?*"

I took one of my deep breaths. "Is the script any good?" I asked.

"Not for me to say, Tommy," Bettye answered. She told me the show was called *Magnum,* and it was about a private detective in Hawaii.

Bettye, also being a writer's agent, said the script was written by Glen Larson and he would be the executive producer.

"You know what I'm going to say next," I told her.

"That you don't really like his shows."

"Good guess."

She said I should at least read it. "And then we'll talk."

Glen Larson started out as a singer with the Four Preps. Their big hit was "26 Miles": "Twenty-six miles across the sea / Santa Catalina is a-waitin' for me." The Four Preps even appeared in the first *Gidget* film.

I liked the song, but I didn't like his shows. His current hit was *Battlestar Galactica*. A kind way to put it was that the show was derivative of *Star Wars*. He'd also done *Alias Smith and Jones,* which was derivative of *Butch Cassidy and the Sundance Kid*. I dutifully read the script. My role was Harry Magnum. Between that name and the title, one could say that Glen's latest idea was derivative of Clint Eastwood's Harry Callahan in *Magnum Force*. Except it wasn't that. It was more James Bond–ish. It's hard to explain, but the whole story seemed to be watching itself. Harry Magnum owned a Ferrari and had a stewardess on each arm, and there were also a couple of Dobermans. There were lots of explosions but not a flaw to be found in Harry Magnum. For someone who would be happy channeling Murray Burns in *A Thousand Clowns,* this was a problem.

"So, Bettye," I said, "I read the script."

"And . . . ?"

"I don't like it."

If you added the circumstances under which it came to me, I hated it. "This isn't right," I said. "I won't do it." And I meant it.

Bettye's reply was something I will always treasure. It was just two words. "I understand."

All right, maybe I didn't understand what I was getting into by saying no. But to this day, I think I understood exactly: What they were doing just wasn't right.

That's what I believe was driving me at the beginning, and it would remain at the core of why I was picking a fight. Actually, Universal was the one who was picking the fight. I had the sense to know they were powerful and well prepared. And so did Bettye.

I had already learned the hard lesson that many agents just aren't concerned about their clients' interests. They don't want to alienate a major studio or network by starting a fight. Most fool themselves into thinking that they can arrive at something that is mutually beneficial, and they can even get indignant if you suggest a conflict. This was enough to drive you crazy. Bettye's words—"I understand"—told me she knew exactly what we were getting into. As far as she was concerned, I had made my feelings known to her, and she was representing *me*. I knew I had an advocate in my corner.

———

I was sitting next to Jim Garner in his souped-up van back at Universal, waiting for the crew to catch up to us so we could shoot the next scene on the new *Rockford* episode. I was pretty quiet, and Jim noticed. Actually, I think he had kinda taken me under his wing. "What's going on?" he asked.

"Nothing."

"Okay."

Then I got started. "Well . . . it's just that . . . Universal is trying to make me do a pilot, and they have no right to do that."

"It's not something you want to do?" Jim asked.

"I hate it."

Jim said something about not wanting to give career advice to anyone, but then he said, "Look. You don't have much power. But if you don't want to do it and they want you, you will never have more power than you do right now. That's all I'm gonna say."

That advice from Jim was like a floating spar in a shipwreck. Jim

Garner always carried with him a genuine humility, and he wasn't going to tell me what I should or shouldn't do. At the same time, when it came to battling major studios, Jim had never ducked a fight. In 1960, Warner Bros. had suspended him because of a writers' strike while *Maverick* was being filmed. That didn't seem right to him. So he fought back, declared his contract void, sued the studio, and won his case at trial. That legal precedent benefited actors for decades. Later in his *Rockford* run, Jim would go to war with Universal. He'd end up accusing the studio of "creative accounting," a phrase that actors and directors quickly rallied around.

So when Jim told me not to overlook the power I had, I paid close attention. None of this was about Glen Larson. Not explicitly. I didn't even tell Jim that Glen had written the pilot, though I did know that Jim and Glen had had their own difficulties. There was a story that Jim had punched out Glen one day at the front gate of the studio for stealing something from a *Rockford* episode. I didn't know whether that was just Hollywood legend. But I knew that when Jim was talking to me, he was sharing something he had learned from his own hard experience. I think the reason Jim's words spoke so strongly to me was that, if he were in my position, he wouldn't hesitate to fight.

—

Bettye arranged lunch at Ma Maison, the place to be and be seen in those days. She was joined by a young attorney who was making his mark in the industry. He was a partner in a show-business law firm that was the new powerhouse in town. The firm was Ziffren, Brittenham & Gullen. Bettye's lunch partner was Skip Brittenham. The third person at the table would be me.

Skip's version of my arrival is a little embarrassing to me, but he loves telling the story and he swears it's true: When I walked into the restaurant and made my way over to their table, he saw a lot of heads turning my way. That was not something I noticed, or at least I chose not to notice.

"Is that him?" Skip remembers asking Bettye.

"That's him," she said.

"Can he act?"

"He can act."

"I'm in."

Skip had already done his homework. Universal was saying they had a right to extend my contract based on the work I had done outside the studio. "Yeah, but they had to notify me . . . *before* the contract expired," I said.

"Legally, you're right," he said. "But they've got about fifty lawyers that will say different. Let me see what's going on over there. Just know this: I will always be on your side."

"We're gonna fight this," Skip said to me when we spoke again. He said he had a plan to free me from making Glen's pilot. "But you can't do anything that will look like you are acting in bad faith during the renegotiation."

———

A couple of days after our lunch with Skip, Bettye was on the phone again. "Glen Larson called," she said.

"Okay . . ."

"He said he wants to take you to Hawaii."

"Why?"

"So the two of you can hang out and have some fun while he rewrites the script and tailors it to your talents. That's an exact quote, 'tailors it to your talents.'" The tone in her voice was more than a little sarcastic.

"I don't want to go to Hawaii with Glen," I told Bettye. "I'm sure he's a lot of fun. He seems like a good guy. But I know me, and if I go over there with him, it's gonna make me feel obligated."

Bettye just listened.

"You gotta understand, Bettye. It's not the character. It's not the story. It's not even what he thinks is funny."

"Okay?"

"It's the character, the story, *and* what he thinks is funny."

"You've got to call him, then," she said. "Remember what Skip said. 'Good faith.'"

When I called Glen, he couldn't have been friendlier. "We'll stay at the Kahala Hilton," he said. "I'll rewrite the script. We'll have a great time."

I had my excuse ready. "I can't. I promised my son we'd finally spend some time together. I'm sorry, but this is family."

"So bring your son!"

This I hadn't expected. Now I had to improvise. "Well . . . he's kinda shy. I won't be able to spend time with him while we're working."

"Have him bring a friend," Glen said.

The next thing I knew, I was sitting with Glen on the beach at the Kahala Hilton, watching my son Kevin and his friend Adam Fowler having fun in the ocean. Glen did most of the talking, and I had on my best acting-in-good-faith face. Glen was a nice guy and a good talker. He talked about Hawaii, life, where we were going to dinner, everything but the project. I'd spent a couple of hours listening when Glen got up and said, "You need anything?"

"I'm good, Glen."

"Then we'd better get to work. You won't believe dinner!"

I signaled the boys. We got in our expensive rental car and headed for the Outrigger Canoe Club, just outside of Waikiki. A high school friend of mine and Bob's, Dennis Berg ("Bags"), had gotten me a guest membership. I joined Dennis and his wife, Tina, on the Hau Terrace overlooking the Pacific and Waikiki. The boys went surfing, real surfing in real waves. Not the tepid little swells in the bay that the Kahala Hilton had created. Dennis and I had Coors Lights in glasses of ice. Tina had white wine. We caught up on things and talked about old times. This was much more my speed. And I needed this time with friends.

Dinner with Glen and a couple of his friends was at Hy's Steak House in Waikiki, I think because he knew I liked the place. I had a great steak with a very nice and expensive Robert Mondavi cabernet reserve because he knew I liked that too. Glen was cordial and charming. He talked about his house in Hawaii and what a great lifestyle living on the islands was.

I enjoyed dinner and the company when I could put aside the elephant in the room. But it was hardly a working dinner. And that was pretty much a blueprint for the rest of the trip: An open tab at the Kahala Hilton for whatever I felt like at any given moment. More dinner at Hy's. Yes, it's easy to fall in love with Hawaii. But that wasn't the point. I already had, long ago, during a two-week infantry exercise with the California Army National Guard and when I discovered the Outrigger Canoe Club on a weekend pass. I remember saying to my friend Dennis Berg back then, as we sat with our Coors Lights in a bucket of ice on the Hau Terrace at sunset, "What a place this is. Too bad I wouldn't have any way of making a living here."

When I flew home with Kevin and his friend, I don't think I was very good company. No problem for the boys, who were having a great time upstairs in the 747's first-class lounge. Thankfully, that gave me time, preoccupation being my constant companion at the moment.

For Universal, this whole brain-damaging game boiled down to just one thing: money. If they could hold me to the expired contract, they could get me at a cheaper, prenegotiated price rather than just saying, "We like your work, and we'd like to start a new relationship with you. What will it take for us to do business?" That's what they should have said. But they were willing to spend tons of money on an extravagant trip to get me on the cheap. That really pissed me off.

It was a long flight back to the mainland, longer than the trip over because of headwinds. And yes, the irony in that occurred to me.

It's funny the things you think about.

The rewrite was waiting for me when I got home. The story was the same; just the jokes were different. I didn't want to do *jokes* for the next seven years. Seven years is what the contract required if the show was a success. While I didn't think this show could succeed, my nightmare was that it might.

I had to do some serious thinking. Sleep never came to me that night. I called Bettye and Skip the next morning. "You say I have to appear to be acting in good faith. Okay. I will consider this project—but only if Glen Larson has nothing to do with writing it or producing it."

"You realize what you're saying?" Bettye asked.

"Bettye, I realized what I was saying the moment I said it."

"You understand what you are risking, Tom?"

"I am well aware of what I am risking. Probably everything."

I knew enough about the industry to understand this much: They were offering me a pilot for my own show. Not a buddy show. My *own* show.

Who the hell does your client think he is? He's never even had a show on the air!

I knew and Bettye knew that's what their response was going to be. Feigned indignation or, just maybe, real indignation. If the latter, they would make it their mission to destroy my professional reputation.

While I don't think I revealed the source, my reply to my friend and agent was "If they want me, I will never have more power than I do right now." And while not doing this might pretty much destroy my chances for success, doing it might destroy my chances just the same.

In spite of everything, I was finding a certain satisfaction in the realization that this was my time. My time to acknowledge that I was a grown-up actor. My time to drive the bus, not just be a passenger. The consequences belonged to me now, and I shouldn't hide from that.

Two questions seemed to dominate my thoughts. The first was *Why now?* I had never even considered the option of turning down something like this before. It never entered my mind on the six pilots I had done. So why now? And *Where did I get the tools?* The tools to confront such powerful interests who were used to getting their way. The answer to that was much easier to understand and appreciate.

From my mom and dad, I certainly had a sense of doing the right thing. I was never a perfect kid. But when I screwed up, my first regret was always that I'd let them down. They gave me the gifts of conscience, consequence, and responsibility. I don't think I will ever fully have an answer to *Why now?* I would have to satisfy myself with the fact that I was ready, I was prepared, and it was time. The questions I kept asking myself on that long flight home told me I was thinking right. And this risk was going to be the price I would pay for the opportunity.

I don't know how long it took for Skip to get back to me, but it seemed like a lifetime. Bettye was on the call when Skip told me I was half right on what Universal's response would be. "All they said was 'Who the hell does he think he is?'" Skip said. "So I told them, 'He's the guy you want to put in your series.'"

He said they were committed to the old contract and they were prepared to go to court to enforce it.

Oh-kay!

Skip said he thought that going to court would be a big mistake. The cost to me would be too high—both financially and professionally. This was not looking good. They had a fish on the hook, and they weren't about to lose it.

"So I'm stuck," I said.

"Hold on," Skip said. "I'm not done." He told me that Universal was prepared to amend the deal.

They would offer three pilot ideas, one of which would be a show called *Magnum* that Glen Larson would have nothing to do with producing or writing. I would have to choose one of the three.

Skip had my trust, as he does to this day. *Who the hell does he think he is?* Well, I sure as hell didn't think I was Paul Newman or Steve

McQueen. And pushing this envelope any further would have been punching way above my weight.

"Okay," I said. "Thank you, Skip. Thank you, Bettye."

My friend George Will, in his terrific book on baseball, *Men at Work,* wrote, "Luck is unpredictable but talent takes advantage of it. Thus the talented have, in effect, more of it." After more than a decade, I knew I had a certain talent. And if I wanted luck on my side, I had to take advantage of it.

———

Time seemed to slow way down after I made my decision. I wasn't going to second-guess myself, but still . . . As my friend Sal said, "You have to allow yourself errant thoughts." That was as true in life as it was in acting. In reality, I got some news pretty quick.

When *Gypsy Warriors* almost sold, the network had ordered some scripts, Bettye told me. "There's a writer Cannell had do a couple of scripts for you. His name is Don Bellisario." Bettye said he wanted to meet with me and would like to rethink the *Magnum* pilot.

Don Bellisario was not your typical Hollywood screenwriter. He came from coal country outside Pittsburgh, where his father ran a bar, and Don grew up hearing stories from returning World War II vets. He enlisted in the Marine Corps after high school and became a sergeant in the pre-Vietnam days. After studying journalism at Penn State and toiling away at an ad agency in Lancaster, he moved to Los Angeles, dreaming of writing for the movies and TV. His big break came when Steve Cannell hired him as the story editor on *Black Sheep Squadron.* Steve thought Don, with his coal-country roots and military background, had a real feel for a slice of America that many East and West Coast writers did not. When NBC canceled *Black Sheep* two seasons in, Steve put Don on the *Gypsy Warriors* scripts.

I knew I'd gone with a writer's agent for a reason!

My friend Bettye McCartt had been doing her homework. Coming out of the Cannell stable, Don was a promising idea. Then Bettye added, "After the network turned down *Gypsy Warriors,* Don went to work with Glen Larson on *Battlestar Galactica.*"

"Oh."

In came those errant thoughts again.

We met for lunch at La Serre, a showbizzy place on Ventura Boulevard in Studio City. Lunch was always packed with industry people. I was sitting across from Don Bellisario, not really knowing how to conduct a meeting like this. It wasn't like I'd ever hired a writer before. I wish I could remember the conversation, but those errant thoughts again . . . I think there was a lot of *fumfering* on my part. I'm sure we talked about being in the military. Don was a marine sergeant, I was a sergeant in the army infantry. I'm pretty sure neither of us bought the idea that being in the military left an emotional scar on all who served, though that view was very much a part of the zeitgeist at the time.

I think we talked about Don's advertising days and doing commercials. I, of course, had plenty of stories about being *in* them. There were no uncomfortable silences or awkward moments, except in my head. I'm sure it was Don who broke the ice.

"So, what do you want to do, Tom?"

"I don't want to beat up Glen," I said. "He has every right to do the show he wants to do. It's just not a show I want to do."

If something is important, you can tell when someone's listening. And Don was listening.

"I want to play a character with flaws," I said. "I had real good experiences on *Rockford.* So I want to do a show, a drama, with humor. I remember Jim Garner saying to a director, 'I don't do comedy. I do humor.' At the same time, Jim never lost the dramatic stakes, the reality."

I remember exactly what Don said next: "Say no more."

—

People who worked with Steve Cannell used to say he could write four scripts at the same time, two with his hands and two with his feet. It turned out Don was fast too. I didn't know whether he'd picked it up from Steve or just had that gift, but a two-hour movie pilot came back very quickly. Bettye said she was sending it to me.

"Is it any good?"

"Not for me to say."

Well . . . it wasn't good. It was *really* good.

In fact, it was the best script that had ever crossed my path.

I called Bettye. The first thing out of her mouth was "It's good, isn't it?"

"No, actually, it's great," I said. "It has story and scope. It has humor. The dramatic stakes are incredibly high. And I want to do it."

"You might want to wait to see the other two submissions," Bettye suggested.

"No. I do not."

"That's what I hoped you'd say, Tommy."

And there it was. Don had written a terrific movie, and it truly was a movie. No happy scene at the end where the main characters prove how much they like each other and why you should tune in next week. It was a story about a career Naval Academy graduate who served as a Navy SEAL in Vietnam and decided to hit the pause button. No, not because of disillusionment or delayed stress, but because, as he put it, "One day I woke up at thirty-three and realized I'd never been twenty-three."

His name was Thomas Magnum.

CHAPTER TEN

Making *Magnum*

I f you were one of the most successful showrunners in network television and someone kicked you upstairs and out, you might understandably hold a grudge. If the person responsible had never had a regular job in nighttime television, you might want to get even. I never got the sense that Glen Larson had the inclination to hold a grudge or get even. I ended up knowing Glen for many years, and he was never anything but cordial and welcoming in our conversations. It takes a big man to treat business dealings for exactly what they are, business. Actually, "Big Man" was the title of the second hit record for Glen's singing group, the Four Preps. I don't have any idea what that means except I like the song.

I always valued the friendship I had with Glen. Sure, he had ownership in the new *Magnum,* and maybe Skip helped smooth things over. But still. The story goes that Glen thought Skip Brittenham did such a good job representing me that Glen ended up hiring him as his lawyer too. Look, I came to know Glen well enough that there was no way he could harbor some secret resentment without me clocking it. Glen Larson is gone now, and I will always see him for what he was, a nice guy.

When casting started for "Don't Eat the Snow in Hawaii," Don asked me to join him. I had never been asked to be involved in the casting process, but Don told me I was playing the lead and my input was important. Every pilot I had done up till then was as support, an ensemble, or a buddy show. *Magnum* was something different. While my character had buddies, I was *the lead*. This didn't really scare me or add pressure. Certainly, lots of worse things had come my way. It just meant that this project was going to be different from the get-go. I did have one concern, but I kept it to myself. I had been on the other side of the desk so many times, I wasn't sure I could separate empathy for the actors from critical judgment. Having spent over a decade in the actors' tribe, I kinda knew this would be a work in progress, and as it turned out, it always will be.

Don made the first choice easy. "I want Larry Manetti to play Rick. I wrote it with him in mind."

"No problem," I said.

I wasn't giving in; I really didn't have a problem. Don had written for Larry in *Black Sheep Squadron,* and Larry had delivered. I had also worked with Larry on my second *Rockford.* And how do I say this? He had something that's hard to describe, but if you could bottle it, you could make a whole lot of money. After Larry came in and got the good news, we went out for a drink, and he told me this story: Before I met him, he was sitting on the soundstage with Simon Oakland, one of those irreplaceable "working actors" our business is blessed with. A tall guy in a white suit came in.

"Simon, who's that?"

"That's the new guy."

"Damn, he's prettier than Elizabeth Taylor."

I don't think I was wearing a white suit, and I sure wasn't prettier than Elizabeth Taylor. But that's my friend Larry.

———

"So, what do you think of John Hillerman for Higgins?" Don said to me.

"Don, I'm glad to see you're aiming high. But John Hillerman, I mean, do you really think he'd do it?" I was well aware of John's work. Peter Bogdanovich's *Paper Moon.* Mel Brooks's *Blazing Saddles.* He worked with Jack Nicholson on *Chinatown*. "He would be perfect, but . . . *come on*."

Don just said, "Let's try."

John Hillerman's interview was pretty short. He had some questions. I was understandably quiet and let Don lead the discussion. "Can you do a British accent?"

"Yes."

"Would you read a scene with Tom?"

"I'd like to work on the accent first."

Welcome news to me. I hadn't known Don was going to ask us to read. At that point, I had never even said any of Thomas Magnum's words out loud. I mean, who would be auditioning whom? I jumped in. "That's fine with me, John."

And that was it. After he left, I spoke up. "Don, I think he wants to do it. He's perfect for the part, and I know you think so too. So why don't we just offer it to him?"

Don was ahead of me on this one too. And that's what he did.

Don also just happened to have an idea for the T.C. role. Gerald McRaney came in for the part. I'm pretty sure I read with him, and Mac was terrific. Then, out of nowhere, Don's friend Phil DeGuere nabbed him for his own series, *Simon & Simon*.

Don seemed undaunted. He told me he had always wanted to try going another way. Not as a second choice but as a different choice. "What about a Black actor for T.C.?"

"I think it's a great idea."

That's when Don brought up Roger E. Mosley. My first thought was that Don couldn't possibly have seen *Terminal Island*, or he never would have wanted *me* as Magnum. Again, Don was aiming high. Roger was doing great work, and I wasn't sure he'd be interested. I told Don about Roger's powerful lead role in the movie *Leadbelly*, directed by the legendary Gordon Parks.

Well, Roger came in. Obviously, I knew him, but not well. I never even had a scene with him in *Terminal Island,* and he always kept pretty much to himself. We read together, and Roger was terrific. He had an imposing physical presence and completely understood the humor in his relationship with Magnum. Happily, he seemed interested in getting the role. I don't remember how, but somehow I got a moment with him alone. The elephant in our respective rooms was clearly on our minds. Roger, as he was prone to do, spoke first.

"We're not ever going to mention that other thing, are we?"

"No, we are not. Not ever."

So, we were set . . . Oh yes, there *was* one other thing. The dreaded network reading. The lead actors had to be okayed by the network. In those days, the CBS execs and the Universal execs sat in the seats of a small screening room, and the actors did a scene in front of them. Actually, we were almost on top of them. I can't honestly remember a lot about the rest of it. Larry, John, and Roger did very well. John's British accent was perfect, by the way. But I'm not sure I exactly made Thomas Magnum come to life. Those errant thoughts were back. The most prominent one came from, yes, the critic on my shoulder whispering in my ear: *They're sorry they ever thought of you in the first place.*

Errant thoughts or not, we were set. And in a very real way, I felt validated. These three talented, gifted actors were on the ascent and weren't about to do a pilot just for a paycheck. I wasn't sure how much they really knew about my work; a lot of it was pretty hard to find. The fact that they were willing to risk their futures by signing on . . . well, it meant a whole lot.

———

Dinner our first night in Hawaii was great fun. John, Roger, and Larry were there. Don was there. Our director, Roger Young, was there. A wave of excitement and optimism filled the room. This was also a seasoned group who had learned, often the hard way, that nothing in our business is certain till it's certain. Nobody wanted to jinx things. One step at a time. So a certain caution tempered the atmosphere just a little. But to be honest, excitement won the night. Secretly, I felt—and I got the sense that everybody else felt—this one was going to work.

When I closed the door of my suite at the top of the hotel, I looked around the spacious room. Actually, it was just one of several spacious rooms. I opened the minibar and took the two little bottles of Johnnie Walker Black—Universal wouldn't mind. I cracked them open and found the ice bucket. No, I didn't have to go down the hall to the ice machine. The ice bucket was full. Turned out it was somehow always magically full.

I had one more day before we started, and that was a good thing. I knew it would be a long time before I could sleep. My head was too full. I went out on the, yes, spacious balcony overlooking all of Waikiki and the vast Pacific. Alone with my thoughts, I wondered if this was "getting there." But you know what? I had already "gotten there" a few times, and it wasn't such a big deal, because there was always somewhere else to go. It was the whole journey that mattered most. All of it. All twelve years of it. And some of my fondest memories were reserved for the struggle, the path that was littered with so many failures.

Fact is, all those years were a blessing. The frustrations and also the failures. The learning part, studying and working on countless sets. The long path had given me time to grow into my *instrument*. Facing this new journey, I wasn't as anxious as I was excited. And I welcomed the uncertainty of it.

———

Our first day of shooting was pretty straightforward. Not easy, but we had a rare occurrence in the making of movies: We started at the beginning. It wasn't a big dialogue day either, mostly physical action. The opening of "Don't Eat the Snow in Hawaii" was used to establish

Magnum's private conversation with the audience. His voice-over narration. It also established his complicated relationship with Higgins. It was John's first day too, not to mention Zeus and Apollo's, Higgins's two Dobermans. Thomas Magnum swims into the beach, moves to the gate of Robin Masters's estate, and picks the lock, all of this based on the pretext of checking security. Once inside, he races toward his real objective, Robin Masters's red Ferrari 308 GTS. He wants to borrow it. As he works to pick the lock on the car door, Higgins and his two companions discover that the gate is unlocked. Higgins sends Zeus and Apollo racing across the vast lawn toward the invader. He glances at the angry dogs and hurries back to the now-urgent task. "Work the lock. Don't look at the dogs. Don't look at the dogs. Work the lock." He looks back at them. "You looked at the dogs!" And he makes it inside the Ferrari just in time.

That took most of our first day. I gotta say, watching John work was just a joy. In that one short appearance, he spoke volumes about Jonathan Quayle Higgins III. And made me laugh many times when I wasn't supposed to.

There was one hiccup in the day's work. No, not the dogs. They were perfect. Happily, I can confidently say it wasn't me either. Film crews try to anticipate anything that might go wrong. This crew was a good one, most having worked on Jack Lord's *Hawaii Five-0.* The problem wasn't me, but it was *about* me. I had never sat in the Ferrari until we did the scene. When I climbed in, an athletic feat unto itself, I discovered my head was hitting the roof. The quick fix was to slouch down in the cramped quarters. I mean, the roof had to be on, or why would I have to pick the lock on the door? But they didn't want me to have to slouch down with the roof on for the whole movie, and there was another part of the problem that hadn't been anticipated. In any spare moment of downtime, we were going to shoot glamorous running shots of the island. Drive-bys. Aerial shots. And the audience needed to see who was driving. So the roof needed to be off. Only when it was raining would we need the roof.

In our last shot of the day, we found the solution. A "magic of film" kind of solution. As I leave the estate, I stop the car and pretend I am undoing the roof, and I slide it backward into its final resting place. Its final resting place was actually in the hands of two prop men on either side of the car. Obviously, they were out of frame. Then I look to the camera, smile, hit the gas, spin the wheels, and drive off. I was well aware I was breaking the fourth wall, as we call it. That can be risky, over-the-top cute, or just plain dumb. But when I looked right into the camera, I got the feeling that Magnum was sharing his little victory with the audience, and it just seemed right. I don't remember if it was in the script or if I improvised it. Either way, Don was smart enough to accept it, or I was smart enough to give a good idea a try—it didn't really matter where it came from. It was a brave choice, and you know what? It worked. And it schooled me in the kind of humor that was so necessary in a pretty serious story about the murder of a friend. That shot is in the opening credits of all the 163 shows we did . . . except the roof part.

———

We worked long days on the movie, trying to get the most out of our two weeks in Hawaii before we returned to Universal to finish filming. Since we were "on location," we worked six-day weeks. Some nights, there was time for dinner. But if you were the lead in a movie where the main character uses narration to share his thoughts with the audience, you were in most every shot. Most nights, there was time only to prepare and then sleep. Some nights, sleep didn't come quickly. It was three hours later on the mainland in Los Angeles. You didn't want to call and wake someone up just to share how your day went. There was one person who had for many years waited up for those calls. But the person with whom I had shared those years of my life was no longer in it; Jacki and I had separated before the opportunity of *Magnum* even presented itself. Still, there's no course you can take in school to prepare you for the end of a marriage. If you knew the *why* of it, you wouldn't have let it happen. But it *had* happened. Things just hit you from time to time, and some nights, I couldn't escape that sense of loss.

Larry asked me to dinner one night. I knew him well enough by now to hear in his voice that it was important. Actors on a project like this are consumed with the work, as they should be. It didn't take my friend long to get to it. "I don't think Don's happy with my work."

"Why, Larry?"

He told me that, after a take, he would see Don whispering in the ear of our director, Roger Young. Then Roger would come over and tell him, "You need to sound more like Humphrey Bogart."

"I just don't think I should do an imitation of a screen legend," Larry said to me.

Larry's character, Rick, ran Rick's Café and wore white dinner jackets, an homage to *Casablanca*. The similarities were intentional. I reminded Larry that he had been in two network series by now and should trust his instincts.

"Yeah, but that's the only note I get."

It wasn't like I could or should get in the middle of this. I already knew Don well enough to know he could be a bull in a china shop. I just made sure my friend knew that I had already done scenes with him and thought he was doing great work. And Larry was never one to see himself as a victim. So he moved on. And we had a great time together, as we always did.

There was a lot of optimism on the set, always of course tempered by not wanting to jinx it. John was terrific. Roger was terrific. And yes, Larry was terrific. Most all of his scenes were with me. So when we heard "Cut!," I would give him a subtle smile and a little nod, and it seemed to bolster his confidence. If my friend was worried, he never let it show in the work.

—

My six years of military service were essential in my understanding of Magnum's career in the Navy. That wasn't an abstraction to me. It was real and tangible from the moment I first read Don's script. I had finished my service as a sergeant E-5 (three stripes), what is referred to as a *noncommissioned officer*. It didn't take much of a leap for me to understand this Naval Academy officer's service—I mean, it wasn't like I had to do a ride-along with a bunch of military guys. I didn't have to do *that* homework, and I could concentrate on what made Thomas Magnum tick. Although, honestly, that would always be a work in progress.

And suddenly, like always, it was over. Don screened a rough cut for me pretty soon after we finished. For some reason, I never freaked out at watching myself, as a whole lot of actors do. A rough cut is just that, a very rough assembly of scenes. But all the work had paid off. The story that Don's script told was compelling, and it would only get more so through the rest of post-production. Sure, I would have liked a couple of do-overs, but it didn't escape me that I had pulled my weight. And I knew, given the chance, I would only do better and better.

Now all that remained was the wait. After six dress rehearsals, I was a seasoned veteran of the wait. But that didn't make the time go any faster. *Best to keep busy.* So that's what I tried to do.

During that pretend-I'm-busy time, Bettye called. She said, "You have an appointment with Steven Spielberg and George Lucas for a picture called *Raiders of the Lost Ark.*"

CHAPTER ELEVEN

It's Complicated

think they've seen just about everybody in town for this role," Bettye told me.

"What's the role?"

"Oh, just the lead."

"Well, it wouldn't be the first time I came in at the end of the line. Can I read the script?"

"No one has. They are being very secretive."

"Okay . . . it'll be worth it just to meet those two guys."

When I walked into the room for the audition, I expected a bunch of key people on the other side of the table. It was just *those two guys.* Steven Spielberg and George Lucas. I didn't feel particularly nervous. I mean, I would have had to be about a half a bubble off of plumb to think this was anything but a long shot.

Now, I'm a little vague on what was said, because they both seemed interested in having a conversation more than conducting an audition. Sure, we talked about work, but other stuff too. Movies I'd seen, where I was from. I was a big *Star Wars* fan, so I'm certain I brought that up. I gotta say, it may have been the most cordial audition I'd ever had. On my drive home, I thought, *Boy, that was pretty cool, no pressure, and having a face-to-face with two people whose work I love. Something to put in my memory book.* And what a great diversion it was from my preoccupation with the outcome of my pilot.

———

When I checked in with Teddy's, they told me Bettye had called. "Good news" was the message.

I called Bettye back right away, thinking it might be news on *Magnum*.

"They want you to test for *Raiders of the Lost Ark*."

"You're kidding."

"I wouldn't kid about this, Tommy."

"My goodness . . . I can't wait to read the script."

"They're not letting anyone read the script."

"Oh . . . Then I'll come to your office and get the pages for the test scene."

"They won't give me the pages for the test scene. All I know is that it will be for the lead. His name is Indiana Jones." Bettye said they had assured her I would have ample time to prepare when I got there.

I got there, and I found they were lighting the lobby of their office, not some soundstage. Steven was quick to greet me, gave me the pages for the test, told me not to worry and to take all the time I needed. I could tell he knew how hard screen tests were. He told me if I had questions, not to be afraid to ask them when we got started.

Oh-kay!

Steven Spielberg is actually going to direct *the test.*

I guess that could have freaked me out. But Steven had been so calm, so intuitive, and so reassuring that the news was fortifying. I'm not blowing smoke. Whether it was real or imagined, his tone communicated a confidence that was contagious.

There was wardrobe waiting for me. The hat and leather jacket helped me understand the period. And it was kinda neat. And the clothes actually fit. Clearly, this was a first-rate outfit who'd done their homework.

I wasn't testing with Karen Allen, who ended up getting the role. A young, very beautiful, very able actress named Sean Young worked opposite me. If I was doing well—and I kinda felt I was—it came from

Steven. This was his set, and the time it took was whatever time he felt was necessary. Nobody looked at their watch or whispered in someone's ear, all things that an actor might pick up on and be distracted by. And it seemed Steven was invested in a positive outcome.

When I drove home, there were no recriminations. Just a sense that I had given it a shot. I have to say my head was full of thoughts. *They're testing a lot of people . . . What if* Magnum *sells? . . . What if it doesn't sell? . . . This is the lead in the next big franchise after* Star Wars, *so the process is going to be a long one.*

So many good things were presenting themselves. I had to just leave it alone. *Raiders* was a big long shot. But all in all, maybe I was finally making it to the majors.

———

"You got a callback for *Raiders*," Bettye told me. "They want to see you again."

"What else did they say?"

"Nothing, not a thing."

So back I went.

"We want you to play Indiana Jones."

I think it was Steven who told me. George had always been kinda quiet. Always thinking, taking things in. But I think I detected at least the hint of a smile on his face.

Look, I don't have a clue how I responded. I hope at least I said thank you.

They said this was a new franchise for them and they thought it needed a new face. And . . . I guess I was *it*.

I think it was then that I said, "I need to tell you that I've done a pilot for a series with CBS, and if it sells, I have a contractual obligation." They looked at each other, kinda surprised. I wasn't sure what that meant until they thanked me for telling them and told me it had been their experience that actors never offered that kind of thing at a time like this, and they were surprised that I would.

"Well, I don't know how I couldn't. So . . ."

I waited for the bad news.

They told me they weren't really concerned. They had a lot of cards to play at CBS—in other words, the network wanted their movies. Not to mention both projects were at Universal.

"Let us worry about that," they told me.

They handed me the script, and Steven said, "Go over to my office, read it, and then tell us what you think."

At that point, I'm sure I said thank you, and I was escorted to Steven's office.

I sat down and turned over the title page. What I saw told me just how protective they were of their material. The writer Lawrence Kasdan's pages weren't just numbered, they were serial-numbered. I put on my best philosophical face, my take-it-easy-this-may-not-work face.

Around page eight my guard just dissolved. *Oh, shit . . . this is terrific.* I wasn't sorry it was terrific. It just made things complicated. It was the part where Indy is being chased by a huge round boulder rolling down the hill after him. I was reminded of when I rode my bike to the La Reina Theatre on Ventura Boulevard in Sherman Oaks and watched the Saturday-matinee movie serials for twenty-five cents. And, of course, it reminded me of the crawl at the beginning of *Star Wars.* The whole movie was right there on the page in front of me.

I kept reading, and it never let me down. Most screenplays leave to the imagination what you might see on the screen. Steven and George, or George and Steven—I wasn't sure who did what, or maybe it was Lawrence Kasdan—anyway, they were telling you what you were *going* to see. And, oh shit, it was terrific.

All of this was going to be, how do I put it, complicated. Extremely complicated. But hey, I had George Lucas and Steven Spielberg on my side. And, of course, I had my trusted A-team in place, Skip and Bettye.

———

I may have been a seasoned veteran of the wait, but I was now faced with the World Series of waits. At least to me, the stakes were that high. I tried to define what I was waiting for in the simplest terms I could. If *Magnum* sold, a good thing, could I do *Raiders*? If *Magnum* didn't sell, a bad thing, at least I could do *Raiders,* a good thing. If I could do both, a very, very good thing. A home-run-in-the-World-Series kinda thing.

Wait, what if I lose both by complicating the process? I was now officially in the weeds. *Stop it, Tom.* Yes, this was a problem, but it was about as good a problem as an actor could have. In my better moments, that was what I held on to—in my lesser moments, clung to.

The wait went on for some time. For more than a month, Steven and George stayed with their offer. And something happened to me that I could not have anticipated. The longer it took, the more I was fortified by the fact that I was the guy they really wanted. I wasn't getting many progress reports from Skip and Bettye. I knew they didn't want to make me crazy with updates. In fact, I wasn't going crazy. I guess I should have been, but I wasn't. And I'm not really sure why. I guess time had schooled me to unconsciously put on my philosophical face. Not outside, for others, but inside myself. Don't know where I'm goin', but there's no use bein' late.

———

Skip had told me, before he first went in to see Bob Daly at CBS, that he felt he could work it out. Working it out meant my being able to do both projects. I wasn't trying to get out of *Magnum,* and Skip would never suggest that I try. And I just wouldn't do something like that. He told me that Bob Daly was a good guy, and he didn't think Bob would want to stand in the way of what was a chance in a lifetime for me. "And that's how I will put it to him."

Skip said George just needed assurance that he could finish *Raiders* even if it meant a small delay in the shooting start of *Magnum*. And Bob would get the benefit of having a movie star signed to a seven-year series deal. Yes, it sounded complicated, but not really. It was as simple as it was complicated. I was simply waiting for a yes or a no.

The wait had lasted a little over a month when I got a message from Teddy's. Bettye and Skip had set up a conference call. I took a very deep breath and dialed in. Skip took the lead, but I knew Bettye so well, I could hear her listening.

"*Raiders* is not going to happen."

"Oh."

"I'm sorry."

"So am I . . ."

———

I thanked Bettye and Skip for trying so hard, as I knew they had. Skip told me that the more he tried to persuade Bob, the more Bob seemed persuaded that he shouldn't give in. Bob told Skip that he didn't want a movie star in his series, that if he let me do *Raiders,* I wouldn't want to do *Magnum* and I would try and get out of it. I, of course, knew I would never do that, but the situational ethics of some in Hollywood had not been my friend here. There were too many stories of actors doing exactly what seemed to be driving Bob Daly's decision. Look, I wasn't the head of CBS, and it wasn't Bob Daly's job to walk in my shoes either.

Skip told me that Bob said he would have been more inclined to say yes were it not for the fact that *Magnum* was their highest-testing pilot by far. Good news at a bad time. He also added that there was no order for *Magnum* at this time. He would announce the whole CBS fall schedule when the network felt the time was right.

How 'bout now!

Somehow I let the frustration pass, only to find out that Bob had told Skip all this needed to be held in strict confidence, which he did, except for Bettye and me. And which I also did. I held my mud. Time to cowboy up and get on with things. But what a hell of a ride the spring of 1980 was turning out to be.

—

"Get on with things" is so easy to say and so hard to do. But then I already knew that. Just as I was experienced in the wait, I had also lived with the disappointment that often followed. It's funny—I think I learned the most from losing the least important role in all six unsold pilots, that giving in to a sense of failure and self-pity was not a place I ever wanted to go again. That lesson had lasted and pretty much prepared me for this World Series of disappointments. I tried to keep my philosophical face. I don't know how I did it, but I did. And over time, with reflection, I think I knew the *why* of it. My growth as an actor always seemed tied to my confidence in my acting. I guess that's why saying to myself, "Tom, you're enough," always seemed to ground me in my talent. Now, Steven Spielberg and George Lucas had in essence enthusiastically said, "Tom, you're enough." And it wasn't just in gesture; I had been *their choice.* Forevermore, I could keep that in my hip pocket.

No, I didn't pretend I was happy about losing *Raiders,* but I was not about to think of myself as a victim. Whether I thought CBS made the wrong decision—and I think they did—that did not mean I was treated unfairly. I had learned many times over by now that life isn't fair, but at least I could be. Nobody made me sign a contract for *Magnum.* At that moment in time, it was the best thing that had happened to me in about a dozen years as an actor.

I caught myself with a little smile on my face when my thoughts wandered to the first scene in the *Magnum* pilot. Only now it was *Don't think about* Raiders, *concentrate on* Magnum. Good advice. My friend Sal Dano had said many times that if you have a problem, don't stare at it with blinders on; get busy and stay busy. It won't make the problem go away, but maybe the solution will come to you kinda *sideways*. In my best moments, that's what I was trying to do.

Bettye called, and I could hear it in her voice. "CBS announced at the upfronts that *Magnum* is officially on the fall schedule. *Magnum* will be on Thursdays at eight o'clock."

Miles to go. So stay level and even, Tom.

I got a lot of calls with congratulations. I gotta say, personal calls are a whole lot of notches above texts or emails. I had a nice dinner with my family: my mom, my dad, Bob, Marti, and Dan. I know, nothing's certain till it's certain. But somehow I felt I wasn't going to get written out of this pilot.

There is very little time for reflection in the life I had chosen, at least if you're living it right. But this time it was earned. I thought again of what my friend George Will wrote: "Luck is unpredictable but talent takes advantage of it. Thus the talented have, in effect, more of it." How lucky I was that serendipity had indeed done its best to smile on me again.

———

It turned out my friend Jerry Reed also had a series for the fall. It was called *Concrete Cowboys. Good for you, Jerry.* Yes, I know, Jerry and I did the movie; at the time, it was just a movie of the week. The producers had no contract with me for a series, so they had recast my part. And I wished them well.

Bettye called. "*Magnum* has been taken off the schedule."

"Say again."

Bettye hesitated a moment. "*Magnum* has been—"

"I heard you, Bettye. I just wanted to . . . Oh, never mind."

"It seems Universal and CBS are at an impasse."

Bettye told me CBS had ordered a show to be shot in Hawaii. And Universal had told them they were going to shoot it in L.A. and pretend it was in Hawaii. After considerable back-and-forth, CBS said they were pulling the show.

"And that's what they did. *Hawaii Five-0* is done, and they want a show in Hawaii."

"So do I. But I know, no one's asking me."

"Well, Skip said just sit tight and hopefully ride it out."

Always expect the unexpected. Maybe I heard that in a movie somewhere, but now I would have to add the phrase to my résumé of cautionary thoughts. Skip told me this was just about money and that Universal wanted a bigger fee for producing what was going to be an expensive show. "These money things usually work themselves out, so don't worry," Skip said.

"I've got nothing else to do, so I just might worry a little bit, Skip."

To me, two industry giants were in a pissing contest, and that meant egos were involved. Who knew what was going to happen? *Always expect the unexpected.* Sitting tight and riding it out became my newest task in what was fast becoming the *Magnum* saga. I only hoped I didn't find myself in the fall sitting home without a job, watching *Concrete Cowboys,* knowing I could have been in it.

———

Almost two weeks had passed when Teddy's told me that Don Bellisario had called.

"We're back," Don told me.

"Great news. Who told you?"

"Our boss at Universal. So it's official."

Don told me that with *Five-0*'s departure at the end of the previous season, we would be based at the Diamond Head Studios they had used and that we'd start shooting maybe mid-July.

Don's tone changed a little. "They want me to change the name of the series to *Magnum, P.I.*"

"That's a horrible title. Did they say why?"

"One of the studio lawyers raised a concern that they might get sued by Clint Eastwood or Warner Brothers."

"Because?"

"Because of the Dirty Harry movie *Magnum Force*. And in Glen Larson's script, you were called Harry Magnum."

"That's ridiculous. The character's name is *Thomas* Magnum."

"Yes, it is, isn't it? But I don't think we can win this one."

I was gratified to hear Don use the term *we*. It implied some form of a partnership in the journey we were embarking on. And I knew that starting a fight about the title would be about the worst signal that I could send to the studio that was going to be my home. Particularly at this moment in time. This was definitely above my pay grade, so I deferred to Don's judgment. But it really was a shitty title.

Clearly, the genius lawyers at the studio meant *private investigator*. But having spent some time in the melting pot that is Hawaii, I knew that *P.I.* is also a somewhat less than flattering abbreviation for *Philippine Islander*. Ever since then, and to this day, I'm pretty sure I have a spotless record of referring to our show as simply *Magnum*.

Don's tone changed a little more. "There is a note that I absolutely have to win on. I'm hoping you'll feel the same way."

Don told me that they'd said the Vietnam flashbacks had to go. That Vietnam was "death," as they'd put it. They said they loved them in the pilot, but the show now needed to "move forward."

"Where is this coming from, Don?"

"They won't say."

"Well, they may have watched the pilot, but they sure didn't *understand* the pilot."

"I'm glad you feel the way I do," Don said.

"I do. I absolutely do. So . . . let's pick a fight."

For me, *Magnum* was not about a car or dogs or even Hawaii, really. It was about four former warriors. Two marines and a Navy SEAL from

Vietnam, and another veteran from conflicts gone by. All trying to make a life for themselves, not because of a rejection of the life that they had lived but, in many ways, as an affirmation of it. The time had come to tell that story. And that's what Don Bellisario had done and done so well.

Don's story didn't hammer a message. It never veered from its obligation to entertain. But the bond those characters shared was there, beneath the surface, for those who chose to look for it.

I didn't think for a moment that everyone at Universal and CBS was united in what was being advocated. But Don and I were as one on this. And with all the frustration I had swallowed, I think I welcomed a good fight. A chance to be proactive about my future.

With no possibility to divide and therefore conquer, it didn't take long for the powers that be to fold. "Don't Eat the Snow in Hawaii" had, after all, been their number one pilot and their best chance of success for the fall season. And the lesson for me, as I hoped it was for Don, was that when we spoke as one, there was no limit to the possibilities.

—

A full season for a series on the three major networks was twenty-two episodes. *Magnum* was picked up for thirteen. While I would have preferred the bigger security blanket, at least I knew what I could count on, worst case. But I wasn't thinking about worst case, so the number didn't dampen my enthusiasm for *Magnum* one bit. However, my newest cautionary thought—always expect the unexpected—tamped me down a little and leveled me out. *Just keep laying bricks, Tom.*

The hard-earned lesson that all those years had taught me was that you can't control the outcome, but you're fully in control of the effort. And I was getting pretty good at the effort thing.

So, what does the actor's handbook say about preparing for a continuing role in a series? Oh, that's right, there really isn't an actor's handbook. So, how 'bout I make something up? Wardrobe and props were to me always an integral part of developing the character.

The only recurring, regular roles I'd had were on *Bracken's World*, which doesn't really count, and then *The Young and the Restless*. In both cases, they dressed me. No one was interested in my opinion, and I didn't have any say in the matter. Now, I had both.

Both those characters were on display in just one event. Now, I had more time to say who he was, where he'd been, stuff like that. And that required a certain specificity. Thomas Magnum wasn't wearing a costume. In other words, it couldn't look like he forgot to take the hanger out of his shirt before he put it on. I had a lot of time over the years to watch a lot of actors, and in my opinion, a lot of them forgot to take the hanger out. So instead of having a few "changes" for the pilot, now I needed to know what was in Thomas Magnum's whole closet.

The hat. John Ford said always start with the hat. Magnum, being career military, was probably a ball cap kind of guy. So, the Detroit Tiger cap was not negotiable. The Tigers in 1980 needed a lot of help, and I had been a natural-born fan since birth. I wasn't compromising my character, just giving him an eccentricity. Anyway, it was my nickel, so why not. I had also taught myself that if you're playing the lead in a TV series, especially a character with the iconic qualities Don gave Magnum, people should be able to close their eyes and literally see the character, kinda like the hat and jacket in *Raiders*.

Part of that was keeping the wardrobe as simple as possible. Simple in the best sense. So, I wasn't about to wear a different baseball cap every week "just to be fair," much to the dismay of my brother Bob and Tommy Lasorda. I felt I did need a second ball cap, and Don came up with the VM02 cap from T.C.'s Marine helicopter unit, one that Roger could wear too.

I also kind of knew Magnum should wear Hawaiian shirts. I wasn't really interested in reminding the viewers we were in Hawaii. I mean, one could consider that obvious. I thought those shirts represented something more important. Thomas Magnum, the Annapolis career officer, had made a startling change in his life. That narrative was critical to the heart of the character. I wanted something that looked kinda like the ones Montgomery Clift wore in *From Here to Eternity*. That retro look. Hawaiian shirts weren't exactly in vogue at the time, and I wasn't about to find them in vintage clothing stores. People were smaller in those days. None of those old shirts would fit, anyway. So, I found someone who was making them in Manhattan Beach. Squeek was her name. I'm sorry, I can't remember her full name because all anyone called her was Squeek. She was terrific and made all the original order of shirts for Magnum under the label, you guessed it, Squeek.

The other essential shirts needed to have a military feel, lots of khaki and OD green. And they needed to have some age on them. Thomas Magnum was not doing all that well as a private investigator.

Most guys on TV don't wear shorts, but in Hawaii most guys do. So, shorts were definitely in his closet. He could have no idea that over time his shorts would be considered short. That's what shorts are, short. Traditional shorts, anyway. And as an authority on Thomas Magnum, I can tell you that he could also have no idea that shorts would mutate into oversize pajama bottoms. And that his response would be to "hold the line" until the pajama-bottom aberration was swept away by the inevitable wave of traditional shorts. And pajama bottoms would be doomed to fashion exile.

As an important prop, the gun he used in the pilot was just right. The legendary designer John Browning's masterpiece, the Colt 1911 .45-caliber automatic, was the sidearm I trained with in the U.S. Army. It was standard issue in the Navy too, so it was a perfect fit. The Colt served to validate the Navy tradition in the Magnum family as it had served the U.S. military since, well, 1911.

It was now mid-June of 1980, and everyone was looking forward to our mid-July start. So, my attention turned to where I would live in Hawaii. This time it wasn't just for a visit.

I was happy and proud that Jacki had the duplex. It was something we had both worked hard for. And I hoped it would give Kevin stability at a time when so much was changing. I, on the other hand, was living in an apartment above the Sunset Strip. Not exactly a luxury pad, but it was nice enough. It's just that living there was not exactly my style. Whether in success or not, I was starting a new life, and I was anxious to get on with it.

As maybe you guessed, Bettye and I had become lasting friends. Leave it to Bettye when she said, "You're not gonna be happy in an apartment." I had always felt she was a lot more "worldly" than I was, so I listened. The plan became for me to go over right away and live in a hotel. Part of that would be on Universal's nickel once we got the official start date. "You need to celebrate this win, so treat yourself and stay in the Kahala Hilton." Her words served to kind of grant me permission. I think it was Bettye who said actors need to celebrate and commemorate their wins because it was kind of a trap in their nature, and certainly in my nature, to dwell on the losses. So, the Kahala Hilton it was, like my last trip except I didn't have Glen Larson's unlimited expense account. Bettye would come over with me and look around for a permanent place I would like. That offer was not exactly in the agent's handbook, but God bless my friend Bettye McCartt because my head was way too full of thoughts.

The first thing I did when I got there was to get a guest membership at the Outrigger Canoe Club, again sponsored by Dennis Berg. I loved that place, ever since my first visit.

The Outrigger was a family club steeped in years of tradition, and my hope was to become a part of that local community. I knew I wasn't going to get any sense of being a local hanging out at the Kahala Hilton drinking Mai Tais with pineapple slices and umbrellas in them. So, the Outrigger became my daily destination. The prices at the snack bar were more in keeping with my budget. If I wanted to splurge, I would go next door to Michel's at the Colony Surf, which was right on the beach, and have breakfast. But I gotta say that the pancakes at the Kahala were terrific. So, I succumbed from time to time. And I felt a certain kinship driving out of my hotel each morning and passing the Kahala condos on my left, home to *Hawaii Five-O*'s Jack Lord.

The Outrigger Canoe Club's mission was to foster and promote the water sports of Old Hawaii. Of course, outrigger canoe paddling was foremost, as well as surfing and swimming. Charter member and four-time Olympian Duke Kahanamoku excelled in all three. But all sports were very much a part of life at the club. Outrigger is credited by many with the invention of beach volleyball, and on the roof above the snack bar and locker rooms were two sand volleyball courts. Having played at Will Rogers and Sorrento beaches in Santa Monica, I hoped to become a part of that volleyball community. Bettye and I had some nice dinners, usually at the Kahala. I had dinner a couple of times with Bags and Tina. Bags is what everybody called Dennis Berg. We always ate outside on the Hau Terrace. It was less formal than the restaurant, and the uniform of the day out there was usually a T-shirt and swimming trunks. It was also cheaper. We'd sit out there with our Coors Lights in glasses full of ice. Friends would come and go, sitting for a while. On Saturdays, the club set up big outdoor barbecues. You'd sign your tab for a steak, chicken, or fish and cook it yourself while, around you, kids of all ages would run around playing in the sand while their moms and dads cooked dinner. The other pastime on the Hau Terrace was watching the sunset. As the sun started to disappear below the horizon, all heads would turn to look for the "green flash." The word was that just as the sun disappeared on certain nights, if the conditions were right, you could see a green flash. On a couple of nights, I heard a few scattered oohhs and aahhs but saw nothing. Did I mention the house specialty? It was one of those stiff rum drinks, fortified with other spirits and fruit, put in a blender and full of crushed ice. It was called a Henry Special, named after a long-time frequenter of the Outrigger bar. A Henry was nothing as pedestrian as a Mai Tai. No piece of pineapple and no umbrella. It didn't need the frills. When you were presented with a Henry, you had entered the major leagues of rum drinks. And a couple of them would definitely enhance your chances of seeing the elusive green flash.

What was it that I said to Bags my first time there when I was in the National Guard? "What a place this is. Too bad I wouldn't have any way of making a living here."

Each night, sooner or later, I would head back to the Kahala and the four walls of a very nice hotel room. Alone with my thoughts, sleep never came easily.

One night, when I got to the hotel, there was a message from Bettye: "I've been trying to reach you all afternoon." There were, of course, no cell phones to ruin your day at the beach back then. But what she told me kinda made my day: "I think I found a perfect place for you. Let's meet for breakfast, and then I'll show it to you."

Bettye's perfect place was just that. It was a small, old, one-bedroom house that the owner, Linda Fisher, had renovated. It was part of a small cluster of homes on Black Point. The point had been formed by the lava flow from Diamond Head way back when. The neighborhood was a modest and charming one with no connection to the fancy side of Black Point. The fancy side was closest to Waikiki and was home to the elaborate estates of Jim Nabors, Alan Carr, and the legendary Doris Duke. On this side, Black Point Road meandered down toward the water and to its dead end. Bettye's pride was on an offshoot, Akulikuli Terrace, that curved its way up the slope a little.

This charming little house with wood siding wasn't on the water, or it wouldn't be in my price range. But it had a spectacular view all the way down the beach in Kahala to Hawaii Kai and, in the distance, Koko Head. And the house faced out to the vast Pacific. All the ships arriving from the mainland passed by Black Point on the way to Honolulu. The story was that the place was originally housing for the commanding officer of Fort Ruger, the military installation in and around Diamond Head Crater. Fort Ruger was established in 1906 by Teddy Roosevelt to defend Honolulu Harbor. It was closed in 1955 with the advent of the Cold War. But the fort was still used for training by the Hawaii National Guard.

Bettye said that Linda Fisher was going to live in the separate bedroom above the garage.

"So . . . well?"

"What's not to like? I love this place."

"I just knew you would, Tommy."

Bettye told me that we needed to close the deal, that rentals were tough to find. "I'll advance you the money if you need it."

"Thank you, Bettye, but I've got some savings. . . . Any idea when we get the official start date so I can begin to get paid?"

She said Universal was dragging their feet as a ploy in their contract negotiations with SAG. "But that's just what they do. *Magnum* is going to happen. Count on it."

A couple of weeks later, ensconced in my new home, I was down at Outrigger having my morning coffee at the snack bar. It was July 21, 1980. I unfolded my *Honolulu Advertiser*. The Screen Actors Guild had called a strike. I looked up at the sky and shouted: "Are you done yet?"

Well, I didn't actually do that. I just wanted to.

———

The strike was designed to affect the filming of the big-box-office movies planned for the holidays and to disrupt and delay the start of the fall TV season. In principle, I couldn't support it. But in reality, no one asked me. I just did not think it could succeed. But it did succeed in disrupting and delaying the start of *my* fall TV season. *Magnum*'s start date was postponed indefinitely.

"*Magnum* is going to happen. Count on it." Bettye's words resonated in a different way now. Yes, it was going to happen, but it was going to happen *sometime*, and I would have no idea if *sometime* was a short time or a long time.

This presented a problem since I had advanced the money for the first and last months' rent plus a significant security deposit. I also had financial obligations to Jacki and Kevin that I wasn't about to ignore. I was determined to ride this out on my own. I wasn't going to take Bettye up on her offer to help, I would never ask my mom and dad for a loan, and I wasn't going to take out a bank loan using my *Magnum* contract as collateral. I had some savings and, while finite, they would give me some time. I would need to think straight through this new chapter of the *Magnum* saga. *Always expect the unexpected.* That cautionary thought had at this point become words to live by.

"If you have a problem, get busy. Maybe the solution will come to you kinda sideways." *Thank you, Sal.* The first thing I did was talk to my landlady, Linda Fisher. I wasn't going to ask her for any special treatment. I had, after all, signed a contract. I told her I would make good on my rent payments. She was in the final stages of her renovation of the house, and I suggested that, being kinda handy, maybe I could do some of the work to help her finish up. Linda agreed and would pay me seven dollars an hour. I had my dad to thank for the "kinda handy" part. Having been a carpenter and a B-29 mechanic, he was skilled in just about anything that needed fixing, and he was patient enough to teach me. And by now, I knew a whole lot more than just how to repair a broken window. Seven dollars an hour was not really going to help much in making my nut, but it would help keep me busy. Somehow, I knew the worst thing I could do was preoccupy myself in the day-to-day progress of something that was very much beyond my control.

Just keep laying bricks, Tom. In this case, maybe even literally.

Ben Johnson would always say, when a scene wasn't going well, "We'll get 'er if the money holds out." Well, Uncle Ben, let's hope it does.

Thomas Magnum must have fallen in love with Hawaii on a stopover before or after a deployment. It was, after all, the place he chose to make home when he "woke up at thirty-three and realized he'd never been twenty-three." And where was I right now? Oh, yes. In Hawaii. All that was left for me to do was embrace the uncertainty of the future and start to live the life Magnum had chosen. No, I'm not talking about spending some time with a bunch of the island's private investigators. And let's be honest, Thomas Magnum was not so good at that anyway. I'm talking about living the life of a "local." That wasn't going to be very hard. I already loved the place.

I knew the answer to my next question without asking it. The Outrigger Canoe Club. Outrigger, after all, in addition to its Hawaiian roots, had quite a few "haole" transplants from the mainland. So, I made the ultimate sacrifice to my craft and started to spend most of my time there.

My day would start with, of course, coffee. Then, checking in with Linda. Doing whatever odd jobs she might have for me. Then on to the club for breakfast at the snack bar, and hopefully to the volleyball courts in time to get the first game as the "nooners" showed up. The nooners were local members who played during their lunch break. After a game, or sometimes two if my partner and I won (two was the limit for nooners), covered with sweat and sand, I would head for the beach and dive into the comfortably warm Pacific. All of this was in full view of the people having lunch at Michel's, at this moment in time above my pay grade. Also, at this moment in time, I was pretty much an anonymous noncelebrity. So, the diners couldn't care less, I was just another swimmer. That was something I knew might not last. And the memory of that time I treasure to this day.

There was a windsock about two hundred yards out from the beach. I would swim out and back. And most often, I would then head for the Hau Terrace soaking wet. I'd sit with some of my new friends and have a Coors Light in a glass full of ice. No, not a Henry Special, not at 1:30 in the afternoon. Sometimes, Dennis Berg would show up for lunch. Bags didn't play with the nooners. He was a much more accomplished player than that. But he was a good friend and a fixture at the club, and he saw to it that I became a part of his circle of friends.

Most afternoons, I went back up to the courts. Not to play, to watch. Afternoons were when the "big sticks" showed up. Outrigger had its share of All-Americans and Olympians. And along with the top beach players always coming in and out of Oahu, those games on A-court were indeed something to watch. Maybe I'd have dinner on the Hau Terrace or grill a steak on my little hibachi on the deck of my new house. Sometimes, Bags and Tina would get me out of the house, and we'd have dinner at some simple, nontouristy, locals place. From time to time I'd get invited to one of my new friends' homes for a barbecue. But you know, it wasn't as a celebrity. I was just a friend of Bags who may or may not be doing a TV show in Hawaii . . . sometime. There really is such a thing as the spirit of aloha.

Bettye was so right. I wouldn't be happy in a hotel. I've always been comfortable having time alone. Time to think. As long as I felt it was my choice, not circumstance. I was living in my own home, a place I was growing to love. Yes, I had my moments. Sometimes, sleep did not come easily. I was, after all, starting a new life in so many ways. I talked to my mom and dad just about every day. But we didn't really talk about my business. They gave me the respect of knowing I was on my own, as I should be. I stayed in close touch with Bob, Marti, and Dan. But that was about it. And I had discovered that if I didn't want to take a business call, I could use the excuse that it was three hours later on the mainland, and it was too late to return the call. Bettye and I would talk, not every day, but she would check in. She told me both sides were digging in, and it looked like a prolonged process. Having made my choice, I felt more than prepared to take anything that might come. Besides, these were good times I was living. And somehow, I knew that in success, these days might soon be gone forever. What was the rush?

—

There was hardly a rush anyway with the entire television industry shut down. Maybe that was just me trying to put a positive spin on an unfortunate situation, but I really don't think so. In my unsold-pilot days, I had small brushes with the idea of celebrity when Esme would send me to different show-business gatherings, premieres, and screenings. I'd show up, and maybe a photographer would snap a photo. Then, some other photographers would snap one just in case I was "somebody," which I was not. If there was a red carpet, I might get a microphone stuck in my face with the question "Should I know who you are?" I mean, how do you answer that? My usual, incredibly creative response was no.

All that changed when CBS announced at the upfronts that *Magnum* was on the fall schedule. I had to do a press conference and some one-on-ones.

This was new territory, something you can't experience until it comes at you. And here it was. The first question was all too often "What's the show about?"

"Didn't you just go to the screening?"

No, I didn't say that. But I wanted to.

I mean, how do you answer that? I would try to be polite and hopelessly attempt to answer. I wasn't very good at that, so my attempt was usually a description of a show I would never want to see. Then, the questions inevitably moved to the personal. This was something I was not prepared for. Maybe that was stupid, but I just never asked myself, *Gee, if I ever get famous, how much of my private life am I willing to share?* Now this question took on an urgency, and I knew I needed to find an answer for it. I considered most of the personal questions to be private, and I was uncomfortable answering them. I was raised to be polite, and I was. So, it was hard not to answer their questions, but it was even harder to do so. I just kind of phumphered around the subject.

"What did you expect? It goes with the territory?" It occurred to me at the time that those who say glib things like that probably have never been there.

I knew, even in failure, *Magnum* would be seen by millions, and my life would change in ways I couldn't imagine. Look, this first encounter with celebrity was just something I dealt with at the time. It didn't leave a scar, but it did leave me with a memory. And that memory would occupy my thoughts for years to come.

———

By September, the strike had taken on a life of its own. And while it is easier to be patient in Hawaii, Mr. Frustration was always lurking close by, if I chose to invite him in. He was a little like the "critic on your shoulder," but not as cunning and smart. Now that I'd found a life in Hawaii, it wasn't really much of a contest most days.

I was having a bacon-and-egg sandwich and my morning coffee at the snack bar, not really knowing if it was a Tuesday or a Friday. I took the rubber band off the *Honolulu Advertiser*, unfolded the paper, and saw it right away: on the front page below the fold, an article with the headline "Spielberg to Finish Movie in Hawaii."

Shooting out of the mainland, George and Steven had worked out a deal where they could continue shooting *Raiders* despite the strike. If you are Steven and George, you get to do those kinds of things. As they should. And good for them.

So, *Raiders* was coming to Hawaii to wrap up the last two weeks of shooting. Well . . . okay. Look, that's not exactly news you just take in stride. But to be honest, looking back, I pretty much took it in stride. I was certainly aware of the irony, but it wasn't like they'd be shooting on Akulikuli Terrace. They would be on another island, Kaua'i. Would that really be any different than if they were shooting in West Covina? I don't think so.

There was one thought that could have had the potential to make Mr. Frustration a worthy opponent. But I pushed it away and didn't allow the idea to form. At least for a while. *Raiders* wrapped shooting the last few days of that month. The Screen Actors Guild strike was still very much a reality. I couldn't push it away any longer.

I coulda done both.

Having some survival skills, I realized that "I coulda done both" was not a chapter of the *Magnum* saga I should dwell on. So, I bought a surfboard. Actually, I had one made. I couldn't really afford one on my budget but . . . *so what!* This was, after all, in a weird kind of way, a special occasion. Donnie at Surfline Hawaii, an Outrigger member, designed it for me. As he put it, "Tom, you're a big guy, so you need a custom job." And when I got to try it out, you know what? I was hopeless. No, not just in need of practice. Hopeless. But at least, like most of the locals, now I had a surfboard leaning up against the wall in my garage.

By October, the Screen Actors Guild settlement agreement was ratified. SAG had been on strike for ninety-four days. It was the longest strike in SAG history. In my opinion, *Magnum* aside, there was no way a new deal could ever make up for the loss of income so many of my fellow working actors had suffered.

———

"Tommy, we're a go. We can start shooting."

Bettye gave me the news. And from Bettye, I believed it. After a ride on a roller coaster, sometimes you need to just settle a bit. In this instance, not required.

"About time."

"More than past time," my friend told me. "Go treat yourself to something, and we'll talk."

"Thank you, Bettye."

The call was short. I was on the beach on the phone extension at the lifeguard stand. It was late afternoon. In October, early in the week, the club wasn't crowded. So, I found a small table on the Hau Terrace just in front of the seawall. The quiet waves would roll in against it and retreat back out to sea. I could faintly hear the Hawaiian trio singing inside the restaurant behind me. I was alone with my thoughts. I had a Black Label on the rocks and watched the sun go down. No green flash, but then I didn't need one. For me, the sun was coming up.

A few of the tables had filled up by now, some with friends. Nobody came over, but then friends have a way of sensing when it's not the time. I'm sure I had another Black Label as I sat there in the evening air thinking about the last year. What a winding road it had been. And there was also something that had been percolating inside of me that I hadn't fully accepted until this day. That the long road had been a blessing. I was thirty-five years old, not the twenty-two year-old who had stumbled on his words at his Fox audition. That "formed" quality I saw in my friend Sam had clearly presented itself. All those years had schooled me, not just in my craft but about myself. That it shouldn't be just about what I wanted to do, but about who I wanted to be, the *person* I wanted to be doing it. Using Kipling's words, "I had met with triumph and disaster" and had at least *tried* to treat those two imposters just the same.

Glen Larson's script gave me the chance to take a risk because it presented an opportunity. I had persevered through the disappointments and delays. Now, I had lived the life that Thomas Magnum might have lived. And because of it, I was fortified and equipped to deliver myself to the uncertainty of this enormous opportunity.

———

I was standing at the base of Diamond Head in front of one of those prefab, steel, industrial buildings. "If it rains hard, you'll have to stop shooting. Too noisy inside. Same thing for airplanes and helicopters."

The voice sounded kinda like it came from Steve McGarrett—and why not? Jack Lord was standing next to me. Jack had reached out and offered to show me around Diamond Head Studios. To be honest, I didn't know what to expect. I had heard he could be "a little grand." By now, I had heard the local story of him getting into an argument with a guest star and telling him to "get off my island." Well, stories told over and over are apt to change and get exaggerated. What I saw was a gracious, respectful, somewhat formal man who chose to be there when he could have been on the beach at the Kahala condos.

Jack seemed very polite by nature and, when you do 281 episodes as the lead in a series, any grandness may very well have been in the eyes of the beholder. And anyway, in show business, it was his island. That he was speaking to me as a peer was, well, fortifying. I didn't want to sound like a fan, so I didn't ask him about *Stoney Burke*, a series he had done that I loved about a rodeo cowboy. I didn't ask him about the wonderful heavy he played in *Man of the West* with Gary Cooper. I didn't ask him about the first Bond movie, *Dr. No*. The first time you meet someone like Jack Lord, whose work you respect, you don't want them to feel like they are being interviewed. By now, this was pretty much a pattern with me. Wishing I could, but feeling I shouldn't. Jack talked about the challenge of combining the crew from the mainland with the local crew. He said a film company on a weekly television series should be like a family. Jack looked right at me and said, "You are in a unique position to make that happen."

Jack in his own polite way was reminding me of a responsibility I like to think I already knew would be squarely on my shoulders this go-round. "And make sure your producer knows you must receive a Hawaiian blessing before you start," he added as he led me toward a small group of bungalows as if he owned the place, which of course he kinda did.

He stopped in front of a bungalow. "That's my office. Space is at a premium here. So, I want you to have it."

"Well, thank you, Jack. You know I've never had an office."

"Well, I think you're gonna need it," he said with a smile.

What a kind thing to do! Jack could easily have kept that space, and nobody would have said a word. But he was passing the torch. And at that moment, I knew it. And I think he knew it. That was so important to me. But you know, it seemed to be even more important to him.

CHAPTER TWELVE

A Beginning

I spent most of my last Sunday as an unemployed actor at the club. But I didn't stay to watch the sunset. I wanted to get back to my place, the small cottage that by now I had settled into and was my home. My new home. My only home. After volleyball and hanging out with friends, the journey I was starting on simply overtook my thoughts. I lit the charcoal in my little hibachi and put on a steak. My mom used to cook me a steak before my basketball and baseball games, so . . . I put a Stouffer's macaroni and cheese in the oven, cracked open a Coors Light in a longneck bottle, sat down in my beach chair out on my small deck, and enjoyed the ahi tuna sashimi I had picked up at the Diamond Head Market.

This was hardly my first rodeo starting a new job. I knew sleep never came easy at these moments in time . . . too many thoughts. Some were already waiting, and some would come out of the blue and surprise me. I kinda said to myself, "Bring 'em on."

I had done a lot of unsold pilots. I was the young sidekick, a fourth or fifth banana, and the rest were buddy shows. But nobody had ever paid me to play *the guy,* the lead actor in a network television series, until now. I stared out at the vast Pacific Ocean. What a wonderful place to be . . . if you can earn it!

Jack Lord had said I was in a position to make the crew a family. I was well aware of that, thanks to my friend and mentor James Garner. Each of them had made that point in his own way, but it was a reminder of my obligation as *the guy* to provide the leadership to help make that happen. There was no school for that, but I'd had Jim Garner as my teacher. I also remembered how many times I had worked on a set where I was walking on eggshells and how many times I had said to myself, "Boy, if I ever have my own show, that is never going to happen."

Time to step up, Tom . . . if you can.

By now, I was upstairs in my small bedroom, staring at the ceiling. I had opened the windows so I could hear the ocean and feel the gentle trade winds.

I have no idea why, but my thoughts brought me to my mom and dad and my big brother, Bob, and me getting in the family car and leaving Detroit for the unknown. My family was leaving to start a new life in California. You don't remember a whole lot when you are almost four. Most of what I remember was arguing with Bob about who got to sleep on the backseat and who had to sleep on the floor. That was an argument I would always lose, so I was doomed to navigate the hump in the middle of the floor. There were no stops for a night in a motel. Dad was intent on driving straight through. Mom's job was to keep us civil and keep Dad awake. Sometimes we got to ride in the front so Mom could grab some sleep in the back. Bob and I would take turns sitting on Dad's lap, helping him steer the car. Another cause for an argument over who got to be first.

So what was all this about?

My mom and dad had taken a huge risk because an opportunity had presented itself. My dad had a chance to start a new career in real estate—on straight commission, by the way. Whatever risk I was facing now seemed like small change.

We moved into a small house in a housing tract in the San Fernando Valley just in time for Christmas in Los Angeles. And you know what? Santa brought a surprise. It snowed Christmas morning . . . Then I fell asleep.

—

Back in Los Angeles, the first day of a new series was pretty much like any other workday except maybe for some handshakes and a few words from the creative producer. But time is money, so that was always about it.

The morning of our first day on *Magnum,* everybody gathered on the lawn in front of our small production bungalow. John, Larry, and Roger were there. The whole crew, mainlanders and locals, were there. The entire supporting staff was there. I was happy that Don was in from the mainland to celebrate the "groundbreaking" of his idea. Don had written and was going to direct this first episode. And in front of all of us was Reverend Akaka to give this new beginning his blessing.

For the last twenty-four years, the Reverend Abraham Kahikina Akaka was the *Kahu* (shepherd) of Kawaiahaʻo Church, the Westminster Abbey of the Pacific, Christianity's mother church in Hawaii. In his early sixties, he carried himself with dignity and strength. He had a strap over his left shoulder that was attached to a small box with a speaker inside, and a microphone was attached to the box. He was a gentle, soft-spoken man with a velvet voice, and he wasn't about to shout his words. I wish I could remember those words because they were so well chosen. But to be honest, my head was too full of thoughts.

I found something from his Hawaii statehood service on March 13, 1959, that is very much in the spirit of what he said that morning to us. "One of the first sentences I learned from my mother in my childhood was from this Holy Scripture: *'Aloha ke akua'*—in other words, 'God is *aloha.' Aloha* is the power of God seeking to unite what is separated in the world—the power that unites heart with heart, soul with soul, life with life, culture with culture, race with race, nation with nation."

There never seems to be time to reflect in this business. All of us had worked so hard to get to this moment, and it was altogether appropriate for us to take the time to reflect on that with hope and gratitude.

—

First days are hard. You can't get to sleep the night before, and when you finally do, you keep waking up, afraid you've overslept. You're anxious, you're nervous—unless you're arrogant enough to think all you have to do is show up and sport a tan. That wasn't me. I was in the anxious-and-nervous category. Even if the work was pretty good, I never felt it was good enough. Second days were better, and the work would progress in that direction till my last day, when I finally felt I'd gotten it right and wished I could start over.

The last couple of years, I had spent some time in director Milton Katselas's acting class. Milton said something one night about dealing with nerves. He said, "When you work, you're bound to be nervous. You have to make friends with that." He said that if your hands are sweaty, you should talk to them. Tell them, "Thanks for coming. You're part of my talent." His point was that if you fight your nerves and try and make them go away, they won't. If you don't welcome them to the party, they can defeat you. And yes, there have been times when I have indeed spoken to my hands and—you know what?—it helped. But the truth is, this really wasn't a first day. It just seemed that way because it had been so long since we'd shot the pilot, and I wasn't as much nervous as I was anxious. Anxious to walk in Thomas Magnum's shoes again. And no, I didn't have sweaty hands.

Our two-hour pilot would serve as our premiere, so we were shooting what would be our first real episode. It was called "China Doll." Don hadn't only written it; now he was going to direct it. There was a style and spirit to the pilot, and Don—probably the only one who had an idea where we were headed—needed to be there to set us off in the right direction. In the episode, Thomas Magnum is hired to protect a valuable vase from, yes, a beautiful Chinese woman, and is threatened by a kung fu killer.

As I have already said, when I try to explain what a show is about, most often I don't want to see it. I mean, who wants to see the show I just described? So I will not do that anymore. The episode is about the *people* put in this situation. It is about T.C., Rick, and Higgins's encounters with a guy named Thomas Magnum. Don kind of validated the spirit of those encounters when he kept telling me, "You gotta see this line I wrote! When you finally come face-to-face with the kung fu killer . . . you see, his name is Ho. And you say, 'Hi, Ho.'" And Don just cracked up.

Look, of course you need a good plot and jeopardy and all the other elements of a good drama. But while I couldn't know it at the time, we were gonna do a whole lot of episodes, and it's hard to separate them all. What I think of most are the "moments." They remain crystal clear in my memory. And it's kinda funny what you remember, whether from the scripts or what happened during production. There was a scene we shot in Waikiki that takes place in the climax of "China Doll." I am closing in on Ho when, suddenly, a shuriken, a star-shaped throwing weapon, flies right by my nose and sticks in the telephone pole next to me. That's the scene. I asked our special-effects guy, Jack Faggard, "Jack, I'm curious. How are you going to rig that effect?"

"I'm not gonna rig anything. I'm just gonna throw it."

Jack was an old prop veteran and as good as they get. But I'd say he was at least in his mid-sixties. He explained, "On your close-up, I'll stand next to the camera a few feet away and throw it. All you have to do is stay still."

Oh-kay!

Jack threw the pointy metal shuriken right past my nose, and it stuck in the wooden pole. One take. Gratefully.

———

Turned out we were still dealing with labor strikes. This one came from the musicians' union, which meant that we couldn't write any music for the episodes. We would have to use stock music from the Universal library. That's not the kind of compromise you want to make on a new show, but it was what it was. We would use old, tired music from old, tired shows to support the drama. We could also use the opening theme from the pilot and music from that. But there was a problem with that—at least, for me, it was a problem. I didn't like the music from the pilot.

"Bettye, what did you think of the music in the pilot?"

"I hated it."

I wasn't about to ask Don what he thought. The composer was his friend. Bettye and I formed a plan. We would use the downtime to slowly, artfully, separately and together, work on Don. Hopefully, we could make lemonade out of a lemon.

———

"China Doll" turned out to be a pretty good episode. But it was going to be hard to match our two-hour pilot, and in fact, it didn't. It had Don's touch for humor and dialogue, but what it didn't have were the emotional stakes and compelling jeopardy of "Don't Eat the Snow in Hawaii." And maybe I was being unrealistic to think it could. Magnum being hired on a case couldn't compare to the murder of a close friend. As for me, I think I consequently pushed the humor and couldn't find an emotional through line.

I'd seen enough television series to know that it takes time for a new show to find its groove. I kinda left it at that. Well, not quite. Why was I kissing my client, for one thing? It's a little hard to make lightning strike in three or four scenes. And this time, frankly, it didn't. Add to that, the main theme and the canned music didn't work for me. So I was concerned—not alarmed, but concerned.

The title of the next show, "Thank Heaven for Little Girls and Big Ones Too," said it all. And Magnum was preoccupied with the big one. It was a Christmas show, to add to its sweetness. Why CBS would broadcast a show on Christmas night was a bafflement and beyond my pay grade.

When I saw the script for "No Need to Know" and read the scene where I kissed my leading lady, it was clear that there was a pattern here. Romance was in the air for Thomas Magnum. *Where is this show going?*

We were shooting a scene on the beach. No, not the kissing scene. That was on another beach. We were between shots, and I was just sitting in my chair, thinking. The director, Larry Doheny, came up to me. He took me aside and said, "Tom, I get the feeling you don't think this script is very good."

"You would be correct."

Larry Doheny had been on more television series than you could count. I liked and respected him. He told me, "When I get hired, I'm just put in a certain slot. There is no script yet. And when one is ready, that's what I get. Maybe it's good. Maybe it's not so good." He explained that on the not so good ones, he had a rule. "I try to find one thing I can hang my hat on. Maybe it's one scene or even just one moment that I can look at with pride. I hope that helps you a little."

His kind advice did help me, and it's helped me ever since.

Fact was, there was plenty to hang my hat on in these first three episodes. I was ignoring what was the heart and soul of the show. Larry, Roger, and John were totally up to speed, and we could build out from there and solve the rest of the puzzle of where this show was going. That was plenty to hang all our hats on.

———

The production side of the show, during both shooting and post-production, was not included in my job description. But you can learn a lot if you keep your eyes open, and, believe me, I was paying attention.

While we were shooting an episode, there was a second unit shooting most of the time too. The show needed a stock library showing the beauty of Hawaii. We needed shots of the Ferrari traveling that landscape and navigating Waikiki. We needed shots of T.C.'s helicopter taking off and landing, and also aerial shots showing why we'd come to Hawaii to shoot our series. Stuff like that.

Our second unit was shooting air-to-air shots that were terrific. Air-to-air meant we had a camera helicopter and a picture copter. Expensive but worth it. They had finished their day in the late afternoon but were so enthusiastic about the footage they had gotten, they decided to get some closer shots on the way home. But they didn't have a camera double for me. One of the camera crew put on my clothes, and they were in business.

They shot T.C.'s Island Hopper flying low along the waves and were getting great stuff. Then the pilot misjudged the size of one of the swells, caught a skid in the water, and the helicopter crashed, tumbling into the ocean. The pilot survived, but the man who doubled me was killed. His name was Bob Van Der Kar.

This tragedy was all recorded on film as he crashed through the windshield into the ship's blades. When we were told, we were instructed not to talk to the press, and of course, no one did. Thankfully, Universal was able to secure the footage and make sure it wasn't seen, so the family was at least given that small comfort and the dignity to grieve for their loss in private. We were shooting our fourth new episode, "Skin Deep," when the accident happened on November 19, 1980, 4:25 p.m., North Ka'a'awa, Hawaii. Larry Doheny was directing this one as well. When we were told, we just looked at each other. Nothing was said; nothing needed to be.

I'm not sure I knew Bob Van Der Kar. Our units worked separately. He was just a good guy trying to make the work better. But maybe you know what I was thinking. *If he hadn't put on my clothes and sat in that seat . . .*

I'd had stunt doubles who'd been slightly injured being me, but nothing like this. And this left me with a feeling that I can't describe to this day. This was certainly not my tragedy, so I guess it wasn't my responsibility. But still . . .

The caption before the closing credits of "Skin Deep" read, "This episode is dedicated to camera technician Robert Van Der Kar, who died during its filming."

—

"Skin Deep" also had a romantic element. But Don wrote it, so I didn't give any notes. It was about a beautiful actress who records her suicide on tape. Magnum watches the tape and begins to fall in love with her. Except it turns out she isn't dead. It's either a takeoff on or an homage to—you can call it either one—the classic film *Laura*. And now that I've described it, you probably won't want to see it. But I digress.

I think it was about this time that I got a script for the next episode. In it, Magnum goes undercover as a gigolo. Well, I didn't want to play a gigolo. I didn't even want Thomas Magnum to *pretend* he was a gigolo. Glen Larson's Harry Magnum had been way too much of a dashing romantic hero. I had said no to that. At some risk, I might add. Now what would be our first five new shows all had some element of that. Maybe a slightly different version, but it wasn't what I'd signed on to do. I'd signed on to the pilot and the character I played in it. My biggest clue to understanding that character was when Magnum says, "One day I woke up at thirty-three and realized I'd never been twenty-three."

He didn't say that so he could get laid every week.

As an actor, you can't *play* romantic, just like a writer can't *write* romantic. That is a result of an audience, and you can't play results. It is in the audience's hands to decide if they find a given character a romantic hero.

I think all this was pretty much a discussion—okay, maybe a rant—that I was having in my head. And I knew I couldn't, so I wouldn't, do this script.

I didn't make the call. Bettye did. She wouldn't let me. Bettye had handled all the difficult moments during what I call "the *Magnum* saga" and handled them with skill and finesse. This moment, so early on in a new series, required the same. I knew moving on to the next script in line would be disruptive for the staff. But if it brought us back to what brung us, the risk was worth the price.

—

I had gotten to know Steve Cannell pretty well during the four projects we'd done together, two *Rockfords* and two pilots, and we had become good friends. I loved his writing and the characters he created. I think it was during our last pilot, *Boston and Kilbride,* that I felt comfortable enough to ask him how he approached his work. Steve had an easy way about him, and when he talked about his writing, he wasn't fancy or grand. He made it simple. Well, writing for television isn't at all simple. Steve just made it sound that way. One of the things he talked about has always stuck with me. "In a one-hour, four-act structure, you don't want fourth-act exposition. So you need to change any fourth-act exposition into third-act supposition by the main character. You don't want Irving the Explainer showing up at the end of your show."

We were doing an episode called "All Roads Lead to Floyd." The guest star was Noah Beery. I was elated he was doing our show, since Noah played Jim Garner's dad in *Rockford.* Anne Bloom played Noah's daughter, who hired Magnum to find her missing, larcenous dad. It was a complicated story that was full of twists and turns. Magnum finally brings the two together.

Noah says, "How'd you know, Magnum?"

Magnum replies, "At first I couldn't figure out what documents your dad had that Mizamura would want. But then, after I talked to Burnside and found out about the counterfeit charges, I figured what he had access to that Mizamura was interested in. Airline tickets! You're validating airline tickets that you're stealing from this office to sell to Mizamura.

"Stop! I can't do this!"

I had become Irving the Explainer.

I wasn't angry, but I was speaking the absolute truth. The whole set got quiet. "I can't do this . . . We have to change it."

The director looked somewhat stunned. His face was pale as he explained, in the nicest tone he could muster, that a change like that would have to come from L.A. I calmly said, "Then I suggest you call them."

It was early evening there and three hours later in L.A. When the director returned, he said, "They've all gone home." I knew that something like this could be portrayed as an on-set tantrum by those who wanted to cover their rear ends. So I remained calm. "Noah, can I ask a favor? Would it be okay for your character to say, 'What are you trying to do, Magnum?'" And Noah, who I knew understood my problem, told me that it was just fine. We picked up the scene from where we left off.

Noah said, "What are you trying to do, Magnum?"

"I am trying to tie up the loose ends—you know, like all those TV detectives."

Over the years, I had done just about every cliché you can imagine, and I wasn't about to repeat them on my show. But I also knew that sometimes you were stuck. And if your *character* knew it was a cliché and commented on it, he was a whole lot smarter.

They could have edited it out in L.A. But they didn't. Probably because it was funny—in the right way, it was funny. We were breaking the fourth wall, just slightly. The *fourth wall* really means the audience. It wasn't the first time we had shared something with the audience, and it wouldn't be the last. It was just one small moment. But to me, it was a big victory, and I was proud that it was handled in a professional way. It also might have put the writing staff on notice to beware of Irving the Explainer.

—

"Tom, we did it."

"What did we do, Bettye?"

"Don's going to change the music." Before I could say anything, Bettye said, "And there's more. He is hiring Mike Post and Pete Carpenter."

Mike and Pete wrote the theme for *Rockford Files*. "Boy . . . this is the best phone call I've had in quite a while. Thank you."

"Thank *you*, Tommy."

I'm sure we probably had a little help. Larry was not fond of the original score either. My friend hadn't minced words: "I hate it, doesn't fit."

Look, the original composer was a fine musician. He just missed on this one. I know this was a tough decision for Don, since he was friends with the composer. I didn't bring that up when I called him. I just thanked him and told him how excited I was and that I thought it was the right choice.

I just knew, if Mike and Pete could capture the spirit of a show like *Rockford*, that we were all in the right ballpark. Bettye told me that with the strike just over, our first six shows would have to have the old music. She said, "Don is figuring out how to phase it in."

———

On December 11, 1980, our show debuted with "Don't Eat the Snow in Hawaii." We ended up number eight for the week. That meant thirty-six percent of the people watching TV that night watched us. And we had a lot to do with CBS winning the week.

We're a hit!

That was the common sentiment when the *Magnum* family, our cast and crew, went to work that day. The mood was . . . joyful. We all still did our work, but each step was a little lighter and quicker. We had worked hard with long hours, six days a week, and the news meant so much. The hard work had paid off, and our future looked bright.

When I got to work, I had a lot of calls waiting for me from our people on the mainland. There were so many that it was hard to concentrate on the work, but I managed. At a certain point, when we were setting up a new scene, I retreated to my motor home so I could be alone with my thoughts. I took a very deep breath. It had been a long road, and I had learned that there is no such place as *getting there*. There's always somewhere else to go. I was not ready to say out loud "We're a hit," if only because I was superstitious enough to believe that might jinx it.

Miles to go, Tom.

That cautionary thought—nothing's certain till it's certain—was very much in play as I sat alone in my room. Could we sustain those ratings over the Christmas holidays, when ratings for all shows declined? Could we grow our show into what it promised to be? I took another very deep breath and went back to the set to the hugs and handshakes we all had earned.

———

It was dark when I picked up Larry at the Colony Surf Hotel. As usual, it was one of those dawn-to-dusk days. And now we were headed for Nick's Fishmarket. I'm sure I kidded him about how his day off was when he climbed into my navy blue Jeep CJ-7. On my schedule, dinner was my only recreation. And who better to have it with than my good friend?

"What's going on, T?"

"Nothing."

"Something's up, 'cause you're not your usual after-work mopey self."

I put in a cassette and turned the volume way up. The opening-title music that I just knew a whole lot of people would soon recognize began to play. This was Hawaii, so the canvas top on my Jeep was home in my garage. Our new music played loudly for all of Waikiki to hear as we drove along the Ala Wai Canal.

Larry was hardly ever a man of few words. "Wow!" That's all he said.

Mike and Pete's *Magnum* theme was so good, maybe some of you remember it. I sure did from the moment I first played it in my motor home.

Actually, I knew Mike Post. He was a friend of mine at Grant High School. Except in those days, he was Mike Postil. I don't think I ever mentioned that to Don, lest it turn into a contest of whose friend had more pull. Grant High in North Hollywood was close to so many studios that, as my years in the business passed, I bumped into a lot of school friends. Some were in props. Some were in the camera department. Some were writers. Somewhere along the line, I discovered Mike Post's love affair with music. Mike Curb, also in music, was someone I played Little League with and knew at Grant. My school also had its share of actors. Micky Dolenz had been in a series called *Circus Boy* and would be in a group called the Monkees. Johnny Washbrook had a series called *My Friend Flicka*. And Cheryl Holdridge, whom I had admired from afar, as I considered her out of my league, was a Mouseketeer.

Larry gave a toast: "To the long fall up." I had a lot of fun at Nick's that night. Maybe too much fun, but so what? I felt we had hit a home run in the bottom of the ninth, and the ten pages of dialogue I would be confronted with when I got home would have to wait.

———

It wasn't until our eighth episode (they were now counting the pilot as two episodes) that I heard our new theme on the air for the first time. The show was called "The Ugliest Dog in Hawaii," and it aired January 29, 1981. Hearing the theme on the air was a nice thirty-sixth birthday present. Except it was still the old theme in the opening credits. The new theme was sneaked in during the show and played in the closing credits. I guess that was Don's way of phasing it in. So be it. That was up to Don, as it should be. Because I loved it so much, I had asked Steve Cannell about the *Rockford* theme. Steve told me that when he and Mike first met, Mike's only questions were about the main character and what he was like. I felt that approach was exactly what our show needed. I was just anxious to see the new theme fully and officially embraced. I mean, I must have played it, full blast, for the whole crew five or six times. Everybody loved it. Well, maybe they didn't appreciate the fifth or sixth time at full blast. But the first four were riveting.

A month later, on February 26, *Magnum*'s twelfth episode opened with the new theme and a much better opening credit sequence. I felt "Thicker than Blood" was our most important episode so far. And it wasn't just because of the music. This was the fourth episode Don had written, and I gotta say, he nailed this one. He brought back the history that T.C., Rick, and Magnum shared in Vietnam, and in doing so, he brought back the spirit of the pilot. Don wrote a story where T.C. is arrested by the Coast Guard for smuggling a marine deserter into Hawaii. He accepts responsibility for what he did wrong to protect the missing deserter. It turns out that the marine had saved T.C.'s life by pulling him out of a burning Cobra gunship. So Magnum and Rick try to help their friend. There, even when *I* describe it, I bet you want to see it. I was happy for Larry Doheny that this one came up in his slot.

Roger's performance was exceptional. He brought a fierce determination to the story, and Don made sure that it fit his character perfectly. "Thicker than Blood" gave our show a new direction, and if we'd been a little more established, Roger would have been nominated for an Emmy.

Roger had already done something for the character and the show that hadn't originally been in his background. He wanted T.C. to work with young kids who needed more of a sense of family. In "Thicker than Blood," there is a heartbreaking scene when he says goodbye to those kids. Roger also wanted T.C. to be a divorced father trying to reestablish the relationship with his family. I don't think Roger has really ever been given the well-deserved credit for bringing that to the audience. Our show was much the better for it.

———

"Don't Say Goodbye" was our fifteenth show and holds a special place for me. Just before we started shooting, it was announced that *Magnum* had been picked up for the rest of the season. That was just three more shows because of the strike-shortened season, but still . . .

Okay, we're a hit. Enjoy the ride, Tom.

So I did, though I was sure, over time, I would find something else to worry about. The episode had a really good cast. Academy Award winner (and my mom in *The Sacketts*) Mercedes McCambridge was playing a blind friend. I was a fan of Andrea Marcovicci's work, and she played my friend's companion. And some guy named Ted Danson played her boyfriend. You know what? He turned out to be a good actor. A really good actor.

The episode was moving along well until . . . Maybe I should just cut to the chase here. I'm on a small cabin cruiser with Marco (that's what I came to call Andrea). Ted appears from below, and he's got a gun pointed at us. (My cliché-detection device was pinging a little bit.) *Oh-kay, I guess he's the bad guy.*

He says something like "We're going on a little cruise. You drive." And he gives me the keys. (Another ping from my device.)

I take the keys. All Marco has left to do is play stunned. I start to climb the ladder up to the bridge but cleverly kick the pistol out of Ted's hand. We tussle, and I throw him to the deck. Then Ted reaches into a compartment and pulls out a big grappling hook. Now, a six-feet-four-inch Ted with a big grappling hook is kinda *checkmate* in a fight—at least for me it was. (My cliché device was now at full alarm.)

Stop! I can't do this!

Marco was at the back of the boat, and I was right in front of her, protecting her from Ted's grappling hook. And I had the keys! "Why can't I just run away? I can push Marco into the water, dive in after her, and yell for the police." This obviously wasn't the first time they had seen me with that kind of determined mindset. So the director, Rich

Kolbe, and Marco, Ted, and I sat down and tried to work something out. Rich was eager for a solution because if we didn't find one soon, the sun would go down, and he wouldn't make his day.

Rich's only point was "Tom, you're a hero. Heroes can't do that."

"Why not?" was all I said.

We picked up the scene from there. I show Ted the keys and say a Magnum-esque "bye." Then I push Marco into the water, dive in after her, and yell loudly to the whole marina, "Call the police!" Ted panics and decides to swim for it, and the poor guy is cut to pieces by the propeller of another cabin cruiser.

This is what I would now call a Magnum-esque solution. And it was not the end of the episode. There were two emotional scenes with Mercedes and Marco still to come. Good, well-written scenes. Look, I'm not trying to have fun at the expense of our writers. This was all very serious business. And the writers could have no idea how the stunt coordinator would visualize the fight. The hardest thing for a writer to do in an episode of television is find a way to end the show when the fourth act's running time is dwindling. We just abbreviated the action scene to get to the heart of what was important and how it affected the characters we cared about. "Don't Say Goodbye" turned out to be a very good episode, thanks to Mercedes, Marco, and my new friend Ted.

—

Fame is a vapor.
Popularity is an accident.
Money takes wing.
The only thing that endures is character.

I think Horace Greeley said that.

"I don't want to be famous. I want to be a good actor."

I said that.

I said it to myself somewhere along the line, and I think I meant it. Those who will never have to go there often brush such thoughts aside with stuff like "Goes with the territory." And, of course, they're right. But it doesn't mean you have to like it. I knew that even if our show failed, millions of people would see it. And I knew my sense of what was private would be altered. *But we're a hit!* (There, I said it again.) As much as I wanted to write my own rules, a whole lot of it does go with the territory.

We were already having trouble shooting outside in Waikiki with the crowds we were attracting. But the life I had found with the local people let me keep that kind of fame at a distance. Hawaii was twenty-five hundred miles away from Hollywood. And in 1980, there were really no entertainment shows on TV. The first big one, *Entertainment Tonight,* wouldn't premiere until September 1981. But fame is a funny thing, and you get used to stuff.

I was going somewhere with Dennis and Tina Berg when Bags said, "Tom, you gotta try this ice cream place. It's unbelievable." Now, I love ice cream (but only chocolate and vanilla). So we went there. But when we got there, the place was in the middle of Waikiki.

"Bags, I can't go in there."

Dennis dismissed me with an "Oh, come on . . ."

The shop was in the back of a little open square, a square full of quite a few tourists. Sure enough, a couple came over to me, and they had their camera ready. The woman said, "Excuse me." Having been through this drill many times, I was just about to say, "Sure, I'll take a picture with you," when the woman said, "Would you take a picture of me and my husband next to that beautiful little palm?"

Fame can play tricks on you.

———

"Thomas, I want you to go to the Golden Globe Awards."

Esme Chandlee, my friend and publicist, was insistent, something she was very good at. The Golden Globes were to be on a Saturday night in late January, and to get there, I would have to get up before dawn on Saturday morning, take the early flight to L.A., race to my room at the Beverly Hilton, change into my tuxedo, and race downstairs to the event. I was less than enthused. I decided to give her my self-pity speech.

"Esme, I've been working so hard and—"

"I know you've been working hard, dolly, but it's time."

"Time for what?"

"You've been in Hawaii too long. Time to be seen. You are in the hit television series of the season, and it's time. Besides, you need to see it."

"See what?"

"You'll see."

So . . . when I had my tuxedo on, I got into the elevator with Esme and took it down to the parking garage, where we got into a limo, drove out the exit onto Santa Monica Boulevard, and turned back into the hotel entrance. We stopped in front of the red carpet. I looked at my friend: It was clear that Esme was in her wheelhouse. She smiled a bright, satisfied smile and said, "Enjoy it." And the limo door opened.

It was mayhem! Lots of flashbulbs, and a big cheer came from the crowd in the bleachers. To be honest, it was a long, loud cheer. I couldn't hear much through the noise, but the word *Magnum* sifted through a few times. I was escorted to a spot in front of a large bank of photographers. They flashed away, all the time yelling, "Tom! Tom! Tom!," so I would look into their lens. Then I was escorted—or maybe pushed—to another spot, where more photographers shouted at me, and then I moved to a third spot—same thing.

I think the flashes put me in a kind of alpha state. I have no idea what that is, but doesn't it sound good? Whatever state I was in, it wasn't

good for what was coming next: a long line of reporters with micro-
phones and video cameramen, and they had lots of questions. Actually,
lots of *stupid* questions. My eyes were having trouble focusing on them
due to my "alpha state," so I have no idea what I said.

When I got inside, the lobby was crowded with people. So I hid in
the bathroom. I needed time to regroup. By now I knew I had done the
right thing by going alone. The last thing Jacki or Kevin needed was to
be checking out at the market and seeing a tabloid with a picture of who
I was "dating." I took a deep breath and went back at it.

Esme took me over to a couple of temporary cubicles that had been
set up. I did a couple of very quick one-on-ones. At least these questions
were smarter. My answers were not.

When you walked into the ballroom of the Beverly Hilton, the tables were set on three levels in a semicircle facing the main stage. The
back row was on the same level as the entrance.

Esme had my arm as we stepped down to the middle level. *Oh . . .
okay.* I would have a great view of the stage and the lower level, where all
the *big sticks* would be. The A-team of the entertainment industry. But
we kept going. She took me over to a table in the back row of the far-left
side next to the stage. It wasn't the best table. In fact, it was the worst
table on the best level. Esme gestured to my seat and left. She had made
sure I didn't have my back to the stage, so I could see and be seen.

That's when I saw it. Next to my place setting was a small box with
a bow on it. On the front of the box was the word CHAZ along with a
picture of me in a white cowboy hat and tuxedo, standing in front of a
Ferrari.

Perhaps I need to go backward here. About two years before this
moment in time, Revlon had hired me to be the face of a men's cologne
called Chaz. They had been wildly successful with a women's perfume
called Charlie. Shelley Hack was the Charlie girl and was soon to replace Farrah on *Charlie's Angels.* Chaz was going to be Charlie's male
counterpart. I had stopped doing commercials at that point because my

acting opportunities had become very promising. In those days, successful actors didn't endorse products, let alone do commercials as someone else. But I was getting a lot of opportunities and not a lot of money, and I had a mortgage. The offer was for fifty grand a year for two years, and I couldn't turn down that kind of security.

Revlon was a first-rate outfit; I had to do print ads and commercials for them. I wasn't really a men's cologne kind of guy, but I was being paid to pretend, so . . . I do have a specific memory of shooting the commercial. I had to shower ecstatically, so ecstatically, so many times, that my chest was, well, sensitive. Then I had to splash Chaz ecstatically all over my chest. And that didn't feel so good. As for the fragrance, it came out of my pores for days.

I looked around my table, and *everybody* had one; I looked around the room, and *everybody* had one. Chaz was the party gift for the A-team. Now, in 1980, the crowd I was hanging with didn't do commercials. I greeted my tablemates, put on my game face, and sat down. I don't think I saw any actors or other card-carrying members of the A-team at my table. If I had, I'd remember. I think my table was occupied by Universal and CBS executives looking to congratulate themselves. To my mind, just as well. I do remember one of them holding up a box of Chaz with a slight smile. "Congratulations," he said.

"Oh . . . thank you," I said with my old *Dating Game* smile.

Before I got out of the limo, Esme had said, "Enjoy it."

I guess I did my best to be a good "celebrity" that night. But enjoy it? Not so much.

—

Sometimes fame can bring you things you never could anticipate. Not only things you should do but things you *must* do. One of those things involved an eight-year-old boy named Kyle Schumacher. He was the son of one of our producer Rick Dumm's best friends. And he was sick, very sick. Kyle had become a huge *Magnum* fan, and Larry and I went to see him at lunch. We both put on big smiles, and Kyle was thrilled. He really knew his *Magnum* stuff and was full of questions. It was hard. There's no school you can go to for this, but maybe we did some good.

Couple weeks later, Rick came to Larry and me. He was pretty upset. "Kyle's dying." That's all he said. When we got there, Kyle's mom and dad put on a brave face when they said, "Thank you." Kyle was in his bed, propped up by pillows. He was very weak. His head was resting on his chest. We put on our smiles when we said hello, though we weren't sure he could hear us. I didn't know what I could say to him. I looked at Larry, who was also at a loss for words. But in the next moment, he reached down and took off the team ring our three characters wore and put it in Kyle's hand. After a moment, Kyle's eyes opened wide. He clutched the ring and slowly looked up at us with a very big smile on his face. Leave it to my friend Larry.

In a letter, Kyle's mom and dad told us their boy was buried with that ring. I will always remember Kyle Schumacher.

———

When I was in my final season of basketball at USC, our coach, Bob Boyd, often said, "You have to play through fatigue." He always made us run wind sprints before we practiced free throws. Coach Boyd was a good coach, not to mention that he had the wisdom to give me a scholarship.

You have to play through fatigue. By our last three shows, that was exactly what I needed to do. Six-day workweeks and fourteen- to sixteen-hour days were catching up with me. At night, I would wonder where I was going to find the creative energy to do good work. My answer would have to be "Show up on time, put a smile on your face, and do your job" (all thanks to Jim Garner).

When you get a script written by Don Bellisario for a second-to-last episode, you expect something special. And that's exactly what I got. Question: What do you call a backdoor pilot episode? Answer: You call it a spin-off. That's what this script was. Well, I guess that's something special.

I gotta say, it hurt a little bit that Don never even ran it by me. No explanation. Nothing saying not to worry, our show was still his top priority. Go with the horse that brung you. That's what I would have done, but I'm not Don.

You have to choose to be offended. That was something I had told myself many times. In today's world, it might be: *Think a second time before you push* send. I settled on: *File it away, keep laying bricks, make the show better, do good work.*

I, of course, talked to Bettye about it, and she was in the same place. Her advice was "Miles to go, Tom."

———

A new series needs time to find its groove. That's what I told myself when Mr. Frustration threatened to get the best of me. I had my shit together in some ways, but in others not so much. I knew my craft and my instrument pretty well. The not-so-much part would be what I called the *business end* of series work. But success had given us the chance to find our groove. And over the course of that first year, I had become more comfortable with this work in progress and the fact that a good television series should always be just that, a work in progress.

The terrific ensemble that Don had put together was pulling its weight. Larry was no longer a character thinking he was Humphrey Bogart in Rick's Café. He was now growing into the role of the manager of the King Kamehameha Club. Roger's character was becoming more three-dimensional while cementing his relationship with Magnum. John Hillerman was Jonathan Quayle Higgins III from the get-go, and his relationship with Magnum was one of those things we could hang our hats on from the start.

When John first met with us, he had said he wanted to work on the accent before doing a reading. It turned out he learned it by listening to a recording of Laurence Olivier reciting *Hamlet*. Technically, the accent was called *received pronunciation*. That's a highfalutin title that translates to "the Queen's English." His accent turned out to be so good that a lot of people, including my English friends, thought he was a Brit. But over a vodka and Fresca (John's beverage of choice) at Nick's Fishmarket, having his linguine and clams with white sauce, he said, "I left Denison, Texas, to join the air force and burned my roots to a charred stump."

John said in an interview that "Higgins thought he was the only sane character in the room and that everyone else was stark raving mad." Whatever was going on in Higgins's head, John seemed to know it instinctively. His portrayal was on point from day one. Even in the pilot, with the stakes so high, his work helped me find where I fit in the complicated equation that was their relationship. He could be Magnum's tormentor, his caretaker, and, yes, his friend when the chips were down. To me, John Hillerman's Jonathan Quayle Higgins III was the part of a lifetime. I'm pretty sure John knew that too. Sometimes I would call him the Great Hildini. That always got a wry smile out of my friend.

———

The Waikiki Theatre was right on the main drag. Driving down Kala-kaua Avenue, you couldn't miss it with its grand entrance, elegant gardens, and fountain. Once inside and sitting in your seat, you felt like you were part of another era. The theater opened in 1936 with Ronald Colman's *Under Two Flags*. The walls on each side had stylish murals, and in front of them were palm trees created just for this Hawaiian movie palace. Down in front, below the screen, was an elaborate organ.

What a perfect place to see *Raiders of the Lost Ark*! And that's exactly what I was there for. It was early June 1981, and *Raiders* had come to Hawaii.

Friends told me not to go, that it would be depressing. No, I wasn't looking for closure. I'm not sure what that even means. I wanted to see the movie, especially *this* movie. If I had any regret sitting there, it was just that no one was playing the organ. I was armed with my popcorn and a box of Jujyfruits. I would hold up each one in front of the previews on the screen to see which color it was. I always saved the black ones for last.

When Steven and George's—or George and Steven's—movie started, I just was carried away. Yes, errant thoughts would try to sneak in, but I had no trouble pushing them aside. I had read the script so many times that I knew it by heart. And when the big boulder started rolling down the mountain after Indy, I remembered thinking in Steven's office, *Oh, shit . . . this is terrific.* And from that moment on, Harrison Ford was Indiana Jones. And Indiana Jones was Harrison Ford. Harrison did such a fine job . . . The one errant thought that never entered my mind was *That coulda been me.* I of course knew that, but somehow it didn't bother me. It was such a good movie . . . I was just happy for Steven and George, or George and Steven. And yes, I was happy for Harrison. He made Indy his own. My only regret was that the what-if was there from time to time, and I wanted to embrace *Raiders* fully like the rest of the audience did.

I've always felt it was important that I see *Raiders.* There had been so much water under the bridge, so many hills and valleys, that I would have felt a coward not to see it. I had a good job, playing a character I loved. So what's to be sorry about? I'm not trying to be noble here, and even I was a little surprised how willing I was to accept it all in the end. I guess maybe I knew something about closure after all.

CHAPTER THIRTEEN

Finding the Groove

O ur first season was a big success, and I say that with nothing but gratitude. We reached almost seventeen million viewers in our shortened season. And *The New York Times* validated that success when they called us and the ABC comedy *Too Close for Comfort* "the most successful new shows of the '80–'81 season."

There's no such place as getting there. There's always somewhere else to go.

And where is that? Most of our shows had been about cases where I was hired, most often by a woman. As in any series, some episodes were more compelling than others. But I felt that formula would put us in too small a box. The one show that promised more was Roger's episode hinting at the past—the story explored in the pilot: Vietnam.

I often gave the note to our writers that Magnum kept making the same mistakes. I wanted to play a flawed character, and I knew audiences liked a character with flaws. But they don't like stupid ones. Thomas Magnum had to learn from each experience and grow from it. Now, this went counter to the standard series formula: the character remains the same each week—just the situations change.

"Well, who said so?"

I didn't actually say that. I just thought it. But all my training as an actor said that was the wrong approach.

I couldn't have felt more strongly that the audience was staying with us because they were by now inside the heads of our main characters. Maybe they needed to find out a little more about them.

Apparently, Don felt the same way. When I got his script for our fifth show that season, I was pretty sure I was right. "Memories Are Forever" was going to be a special two-hour episode. (Success does have its rewards.) When I finished reading it—boy, it was good! We were breaking new ground. Magnum is sitting alone in a café by the water, sneaking pictures of a couple across the room with a long-lens camera. He doesn't really like working divorce cases. Bored, he trains his camera on an elegant sailing yacht passing by. His lens catches a glimpse of a woman. She looks exactly like the woman he married in Vietnam—except that woman had died there. That's all I'm gonna say because . . . I'm not Don Bellisario.

"Memories" aired November 5, 1981, to great reviews. It's a complicated story, and Don artfully uses flashbacks and mystery to tell it, very much like in the pilot. It is, yes, romantic, very dark, and ultimately tragic. It puts the audience inside Magnum's head. And it sent me on a new path. Memory would inform Thomas Magnum's story. His past would play an active role in his present.

I was already running on fumes when I did "Memories Are Forever." But that episode gave me a huge lift, like I had taken some sort of "cosmic nap."

I'm not saying we should have done a show like "Memories" every week. That wouldn't be in the spirit of what our show promised. Not to mention that we couldn't afford it. But the fact that we *could* do a show like that from time to time meant we were on our way to finding our groove.

———

Always expect the unexpected. Maybe it was time I adjusted my thinking on what had long been a cautionary thought. The unexpected just might be a good thing. With *Raiders* gone, I assumed my future would be as a "television actor." Hardly a cross to bear. The business was really quite structured in that way in the early '80s. We were back to the unwritten rule that television actors didn't do feature films and film actors didn't do TV and no one got to do both . . . certainly not lead actors.

Somewhere in the middle of the second season, I got an offer for a feature film. The lead in a feature film. Go figure. And Bettye assured me it was a legitimate offer. It was an action-adventure film called *High Road to China.*

"Who else is being considered, Bettye?"

"Just you, Tommy. If they don't get you, the picture won't go."

"But I'm already working."

"They'll wait till you finish."

"Oh . . . What about the script?"

"It's already on its way to you."

"Is it any good?"

"Not for me to say."

High Road to China was indeed a very good script. It made me want to turn the pages.

"Bettye, this is a big picture. Do they have the money?"

"The budget is twenty million."

"Yeah, but . . ."

"I checked. It's real."

There was a certain irony in the twenty-million number, as that was also the budget for *Raiders.* Always expect the unexpected.

It was to be produced by the Golden Harvest Company, distributed by Warner Bros., and directed by Brian G. Hutton, who directed the Clint Eastwood films *Kelly's Heroes* and *Where Eagles Dare.* The character I would play wasn't even close to Indiana Jones and hardly Thomas Magnum. That fit my appetites just fine. Patrick O'Malley was a hard-drinking former World War I pilot, hopelessly trying to make a business out of chartering his two biplanes, named *Lillian* and *Dorothy* for the

Gish sisters of silent-film fame. He is hired by a very rich, spoiled woman who is desperate to find her father, lost somewhere between Istanbul and China. Not exactly a couple of naturally lovable characters the audience would instantly warm up to. But that's what movies are for. I was excited about *High Road to China.*

The film was to be shot on location in Yugoslavia for a little over three months. So I would need to get there right after season two ended.

———

When I arrived in Zagreb, Yugoslavia, my driver, Josip, introduced himself, and I got in his car for about a two-hour drive. As we made our way through the city, I do remember it seemed a little utilitarian—kind of, I don't know, "gray." Yugoslavia was a Communist country then, even after the death in 1980 of Tito, its longtime dictator.

The Ambassador Hotel was in Opatija, a charming town on the Asiatic Coast. My makeup man, Lon Bentley, and my stand-in, John Nordlum, were waiting to greet me when I arrived. I had a strong deal on this movie and had been able to get them on the picture too. After all the other official greetings, the first thing I said was "Is Bess here?"

I had seen Bess Armstrong in a movie called *The Four Seasons,* and she was terrific; she pulled her weight with the likes of Alan Alda, Carol Burnett, Rita Moreno, Jack Weston, Len Cariou, and Sandy Dennis. Bess came down, and we had drinks at the hotel bar. We had never met, so we were both full of questions. As is often the case in our work, you shake hands and say, "How do you do?"—and the next day you're working in a romantic comedy together. We had a great time that night, and it became clear we spoke a common language about our craft, which I had kinda figured after seeing her work. I would have a couple of days, which I very much needed, while Bess shot the scenes that introduced her character. Then I was off to the races, being in just about every shot for the rest of the movie. I didn't mind. I was in a big international production, and I was getting paid to be there. Our crew was a melting pot, 145 Yugoslavs, 60 Brits, 15 Italians, 10 Americans, and 1 Frenchman. When they said "action," it was shouted in multiple languages. It was a helluva ride.

I knew Jack Weston's work from movies like *Wait Until Dark* with Audrey Hepburn and *The Thomas Crown Affair* with Steve McQueen. He was in *The Four Seasons* with Bess and was terrific opposite Rita Moreno. Jack was playing Struts, O'Malley's copilot and enabler. When I met Jack that night, he said, "I'm doing the Jack Oakie part." Jack Oakie was famous for playing the sidekick, or what we in the business call the *second banana,* and that is no small thing. Second bananas have a whole lot to do with making movies work.

I also found out that night that our director, Brian G. Hutton, wasn't at all what I'd expected from his rather formal billing. "Oh, I used to be the actor Brian Hutton, and when I started directing, I wanted something a little grander. So I put in the G." The explanation came out with a distinctly New York accent. He was dressed—as always, I would later find out—in black jeans and a black cashmere V-neck sweater with holes worn in the elbows. He told me he'd put on his best, his "A sweater," to meet me. I would find out there were also B and C sweaters, just like the A sweater but with more holes. Brian was a genuine, one-of-a-kind character.

All of this was a lot to take in after my long trip. Lots of introductions and handshaking. Brian, being an actor first, was making sure I had a little fun. He told a story about directing Elizabeth Taylor in *Zee and Co.* with Michael Caine: Elizabeth stopped in the middle of a scene; she wanted to go to the bathroom. Brian said to her that he was "astonished that the great Elizabeth Taylor needed to go to the bathroom because I thought fairies came and took it away in toothpaste tubes."

Elizabeth responded with a hearty laugh, and Brian did her next picture, *Night Watch.* After those two movies, Brian took a long hiatus, from 1973 to 1980. He had lost his enthusiasm for the work. As he put it, "A gorilla could have made those two movies. All I had to do was yell 'Action!' and 'Cut—print!' because everyone was doing what they had to do."

First days are hard. And this one was no different. I was going to be *the guy* in this movie, but inside, I was just a kid from Sherman Oaks. While my driver brought me out to the location, I had alternated between overrehearsing my lines (which I knew cold) and telling myself, *You're enough.* Which, for some reason, was always a comfort. Once I was on the set, I met the rest of the crew. I don't think the Yugoslavs had a clue about my show. The Italians did and called me *Manyum.* All the Brits in the camera crew knew as well. I was introduced to Ronnie Taylor, our cinematographer, who had just come off *Gandhi.*

Oh, and did I mention it was freezing? I didn't know what it was Celsius, but I did know it was about twenty degrees Fahrenheit. We were doing the scene where Eve Tozer (Bess) meets O'Malley to hire him. Kind of important. Bess is dressed in a flimsy but elegant flapper dress from her night on the town. And I am a very hungover Patrick O'Malley, lying on a hammock wearing just trousers and a long undershirt, half asleep. Eve is no shrinking violet. She can handle a gun and fly a plane. She throws a glass of wine in my face to get my attention. Except the grape juice had frozen by the time Brian said "Action." Look, it's never gonna say in the credits that it was their first scene and it was freezing cold or else they would have been better—you just press on. I knew that lesson, and so did Bess. We both chewed on ice so our breath wasn't steamy. The prop department heated up the grape juice, and I didn't have to *pretend* I was shocked when she threw it in my face. In solidarity, Brian wore only his jeans and sweater during the scene, his B sweater.

Brian G. Hutton was quick to laugh and loved to tell stories. This helped all of us, actors and crew, get through a very tough day. Once, when we were about to roll the cameras, Brian stopped the process to tell a story. The assistant director, Bert Batt, a Brit who knew Brian, tried not to roll his eyes or look at his watch. All the while, Brian explained in great detail the trouble he had directing Faye Dunaway and Frank Sinatra in *The First Deadly Sin*. His long story short, Frank wanted to be done after the first take, and Faye didn't even warm up until take thirty.

I had always loved Brian's movie *Kelly's Heroes;* now I was seeing how his touch was all over it. His cast of Clint Eastwood, Donald Sutherland, Telly Savalas, Don Rickles, Carroll O'Connor, Gavin Mac-Leod, and Harry Dean Stanton were all so good, yet so different. Brian put them all together and let them do their thing and found not just the drama but the humor. He was absolutely fearless about finding the humor in even the most serious moments. And I could see that at work on our first day. All I can say is, by the end of the day, Brian G. Hutton had my absolute trust. I was in the right project with the right guy. And I was so happy to be in his movie.

———

The Ambassador Hotel was mostly filled with a lot of our cast, crew, and production staff. There was always company in the bar to hang out with. Being in the Communist world, we were all cautioned that there were rolling power blackouts, and you didn't want to get caught in the elevator. I asked my already indispensable driver, Josip, how to say, "Please make love to me in the elevator." I probably spent way too much time teaching my tablemates in the bar: *"Molim te yebame uliftou."* Just in case.

We were shooting exteriors, and the days early in the year in that part of the world were still pretty short. So there was always time for dinner. Most often it was Jack; Lon Bentley; our set photographer, Emilio Lari; and me. Sometimes Bess would join us. Emilio was a great guy and great company. He would joke, "I am very famous in my country." He might have been joking, but he *was* very famous in Italy.

The food in Opatija was great. A lot of restaurants didn't have refrigerators, so they showed you the platter of fish, langostinos, calamari, and mussels, all taken from the Adriatic that morning. Josip always steered us in the right direction, usually to simple family-owned places, and we couldn't have felt more welcome. The people in Opatija, just like our local crew, were friendly, hardworking, good people.

I don't want to say money was no object, but it kinda wasn't. My per diem was negotiated in U.S. dollars, but we were paid in Yugoslavian dinars. I think the exchange rate was about ten dinars to one dollar. The cost of living in Yugoslavia was very low; that's why the producers chose it. Let me put it this way: I had a lot of dinars. I don't really know if Golden Harvest was being sneaky or if they'd done it just because they could (which is also a little sneaky).

On a lot of days, we got to entertain ourselves with the air show above us. We could watch our aerial unit doing their thing: low-level fly-bys across the landscape and the aerobatics of the artful ballet between *Lillian* and *Dorothy*. There was, after all, a romance evolving between Eve and O'Malley. David Perrin was my flying double and a great guy. He was absolutely fearless in his biplane, a Stampe SV.4. He was a very modest man, but I'd heard he was incredibly well respected in the flying community in England. Dave always made me and O'Malley look very good.

We were shooting mostly in sequence, rare for a film but great for actors. The story, traveling across six countries, required building sets for each new location. Each set was expansive and incredibly detailed and accurate. That way, Brian and Ronnie Taylor could point the camera in any direction they wanted.

I was coming down the stairs from my room on the third floor. I had an early call, so I was avoiding the elevator. When I got to the lobby, the second assistant director, Chris Carreras, said, "Enjoy your breakfast." He explained that, overnight, the powerful "bora winds" had blown away our Afghanistan tent city, and the crew had to shut down for at least a couple of days to resurrect it. Jack, Bess, Cassandra Gava (who played Alessa in the Afghanistan and Katmandu sequences), Lon, and I crammed into the car and headed for Venice, about four hours away. I think I mentioned that I had a lot of dinars. We all did. Except you weren't allowed to take them out of the country. When we got to the border, my driver, Josip, told us to stay in the car while he got out. He had a "conversation" with the Yugoslav border guards. We never had to get out of the car, just gave a big smile and a wave, which the guards returned as we crossed into Italy. Josip told us we could get the best exchange rate in Trieste, a town close to the border. We still took a bath on the exchange into lira, but we didn't want to end up stuck with the less than formidable dinars at the end of the picture. We had an espresso at a nice café, and I gotta say, there were a lot more smiles on this side of the border. And then on to Venice.

———

Jack was kind of our tour guide in Venice, having been there before. We stayed at the Gritti Palace, a wonderful sixteenth-century former palazzo on the Grand Canal. The only reason there was room for us was that it was off-season, so the city wasn't crowded. We ate at the famous Harry's Bar. It opened in the 1930s and had a reputation for being very friendly to Americans. It was a favorite of Katharine Hepburn, Gary Cooper, Orson Welles, Humphrey Bogart, and Ernest Hemingway. We ate there both nights, hoping maybe some of that history would rub off. Then we raced back to Opatija.

Brian continued to be true to his nature and instincts. No matter how serious or threatening the scene was, he would always come up with a "button" for Jack. When Eve, Struts, and O'Malley are confronted with the ruthless Suleman Khan (Brian Blessed), they are not sure if they are guests or captives. Suleman Khan commands, "You will be my guests for dinner." Jack, out of the side of his mouth, quietly says to O'Malley, "Does that mean he is going to feed us or *eat* us?"

———

The weather turned warm, and I was looking forward to a cold beer in the bar that evening. There were more of our people in the lobby than usual. They were clustered in small groups, but the room was quiet. Fred Weintraub, our producer, came over and gave me the news. My plane had engine trouble. So Nigel Thornton, our helicopter pilot, was ferrying a mechanic, Jason Anderson, and my stunt pilot, David Perrin, over to the airfield to get *Lillian*'s backup. They never arrived and were missing. The next day's work was canceled while a search was conducted. That was a long night. A lot of us stayed around and waited late into the evening, each lost in our own thoughts . . . and prayers.

The next morning, most of the crew went out to the airfield to wait. When some of the search team came back and walked across the tarmac toward us, we knew. You could see it in their body language. All three of our friends had been killed. Apparently, they were flying in a canyon and didn't see an electrical cable strung across it.

Dave Perrin hated helicopters. He felt they violently opposed the laws of physics. And I guess they do. Since the *Magnum* crash, my friend Boris Sagal, who directed me in my first pilot, had been killed in a helicopter accident while scouting locations in Oregon. And now this. I sit here, pen in hand, trying to explain my emotions . . . I can't. I think I was gifted and cursed with a hyperactive sense of responsibility. This was not my fault, but so what? David Perrin was wearing my clothes. If I was looking to find closure, forget it.

———

Time passed slowly for a while, and of course, errant thoughts would creep into the work. But in the film business, the work is waiting for you every day, and you owe it your commitment every day. It was the life we had chosen.

In Katmandu, O'Malley and Struts go to see the village wise man. They hope Zura can tell them where Eve's father went after visiting his village. But the old wise man speaks in riddles. They manage to glean enough to know her father is in a village in China. Struts asks, "Anything else you can tell us, Zura?"

"The oxen are slow, but the earth is patient."

Jack rolls his eyes and pulls O'Malley out of there.

To my great regret, we were running out of Jack time. When *Dorothy* is destroyed in an attack, Eve will have to fly with O'Malley to China. Struts will have to stay behind. Our goodbye scene was easy to play: It was also Jack's last scene in the movie. Jack would be a friend for life, and I knew it. We both had to avoid our own sentiments. These two characters would never allow that to show. A lot is said, but when it's time for goodbye, Jack says, "And one more thing, O'Malley." It appears he is giving in to the sentiment when he says, "Always remember . . . the oxen are slow, but the earth is patient." And he gives me a big hug. My friend Jack ad-libbed that line. It stayed in the movie.

———

Who the hell is this guy Wilford Brimley, who's playing Bess's dad?

"He's the guy in *Absence of Malice* who comes in at the end of the movie and steals the show."

Brian was talking about the Paul Newman and Sally Field movie that Sydney Pollack had directed. A lot of people, or at least a whole lot of actors I knew, were talking about "this guy" Wilford Brimley. Then I remembered I had seen him in *The China Syndrome* and *Tender Mercies*. I just never knew his name.

"You're kidding me . . . Wow." That's all I said.

———

Eve and O'Malley land in the village in China in the middle of a war. Bradley Tozer (Brimley) is trying to save the village from a Chinese warlord. Brian gives Eve's father a grand visual introduction. He appears in a doorway as if walking out of the flames from the iron forge behind him. After all, this *was* what the whole journey was about, so leave it to Brian. Bess's performance in their reunion scene was wonderful. This strong, resilient woman became a little girl when she called him "Daddy" and then ran to embrace this powerful man.

The best way to describe Wilford Brimley's work was that it was honest. Every word that came out of his mouth was absolutely authentic. More so than any actor I have worked with to this day. And it very much reflected who he was as a man. He meant what he said and said what he meant.

I couldn't have asked for a better scene partner than Bess. She was generous as an actor, very collaborative, and never competitive. I guess I had a crush on her from the beginning. I think Bess, who was otherwise occupied, had figured that out. She was very gracious in making sure it didn't interfere with the work, which made it easy for me to do the same.

Lon Bentley, Wilford, and I went over to Trieste one Sunday. We exchanged our dinars and had a late lunch in the same café we had visited before. Lon and I mostly listened that afternoon. Wilford had been a blacksmith by trade and, by his own admission, a skid-row drunk, a stuntman, and a bodyguard for Howard Hughes. He was fiercely proud that, of all the people in Hughes's inner circle, he was the only one who wouldn't write a book. He told us a lot about that time, but they were things to be told among friends, not to be broadcast to the world. At some point, I ordered a Scotch. Bill asked me for it. He took a long, deep sniff of it and handed it back to me. "Thank you" was all he said.

And then our movie was over. It seemed like an eternity but was really just a moment in time. I would do two more movies with my friend Bill Brimley. He and my friend Jack are both gone now. I do so miss them.

———

You have to play through fatigue.

I hadn't planned on *High Road* going three weeks over schedule, and by the time we wrapped, I was overdue in Sonora, California. For some reason, I felt I had to push the envelope and take on one more project before I went back to *Magnum* in the summer. Actually, there was a very important reason. During *The Sacketts,* Ben Johnson, Jeff Osterhage, Louis L'Amour, Sam Elliott, and I had made a pact that, if we got another chance to work together in a western, we would all show up. With Louis's Sacketts tied up in some kind of litigation, he created a new family, the Travens, in his next book, *The Shadow Riders.* CBS jumped at the chance to make it a movie. So our band of brothers, and, oh yes, a new sister, Katharine Ross, were all in Sonora. They would have to start shooting without me until I got there. I would have only one day in L.A., then up to Sonora. Well, whatever it took. *The Shadow Riders* was not only a sacred trust but a dream come true. Maybe that was better than a rest.

If I had to walk into a movie with no time to prep, I was in the right one. The company had been shooting around me for three days, so I had a full first day. But I was surrounded and supported by a crew who included many friends. My beloved horse Utah was retired, but the wranglers gave me a tall, leggy sorrel named Reno that Glenn Ford rode in *The Sacketts.* Jim Byrnes had again written a great script, and I had only one note: I wanted to do at least one scene with Katharine. Jim obliged.

Dennis Durney, my friend since Fox, was one of the producers. He helped me get my son, Kevin, a job with the wranglers. That time with Kevin was irreplaceable, not to mention that he got an education in the care and feeding of horses. The wranglers pushed him pretty hard, as they should. He was working before dawn until after sunset.

In Andrew V. McLaglen, we had a great director who was steeped in the western film tradition and was the son of legendary actor Victor McLaglen. He had directed the likes of John Wayne, Jimmy Stewart, Dean Martin, William Holden, and Kirk Douglas. I could stand straight next to Andy. He stood six-eight. Harry Carey Jr.—or Dobie, as we called him—played my father and was a card-carrying member of John Ford's stock company. The great Jane Greer played my mother.

The chance to work with Sam, Jeff, and Uncle Ben not once but twice was the kind of thing most actors never get to do, no matter how much they want to. I treasured this time. After we finished, Louis L'Amour gave me a leather-bound edition of *The Shadow Riders.* He signed it: "To Tom Selleck. You make my people <u>live.</u> What more can I say? Louis."

What a great ride we all had.

CHAPTER FOURTEEN

In the Groove

W hen I got back to Hawaii, I had some celebrating to do. *Magnum* had received an Emmy nomination for Outstanding Drama Series for the 1981–82 season, along with *Hill Street Blues, Lou Grant, Fame,* and *Dynasty.* Go figure. Action-adventure shows that include humor in their obligation to entertain aren't supposed to be taken seriously. And go figure, I was nominated for Best Actor. No, that's not false modesty. It was just completely unexpected for the same reasons as above. I knew by now I *was* good and getting better all the time on that endless journey that is so compelling for an actor. And there was another thing. Leads, particularly the kind of leads I was being asked to do, should look easy. They're not. But since you're kind of the audience's representative in the story, you don't want them to see *the work.* And if the viewer says, "Oh, he's just playing himself," well, that's the goal. Because you're not. And that my fellow actors recognized it meant so much.

The nomination was certainly fortifying but at the same time a little overwhelming: to be on the list with the likes of Ed Asner, Daniel J. Travanti, and John Forsythe. Oh, there was one more name on that list—to me, by far, the most important one—James Garner. *My goodness, who woulda thought?*

When your show is submitted for Emmy consideration, you have to pick one episode for viewing. Guess which one I picked. And my guess was that Don did the same for the show. How could we not? "Memories

Are Forever" was kind of Don's and my secret weapon. For a show that had faced so many obstacles and was in only its second year, recognition by our peers was indeed cause for celebration. Don and I shared that celebration along with our memories of the path that had brought us here. And when he showed me his script for the two-hour third-season premiere, all I could say was "Don, it's a home run."

———

"Did You See the Sunrise?" was a deep dive into Magnum's past. T.C.'s as well. Like "Don't Eat the Snow in Hawaii" and "Memories Are Forever," it revealed that this carefree, fun-loving private investigator was taking a holiday from his history. He was not trying to bury his past; it was very much present inside him. But it did not haunt him. It informed him.

This episode was emotionally a heavy lift for me and even more so for Roger. I was proud of the work we did, and I know Roger was too. Don's script had a lot of complicated twists and turns—somehow he made it complex but not confusing. Each new twist was clarifying. Magnum's story broke very new ground.

"Hey, let's go up the Pali Highway and see the sunrise."

Mac, Magnum's Navy friend and reluctant confidant, has joined his sometime friend and his date for a late-night party at a club. It turns out to be an all-nighter. And just as the sun is starting to come up, Mac, who had always wanted to drive the Ferrari, goes off to get it. When he starts the car, it explodes, killing him.

We find out in flashback that Magnum and T.C. were POWs in Vietnam before they escaped to rejoin their unit. We see them along with two other team members. Each of them has been forced to constantly stand in extremely confining bamboo cages, hanging from a tree. They are being interrogated by Ivan (Bo Svenson), a Russian KGB colonel and a specialist in psychological ops. He gets no help from Magnum or T.C. and moves to T.C.'s helicopter gunner. He calmly takes out his

Soviet pistol and deliberately shoots him in the femoral artery. Magnum and T.C., helpless, are forced to watch the marine bleed out.

Magnum supposes his way to being certain that Ivan is in Hawaii and behind Mac's murder, the Russian thinking he would kill Magnum. And Ivan is set to leave the islands under diplomatic immunity.

Magnum (in narration) says, "That wasn't good enough."

He intercepts Ivan's car on the way to the airport and walks him into the depths of the jungle. Magnum stops about ten feet away, and Ivan turns to face him. He opens his coat to show he is unarmed and takes out a cigarette case.

Ivan says calmly, "Cigarette?"

Magnum is stone-cold still, his eyes fixed on Ivan. He says nothing.

"If you're going to shoot me, do it now . . . You won't. You can't. I know you, Thomas. I had you for three months in Duc Hue. I know you better than your mother. Your sense of honor and fair play. Oh, you could shoot me if I was armed and coming after you, but not this, Thomas . . . Never."

Thomas Magnum speaks. "Ivan."

"Yes?"

"Did you see the sunrise this morning?"

"Yes. Why?"

Thomas Magnum raises his service automatic and fires.

Our audience had never seen this side of Thomas Magnum. The Navy SEAL who knew war. Clearly, this was not the first time he had deployed what he would call swift justice. But they had never seen him like this: standing straight and motionless like a hunter, eyes fixed on his prey. *I* had never explored this side of Thomas Magnum. I was crossing to the other side of his street. As always with each episode but more so in this instance, I was able to make him (how did I put it way back at Fox?) more fully formed.

As for the morality of the act, I was satisfied that Thomas Magnum did the wrong thing for the right reasons.

Down these mean streets a man must go who is not himself mean, who
is neither tarnished nor afraid. He is the hero; he is everything. He
must be a complete man and a common man and yet an unusual man.

—RAYMOND CHANDLER

———

I'm not sure when I stopped picking Kevin up at the Honolulu airport,
or anybody else, for that matter. It had become impossible for me to get
in and out of there without drawing a crowd. When you are a local living in a tourist destination, you can spend a lot of time dropping off and
picking up friends. So not being able to go was a relief in that respect,
though it would have been nice to be able to extend myself to family.
But that couldn't happen anymore. Kevin was okay with it. The crowds
just took away from beach time. Kevin had embraced a lot of the culture
of the Outrigger, and that was a good thing. He was showing a promising talent for volleyball, which would grow into him becoming an all-
American and winning two national championships at USC.

He was squeezing in one last trip before school started. I was still
working six-day weeks and getting up early but could always get one of
our drivers to pick him up at the house and drive him down to the club.
He more than knew his way around the place and had lots of friends
there. I knew he'd be okay. He'd been around a lot of movie sets and
knew that hanging out on them was like watching paint dry.

We got up early on a Sunday and were going to head down to the
club for breakfast at the snack bar.

"Hey, Dad, I just got my learner's permit. I already know how to
drive, but I was hoping you could teach me how to drive a stick shift."

There are a lot of rituals that, as a parent, you become aware of
and value. I had missed a whole lot of them with Kevin. Sure, if I was

in L.A., I was able to go to a graduation or a Little League game from time to time. But that's just being an occasional parent. A dad teaching a son to drive was, happily, a moment I wouldn't miss. "Sure, Kev," I said. I backed my Jeep CJ-7 onto Akulikuli Terrace, got out, gave Kevin the wheel, and climbed into the passenger seat. I proudly explained the gearbox and how to coordinate the dance between the accelerator and the clutch. There was the inevitable *lurch forward, stall—lurch forward, stall.* But Kevin got the hang of it all quickly. Either I was a great teacher or, more likely, Kevin was a quick learner.

The proud parent, I said, "Okay, drive me down to the club."

Kevin was nervous. So, going down Black Point Road, I had him stop, then restart and put it back in gear. We did that a couple of times, and Kevin was perfect. We turned down Diamond Head Road and headed for the Outrigger.

The Outrigger had a three-story parking garage. (Parking was at a premium in Honolulu.) I told Kevin to go slow and drive up to the top level. There weren't a lot of cars up there, and I didn't want to overload my new driver. Kevin pulled flawlessly into a parking space.

"Good job."

"Thanks, Dad."

Kevin let out the clutch. The Jeep lurched forward and over the concrete-bumper stop to the steel-cable barrier, broke through, went over the edge, and we headed straight down toward the alley three stories below.

Now, things were kind of in slow motion, and I thought, *I can't be that lucky twice.* The Jeep had no roof, there were no seatbelts, and we were just wearing swim trunks and T-shirts. I really don't remember landing, just Kevin saying, "Are you okay, Dad?" "Yeah, I think so." We both slowly climbed out of the Jeep, which was standing on its nose, the rear end pointing straight up from where we'd come. We were somehow both in one piece. Then I saw what had probably saved us from our three-story drop. The back alley at the club was where they stored their best eight-man outrigger canoe. It was out on the ocean that morning, and we'd landed on its trailer. I think that trailer and its heavy-duty suspension system absorbed a lot of the impact. I guess I *could be* that lucky one more time.

We both had scrapes, cuts, and bruises but were moving around. Kevin was telling me he was sorry. I was telling all the members who had gathered round that I was sorry. The ambulance gave me an okay but wanted to take Kevin to the hospital to check him out. He had gotten the worst of the impact, probably from the steering wheel. But, thank God, he checked out all right. I called home as soon as I could get to a phone. My mom and dad were already aware and very worried. They had been fielding calls from a whole lot of people who'd heard on TV and the radio things like "Tom Selleck in serious car crash. Details at eleven." Shame on the media.

The consequences could have been a whole lot worse if the outrigger canoe had been on its trailer. It was probably the club's most prized antiquity, going back to its origins. It was a sight to behold, made entirely of koa wood. Its loss to the club surely would have meant *my* loss from the club. As it was, I got a whole raft of shit, usually in the form of "The Tom Selleck School of Driving." And Kevin's buddies made sure he was forever saddled with the nickname "Evel Knievel."

———

Great news. Don announced he was bringing a new producer over to Hawaii. Charles Johnson had made his bones on *The Rockford Files,* quickly moving up the ladder to producer. When Steve Cannell had been developing *Boston and Kilbride,* I'd liked hanging out in the *Rockford* offices. So I had bumped into Charles many times. He would come through looking like he was going somewhere else. But he always had a smile on his face and stopped to say hello. He was smart and gracious, and since he was coming out of that exceptional group, his arrival was indeed great news. Charles would work with Don in L.A. for a few shows and then be our producer in residence for the production in Hawaii.

It was probably Bettye who told me the news, and while she didn't go into the details, she was probably the orchestra conductor on this critical change. She had Don's ear, and he might have thought he was using her to take my temperature. But she was skillful and crafty, so she probably just let him go ahead and think that.

Don wrote four scripts that year. But did I mention we were doing twenty-two? If he'd been shepherding the other episodes so that our promising writing staff could understand his vision, that would have been one thing. But he was now running another show, *Tales of the Gold Monkey,* at the same time. Clearly, his collaboration was at best sporadic. I'm sorry, I just didn't think you could be a part-time showrunner.

I won't say that was the last straw. I was learning there is never a *last straw* in series television. But this one really hurt. I'd also learned that "being hurt" isn't a productive emotion to dwell on in series television. Now, Don had written another spin-off. And this one didn't even resemble our show; it was told from another character's point of view. That is something our show just did not do. Maybe Don knew by then that *Tales* wasn't going to be renewed, I don't know. Maybe that was a common condition with showrunners, I couldn't know. I guess you *could* make a lot of money that way.

"Tom . . . I have created a show that is consistently in the top ten. We have grown our audience each year. That show has received an Emmy nomination, and your work has earned you one. What more could you want?"

Everything Don said was absolutely true. But that conversation never happened. It was me trying to walk in his shoes. I guess it was my way of talking myself off the ledge. I found I was having more of these conversations with myself. Other than on special occasions, Don was in L.A., and I was on an entirely different landmass. If we were in the same city, I would be seeing him just about every day. So, if we'd had that conversation, it would have been in the course of everyday events, and we could have had communication without a sense of confrontation. That was hardly Don's fault.

I had long since taken off the training wheels on what I felt was my role in a successful show. So I knew there was a problem in structure and process that was growing. In Hawaii, the cast and crew were in the trenches and paying a heavy price for morning-of script changes. Everything was written in L.A., and if those new drafts didn't make the eleven o'clock Pan Am (the last flight of the day), we would be rowing the boat without a paddle the next morning. In L.A., they were probably saying, "What the hell do those people over there expect?" We desperately needed more of a connection to the mainland. If Don and I had been in the same room, I would have said, "First of all, thank you for all you've done for the show. What more could I want? Maybe . . . communication. Consistency. And the confidence to know that we're not leaving a lot on the locker-room floor. Don, respectfully, our show needs more of *you*." My hope was that Charles Johnson would see the growing dysfunction and start to restore a sense of collaboration among a talented company of the like-minded separated by an ocean.

———

On March 18, 1983, *High Road to China* had a big premiere in Westwood. Universal and CBS were kind enough to give me a day off so I could get to L.A. for the weekend. What was it like? I honestly can't tell you. No, it's not that I *won't* tell you. It's just that it was all a very large blur. And it's not like I kept notes. I vaguely remember getting out of the limo as Esme said, "Enjoy, dolly." "You gotta be kidding, Esme." There was loud, long cheering from a big crowd, lots of flashbulbs, lots of interviews, and inside in the lobby, pretty much the same thing. There was no place to hide. I was completely unaccustomed to being the guest of honor at a big Hollywood movie premiere, and the alpha state I had experienced at the Golden Globes had graduated to kind of a trance. I do remember watching the movie, sitting next to Brian G. Hutton (the director, not the actor). The audience laughed at all the right parts, and Brian laughed with them. The audience applauded at the end, not politely but enthusiastically. When we were getting up before the chaos started again, Brian took my face in his hands, looked me in the eye, and said, "You're a good actor. Always remember that." That made the trip worth it.

Larry sometimes worked only a couple of days a week on *Magnum.* He made the trip to the premiere to support his friend. He and his wife, actress Nancy DeCarl, made dinner for some friends and me at their home in Studio City. At some point, Larry said, "Let's go for a ride, T." He drove me down Ventura Boulevard and parked across the street from the Studio City, one of my movie-house hangouts as a kid. At the premiere in Westwood, I never got to see the theater marquee. Now there it was. My name above the title, *High Road to China.* And there was a line going down the street and around the block.

"Congratulations, pal."

Larry rolled down the window, and we both started yelling, "Thank you! Thank you!" The people in line didn't really know where it came from and didn't know who said it. No alpha state here. It was a moment in time that is still crystal clear in my memory. Kinda like a film actor's substitute for a theater actor's standing ovation. And for a bricklaying worrier like me, a moment of pure joy. *High Road to China* was the number one movie that week.

High Road was greeted with what they call *mixed reviews.* Look, I was proud of our movie and the risks Brian had been willing to take to give it its own sense of style. Feature films are special, and they should be. I was trying to launch a film career while I was doing a more than successful TV series. A lot of actors may have been in a series earlier in their careers, but as far as I could figure, no one else was trying to do it at the same time. I don't think that made me special, just that the business was starting to change. I knew I would be facing a tough jury, and I would have to earn my place. But I did not appreciate the reviews that dismissed the movie as a *Raiders* knockoff. It wasn't.

My bosses at Golden Harvest weren't exactly helpful. I think I mentioned they could be a little sneaky. In fact, they were. I had a conversation with an enthusiastic member of the Warner Bros. distributing team. He told me our film had grossed somewhere around fifty or sixty million dollars. A serious number in those days. I had a strong deal on *High Road* and a small percentage of the gross. That's way too complicated to explain. But when Golden Harvest announced the final tallies, they said the film had grossed only $28,445,927, which made it the twenty-seventh-highest-grossing film of 1983. Pretty good, but not exactly helpful. To this day, I think that was total bullshit. Well . . . keep laying bricks, do good work.

———

Back when I was doing *The Young and the Restless* at CBS Studios in Hollywood, I would go across the hallway to the stage on the other side, sneak in, and watch Carol Burnett and her talented cast rehearsing for their weekly show. I was a huge fan of *The Carol Burnett Show*. It was required stay-at-home viewing, along with *The Rockford Files, The Mary Tyler Moore Show,* and *Newhart.* Around the time *Magnum* started, I was at some luncheon at the Beverly Hilton. I think it was for Esme's Hollywood Women's Press Club. Anyway, I was walking across the lobby with Esme, and I saw Carol Burnett talking to some people in a small alcove off to the side.

"Esme, Carol Burnett's over there. How could I meet her?"

"Just go over and say hi. Carol won't bite."

So I went over, stuck my head in, and blurted out, "I love you." Carol gave me a surprised look, then a smile. "Well, I love you too." I got a little embarrassed and got out of there. And that was it. My brush with greatness had passed.

Right after *High Road* opened, Esme called. "They want you to present an award at the Oscars a few weeks from now."

"Who's they?"

"The Academy."

"Oh."

"It will be presenting Best Film Editing with Raquel Welch."

"But I'm still working."

"I will make them understand."

It was obviously worth the trip and what would be another quick turnaround. Boy . . . things were happening fast. On March 18, my first film opened. Less than a month later, on April 11, I was invited to present at the Academy Awards. Go figure. I wasn't about to say I was a member of the elite feature-film club, but they sure as hell were inviting me to knock on their door. Some of the other presenters were Bob Hope, Charlton Heston, Olivia Newton-John, John Travolta, Sylvester Stallone, and Cher. Carol Burnett was presenting Best Picture. The night would be hosted by Liza Minnelli, Dudley Moore, Richard Pryor, and Walter Matthau.

I did have one problem, even if it was one of conscience. My divorce was final, but I was becoming increasingly aware of the debris that comes with fame. With each tabloid story about whom I might be dating, Jacki and Kevin would have "friends" saying things to them like "I don't want to upset you, but have you seen this?" I simply did not want to bring a "date" to the Academy Awards.

Carol Burnett was also going through a difficult divorce. I thought maybe she and I could go together. I had gotten to know Carol much better since that first meeting. Otherwise, the idea never would have even occurred to me. And I guess the fact that we were both presenting made me feel she would know the invitation was coming from a peer. Esme thought it was a great idea, and Carol's answer was yes.

I gave Carol my hand while she got in the limo and closed her door. As I walked around the car, my mind was racing a little bit. *What am I gonna talk about?* I had already told her the *Y&R* story; we had talked about the "I love you" moment quite a while ago. I climbed in, and Carol immediately struck up a conversation. I don't remember what we talked about, but she sure put me at ease. Carol is good at that. So we headed downtown to the Dorothy Chandler Pavilion.

The Academy Awards were very different back in 1982. This was an elegant, dignified, worldwide event. It wasn't so much a TV show as a chance for the audience to eavesdrop on our industry's big night. The pictures nominated were all exceptional, well received by the public as well as the reviewers. They were Steven Spielberg's *E.T.: The Extra-Terrestrial, Missing* with Jack Lemmon, *Tootsie, The Verdict,* and *Gandhi.* Quite a year.

Carol and I got out of the limo, and there was a loud cheer from the crowd. We smiled and waved. Carol had a sincere affection for her audience, and it showed. Esme told me later that we had received one of the biggest crowd reactions. I was touched by the warm reception and, along with Carol's grace in handling it all, that helped me ward off being captured by Mr. Alpha State. This was a big night for Carol, presenting Best Picture; she got the first questions. Since I was the new guy at the Oscars, I welcomed that. A lot of the questions were actually about the work. Maybe more so for Carol than for me. But at least the slightly stupid "Who are you wearing?" had not yet infected the proceedings. Once we were in our seats, all we had to do was watch and wait to be pulled out for our presentations. Happily, I got to applaud Ronnie Taylor, our DP from *High Road,* when he won Best Cinematography for *Gandhi.* I had met Raquel Welch at our rehearsal, and she was welcoming and charming. Now I was standing with Raquel backstage, and she couldn't find someone to check her makeup. Lon Bentley had come over with me from Hawaii, so he checked her out and fixed her up. Not a difficult job. Then out we went. No brain farts in our presentation, which made it nice for the winner for Best Film Editing, also *Gandhi.* Our job wasn't quite over. We walked the winner to the press room, posed for some pictures, and answered a few questions. I got back to my seat in time to sit with Carol for a while. I remember squeezing her hand as she left for her presentation.

I had known my good friend Dani Jansen since I had been separated and she was getting over the loss of her husband, David. Dani asked Carol and me to a small get-together after the awards. Carol also knew Dani, and we had a great time. Lots of interesting people. That whole day was quite a deal. But to me, the nicest thing to come out of it was that Carol Burnett was now just *Carol.*

———

After the 1981–82 season, I got the official go for my summer job: a feature film called *Lassiter,* to be shot in London at the beginning of May. It was again for Golden Harvest. To be honest, I wasn't crazy about the Golden Harvest part. But I felt it was important to follow up the success of *High Road* with another feature film. I had to choose between offers that would fit in my *Magnum* hiatus. And *Lassiter* was a really good script, so a great opportunity. Also, Al Ruddy would be producing this time. Bettye had worked with Al on *The Godfather,* and that, I hoped, would be the difference this go-round.

The reason it took a while to set a start date on *Lassiter* was I needed to be guaranteed at least three days off starting May 19. I had been asked to introduce Bob Hope for his eightieth-birthday celebration at the Kennedy Center in Washington, D.C. The invitation was not something Esme conveyed to me; Bob Hope called me personally and asked me himself. I was flattered, of course, but not really surprised, because this was not the first time I had gotten an ask from Bob Hope. The first year

of *Magnum,* he had called me directly to ask me to be on a TV special
he was doing.

"I'm sorry, Mr. Hope. I'm stuck working in Hawaii."

"We'll work that out, Tom."

"But I don't sing or dance, and I'm not funny."

"Don't worry, we'll just do five minutes of stand-up."

Just five minutes of stand-up with Bob Hope. Oh-kay!

In both cases, what he wanted me to do was pretty scary. Inside, I
was still the kid at Grant High School who was afraid to get up in front
of everybody in speech class. But when Bob Hope is on the other end of
the phone line, how do you say no? Clearly, Mr. Hope was well aware of
that. "Looking forward to it. See you there, Tom." And that was that.

I was excited about *Lassiter* but had one regret: I would miss playing in the 1983 AAU National Volleyball Championships in Memphis,
Tennessee. Of course, work comes first, and we all have to make those
kinds of trade-offs. I had been playing with the Outrigger Canoe Club
team for the last two years. This was serious six-man Olympic-style volleyball in the thirty-five-and-older division, and I had earned a spot on
a team full of ex-Olympians and college all-Americans. We had lost in
the national finals the year before and now had a chance at redemption.
I know I was in a hit TV series. But for someone whose entire athletic
career in high school, junior college, and college had been spent on losing teams, the chance to win a national championship was a very big
deal. The dates of the tournament surrounded the Bob Hope event. So I
called my friend Dennis Berg, who was also on the team and our coach,
and asked him, "If I could make it work, Bags, would it help the team?"

"Make it work if you can. We need you."

We need you. That was all I needed to hear.

I started to work on a plan. A secret plan. Because I couldn't very
well tell the *Lassiter* people, or anybody else, for that matter, that I would
be playing in a serious athletic competition while in production.

Bob's birthday event was the night of the twentieth, and the tournament's last day of competition was the twenty-first. That was the day of the semifinals and finals. I was confident our team would make it at least to the semis. After the event, how could I get from D.C. in the middle of the night to Memphis, Tennessee, so I could play in the semis the next morning? Charter a plane! Thankfully, I had something in my hip pocket. After the success of *High Road,* the heads of Warner Bros., Terry Semel and Bob Daly (yes, that Bob Daly, the one who said I couldn't do *Raiders*), called me and said Warner wanted to be in business with me, and offered me the use of the Warner jet when I needed it. So I chartered the Warner jet. My secret plan would have to be carried out with commando-like precision. But it could just work.

That was the real reason I had asked for at least three days off. Even Bettye and Esme didn't know about the extracurricular part. They would have brought in Skip, who would have told me I could get sued if I got hurt. While it was surely not my finest hour in terms of being a professional actor, come on! How many athletes ever get the chance to play for all the marbles? I packed an extra suitcase before I left for London, a suitcase full of my volleyball gear.

———

I was very excited about *Lassiter.* It was a period piece about a high-end jewel thief in late-1930s London. We had an excellent cast. Jane Seymour, who was so good in *Somewhere in Time* with Chris Reeve. Bob Hoskins, who I thought was absolutely riveting in a movie called *The Long Good Friday.* And Lauren Hutton, the more than famous model who was now doing really good work as an actress in films. My friend Roger Young, who had continued to do great work since our *Magnum* pilot, would direct. That was a big help because I knew we spoke the same "language," and as usual, I didn't have much time to prepare. No table read with the cast, no prerehearsals. There was no time. My preproduction meetings were spent with the wardrobe, prop, and makeup departments. I brought my longtime makeup man Lon Bentley with me, and he and I worked on a haircut and overall look that fit the period. I was happy with the results, as were Roger and Al Ruddy.

Founded in 1841, Bermans & Nathans was the largest established costume supplier in the world. It was also the most famous, winning thirty-seven Best Costume Academy Awards for pictures like *Star Wars, Lawrence of Arabia,* and *Titanic.* I was excited just stepping through the door when a distinguished, well-dressed, polite gentleman said, "This way, Mr. Selleck." He walked me to one of their famous fitting rooms. It was quite spacious, and there were three people there: a tailor, the Bermans & Nathans costumer, and our costume designer, Barbara Lane. There were all sorts of fabrics laid out on a large table. They told me they wanted to design a whole closet for Nick Lassiter. Tuxedos, dress suits, sport suits, sport ensembles, shirts, shoes, and some great hats. As a former clothing salesman, I was in heaven. That was a full day, but I didn't mind. The tailor took every measurement you could imagine. I think they were surprised I knew "the tailor's language." I was proud of that. I did get stumped once.

"And which side do you dress on, sir?"

"Excuse me?"

They hesitated a bit, made a few gestures, and I finally got it. They were referring to which side I preferred to put my *business* on. I've never missed that one again.

To this day, when I get iconic roles like Nick Lassiter, the thought always creeps in that one of our great leading men would have been better casting. Whether it was John Wayne, Jimmy Stewart, Gary Cooper, Humphrey Bogart—well, you get the idea. With *Lassiter,* that would be Cary Grant. The thought didn't really defeat me as much as it reminded me that I'd better find another way to play the role. My way. And that would be enough. Cary Grant had played an elegant cat burglar in Hitchcock's *To Catch a Thief.* And our film was a caper movie very much in that spirit. Well, there've been a lot of caper movies and a lot of westerns and a lot of detective movies. What distinguished ours most was it took place in prewar London, and Nick Lassiter was sneaking around the rooftops of the city to steal jewels from Hitler's German embassy. And the story had its own very clever plot twist at the end.

Another thing that has stayed with me to this day is that I always get a bit intimidated in a scene with a crowd of extras. These essential background artists know their stuff. I get a little paranoid that they'll judge my work and say, "And he gets paid big bucks for *that*?" The answer is not to never play crowd scenes; the answer is to put those ideas into a small box with all the other errant thoughts and lock it up.

The shooting was going pretty well. Our cast seemed up to speed from the get-go. I was somewhat up to speed, which was pretty much my way of thinking in every lead role I had ever done. Everybody was happy with the dailies, and even if there was room to grow, I was happy too.

We were shooting one of my first scenes in the script after the opening cat-burglar scenes. Our set people had done a terrific job creating a huge casino out of a big ballroom in the Dorchester Hotel. It was all very elegant. Everyone was in black tie, and some were in white tie and tails. This was going to be a visual introduction to the sophisticated side of Nick Lassiter. I would come in, be greeted by the host—who clearly knows Nick—light up a cigar, and go down a long, sweeping stairway into the crowded casino. There were a couple things I knew I should not do. Don't look at the cigar when you light it; instead, be checking out the room. And don't look down at the stairs; instead, be checking out the crowd in the casino below. Either one would detract from the audience's sense of a kind of bigger-than-life quality this character needed. So I lit the cigar, *check*. I started down the stairs as if I owned the place, *check*. And I tripped and fell in a less-than-bigger-than-life way. As professionals, the extras remained in character, but I knew they were laughing inside. I got up much more embarrassed than bruised, which was greeted by applause from the entire company. I laughed and applauded with them. I wonder if Cary Grant ever fell down the stairs. The fall was not in the picture.

———

I guess nowadays most people don't know what it was like to fly the Concorde. In its era, it was a travel marvel like no other. You could fly from London to D.C. and arrive two hours before you left. And the Concorde was a crucial part of my secret mission.

I'm pretty sure I told Esme and Bettye just before I left, because I might need them to run interference if something went wrong. I knew that once my driver, a Cockney fellow named Tommy Lee, picked me up, the die was cast. Risk is the price you pay for opportunity, and after all, my entire athletic legacy was on the line.

Once I was on board, phase one had been successfully executed. Phase two required a total commitment to helping make Bob's birthday worthy of this industry legend and friend to every veteran. It was a celebration he had earned. *So get that volleyball stuff out of your head, Tom.*

After my caviar appetizer, I pulled out my script for Bob's introduction. Actually, it was not just an intro. It was a somewhat lengthy biographical piece. I knew from my limited experience not to try to memorize anything until I could rehearse at the Kennedy Center and see the venue. About that time, my airship kicked into high gear, pushing me back against the seat. There was a display on the Machmeter in front of us, and we were transfixed as it rose past Mach 1 (no, we didn't hear the sonic boom) and steadily rose until we hit Mach 2. A cheer came up from the rookie passengers, and we settled into our elegant dinners. Yes, if you were six-four, it was a little cramped. But so what? The flight was *less than four hours*. What a way to travel. I'm sorry if you missed it.

I never could have embarked on this secret mission without my assistant, Pualani McGinness. I had hired her in the middle of season three and trusted her completely from the moment I met her. She was a local girl and had brought order to the chaos that had surrounded my workdays on *Magnum*. Pua was also an Outrigger member and knew pretty much everyone on the civilian side of my life in Hawaii.

I got to the famous Willard Hotel (the place where Lincoln slept) in plenty of time to make the rehearsal. I had seen the Kennedy Center before, but only on TV. When they showed me where I would be onstage, I was grateful there was a podium so I wouldn't have to worry about what to do with my hands. There was a small level below the balcony, and in the middle of that semicircle was the president's box. That's where President Reagan, First Lady Nancy, and Bob Hope and his wife, Dolores, would be facing me. This was good to know but hard to get my apprehensive mind around. I also learned I would later introduce Tommy Tune and Twiggy, who would be premiering a number from their Broadway show *My One and Only*. That would be the easy part. When I got back to the Willard, there was a message from Pua: "Bags says things going well in Memphis." A long day, and I tried very hard to get some sleep.

—

I think I slept until late morning, and I really needed it. I had a big breakfast from room service and went to work on my speech. I knew there was a prompter, but why not know it cold, so I could take my eyes off the stupid device and actually look at Bob and Dolores and the president and the first lady from time to time? My call time was at about four in the afternoon, very early for an evening event. But they always wanted to make sure everyone in the show was in the building in time for any last-minute notes. So I got into my tux early and still had time for a couple of phone calls. I know I called my mom and dad, like I always did. "No, Mom. It's not tonight. They're taping it for the twenty-third." Then I called Bags. He said, "We're in the semis. We'll play around ten o'clock tomorrow morning. Can you make it?"

"I'll be there."

Now, put that away, Tom, and do your job.

The show was opening with a taped conversation between Bob and President Reagan. Then Lynda Carter would sing songs from Broadway shows but with special lyrics. I was after her. Lynda was singing, my knees were shaking, and yes, my hands were sweating. This time I spoke to them both: *It's his eightieth birthday, for God's sake. Don't screw it up.*

Lynda finished, and I heard my name. I took a couple of deep breaths, breathing being necessary for my task at hand, and out I went. If you want to know how I did, I'm sorry, I'm afraid I can't tell you. It was just another blur. I at least know I got through it without any major glitches. I enjoyed being in the wings and watching the rest of the show. And everybody went out onstage with Bob during the finale. *That* was neat, being out there with Lucille Ball, George Burns, and that whole group. So many people I would have liked to meet and talk to, but these kinds of events never seem to work that way. Everybody's off and on their way. I did get to meet and have a brief conversation with two people who had come backstage—President Reagan and First Lady Nancy. The official photographer asked for a picture, so the three of us came together for the photo. I had taken so many pictures the last couple of years that I automatically put my arm around the woman next to me, in this case Nancy Reagan. Not really appropriate. But the Secret Service didn't come in and tackle me, and Nancy didn't seem to mind. So that was the picture. I wish I had a copy.

There was a reception afterward that I felt I should attend. Lots of pictures there, only the people put *their* arms around *me*. I still remember one guy who was very patient in the group surrounding me. That patience stood out in the crowd. When I got a chance, I turned to him. He gave me his card. He was with the Defense Department. I shook his hand.

"Tony Makris," he said. "Nice to meet you. I don't need a picture. I just want to ask you one thing. You kill that Russian?"

"You bet I did."

He just smiled and walked away.

It seemed, at the height of the Cold War, that "Did You See the Sunrise?" was having a very big effect on a whole lot of people.

———

Naval Air Station Memphis was a quick ride from the airport, so I got to their gym with time to spare. I think Tina Berg, Bags's wife, was waiting outside and took me to the rest of the team sitting in the stands, watching what they call the consolation game, which decided third and fourth place. I had only a couple of hours' sleep, having gotten up before dawn to fly to Memphis, but I was not thinking about sleep. As I went to the locker room to change into my uniform, Bags had told me I would be starting as an outside hitter.

There was a tradition on our team that the newest team member would have to carry the bag of volleyballs and make sure they were at the court in time for warm-ups. Well, I was the rookie, so that was me. I had done my duty in the early part of the season. But for some reason, as the crowds grew, I would be waylaid, and the volleyballs started arriving later and later. Quite a while ago, that tradition had been abandoned so I could sneak onto the court for warm-ups. I was more excited and energized than nervous and tired. We handled the semis pretty comfortably. Now we would play for all the marbles against the team that had beaten us last year, Legends of San Diego, a welcome chance at redemption.

They kicked our ass in the first game, 5–15. The finals were best two out of three. Our backs were against the wall, but at least we had the crowd on our side. I'm not a sportscaster, so here's the rest: We dominated the next two games, 15–8 and 15–7. We were the 1983 AAU National Volleyball Champions. Everybody's arms went straight up in the air, there was a split second of a private moment, then the team came together jumping up and down in a collective hug. A simple, joyous human reaction that I had seen so many times on TV. I don't know, maybe that's kind of a tribal thing.

Then I had to separate from the team, change in the locker room, get in the car, and get to Dulles Airport in D.C. for phase four of my plan, catching the Concorde back to London. I missed the rest of our team's celebration and the award ceremony. I was still on a mission. But that was okay. When I got on the Warner jet in Memphis, there was a cooler full of Coors Light in longneck bottles and an unlimited supply of potato chips, pretzels, and Snickers. To this day, that was the best trip I would ever have on an airplane.

I found a pay phone in the Concorde lounge in D.C. and called Bags. "How was it?"

"Great. John Stanley was MVP. Dave Shoji and Tom 'Mad Dog' Madison were first-team all-Americans."

"That's great, Bags."

"And, oh yeah, *you* were selected honorable mention all-American. Congratulations."

Go figure.

CHAPTER FIFTEEN

You Never Know

had been pushing the envelope very hard, so I expected a tough week on the movie. Actually, it was a great week. I was sky-high and, no, not from the Snickers. Plus, I had a secret between me and myself. I mean, it wasn't as if the London *Daily Mail* was gonna sniff out the story from the local Memphis newspaper or the Outrigger newsletter. I do think I told my friend, neighbor, and makeup man Lon Bentley. He was a good secret-keeper. And I really needed a chance to celebrate my secret. Something had been on my list since the Great Hildini had told me, "When you're in London, you've got to see *Cats*. It's terrific and totally unique." So I asked Lon, "If I can get tickets, you wanna go see it and get dinner afterward, my treat?" The show was sold out, but Brian Blessed, my castmate in *High Road to China,* was now in *Cats,* and he helped me get house seats. After work, off Lon and I went to the New London Theatre.

If anything, John Hillerman had undersold just how good *Cats* was. Like he'd said, it was terrific and unique, but I didn't expect to be absolutely blown away and inspired by it. In the New London Theatre, the show was in the round, so the audience was practically a part of the cats' world. A lot of the cats came into the aisles at the beginning and interacted with the audience. They were all in very individual costumes, and each was very much their own character. Yeah, sometimes they might have been standing on two legs. But between their costumes and their own individual cat makeup, you had no idea what they looked like as humans, so you suspended your disbelief and accepted each character. I was now along for the ride and joined this strange world. I was eager to go on their journey. Most of the musicals I'd seen had a pattern: The leads acted and sang, the dancers danced, and the chorus sang and danced in unison. I had never seen a show with this kind of constant movement, and everybody could sing and dance *and* act. Even in the big numbers, where everybody was singing and dancing, they may have been doing the same steps, but each one of them did it in their own way. They never abandoned their characters. Finding my character was always my first priority as an actor. So I knew how much time it must have taken to prepare and develop this ensemble of individuals.

Of course, a performance of the song "Memory" was, well, memorable. But there was another number that stood out for me, maybe because it was so athletic. "Mungojerrie and Rumpleteazer" involved two cats in constant motion. It was an up-tempo number, and this couple of cats somehow managed to dance and do acrobatics while singing the whole time. It was also charming. You know a show is good when it ends too soon. Lon and I stood with the rest of the audience for several ovations, and he leaned over and said, "Let's go see Brian."

Brian Blessed played Old Deuteronomy, the wise man of this tribe of felines. Brian had a larger-than-life quality that he displayed in this show and in *High Road.* The three of us had a great time reminiscing. He shared a dressing room with another featured actor, Stephen Tate, who put up with our stories and joined in the conversation. But when Brian changed the subject to his passion for mountain climbing, Stephen excused himself quickly. Brian was fully alive as he explained the skill, the excitement, and the danger in scaling a mountain. He shared his ultimate goal, Everest, with such reverence that we knew there was so much more to *that* story. And there was.

When we left the dressing room, everybody was gone. I had hoped to meet the rest of the cast to tell them how much I'd enjoyed their work. Actors never get tired of hearing that, and they sure had earned it.

And to be perfectly honest, I hadn't had much time for a social life the last couple of years, and . . . you never know.

But still a great night. Lon and I had long ago become good friends, and we had a nice dinner and a bottle of Brunello at an Italian restaurant called Sambuca.

———

I felt *Lassiter* was going really well, and Cary Grant aside, I was doing good work. Wardrobe is always an important part of the character, and in a period piece, maybe even a bit more important. And what a wardrobe I had. This made it much easier to literally walk in Nick's shoes. Or maybe he was walking in mine. Or, most likely, a little bit of both. All good things. I got my second of three shots. We had an action sequence where I swam in the Thames, and the insurance company wouldn't approve it without them.

I had decided that I wanted to see *Cats* again. No, not from the shots. The quality of the work by these fellow actors was, I don't want to sound corny, but inspiring and fortifying. I just couldn't imagine how they did what they did every night. So I dragged Lon along, and off we went. I kinda knew he wouldn't mind.

Paul Mills, the stage manager, made getting in and out a lot easier. He put us in a small VIP room. And when the lights went down just before the show started, he showed us to our seats. At intermission, before the lights went up, he pulled us out and back to the VIP room and so on. His courtesy was welcomed, and it gave me the privacy to avoid distractions from the audience.

From the moment the music started, it was there again, the commitment. As the show progressed, I realized that what I'd seen that first night wasn't a one-off. They actually did this every night, and when Mungojerrie and Rumpleteazer came up, it was clear they actually did *this* every night. And something else happened—no offense to Mungojerrie, who was brilliant—I noticed I was focusing more on Rumple-teazer. She had a kind of unique energy, a feistiness and a joy. Not to mention she looked pretty good in a leotard. As the show progressed, I was kind of isolating my focus more and more on Rumpleteazer. She was a professional and never broke character and played to the entire house. But near the end of the performance where the whole cast is sing-ing out to the audience, Rumpleteazer stopped and stared toward where I was sitting for just a split second and then moved on.

"Lon, did she just look at me?"

"She sure did."

When we went backstage, Lon suggested we pop in on Brian again as a courtesy. That was okay with me, because it was a good excuse for getting backstage and . . . you never know.

Well, Brian started again. I kept nodding so he wouldn't know my head was asleep. He was somewhere around crampons and carabiners when I interrupted him. I pointed to a picture in my program. It was a picture of Rumpleteazer. "Who is that?"

"Oh, that's Jillie Mack. I don't know, but she's probably crazy about you. As a matter of fact, all the girls are. But I know you get that all the time, so I told them all to stay away."

"Oh."

On the way out of the theater, I summoned all my strength and cour-age and asked Paul, "Is it proper to call a member of the cast backstage?"

"Oh . . . Sure, I'll give you the number."

———

I was in Carmarthen, Wales, in a seventeenth-century farmhouse in the early evening, sipping what my friend Doug called a brown drink (Glenmorangie single-malt whiskey). Doug Plowden and I had been best friends from junior high all the way through college. After I went into the army, we had drifted apart, Doug having his hippie period and traveling. I did not have a hippie period and chose another path. But with true friends, no matter how much time passes, it's easy to pick up where you left off. Doug and his wonderful wife, Tessa, a Brit, had rehabilitated the old house and now were farming the property here in Wales. They loved entertaining and had a few friends over from some neighboring farms. Doug and I had moved away from the rest of the group and were sitting in a couple of very comfortable old chairs.

"Why not? Why don't you just call her?"

"Doug . . . I decided that's not a very good idea."

"That's ridiculous. Come on."

Doug took me upstairs to his bedroom, where he had an extension phone. I was staring at the piece of paper with "Jillie Mack" on it and the backstage phone number. He took it away and dialed the number. Doug was the guy who used to have to call and set me up with someone on a double date because I was too shy to ask.

"Jillie Mack, please."

He handed me the phone. But he didn't leave. Doug sat down in a chair opposite me. He was enjoying the hell out of this. Did I mention he had always been a champion kidder? I sat down on the bed, and a voice came from the phone: "Jillie Mack."

"Hi . . . my name is Tom Selleck. I'm a friend of Brian Blessed . . ."

"Yeah?"

"I . . . saw your performance and I . . ."

"I'm about to go on. Would you like to take me out for a cocktail?"

"Yes!"

———

I had never watched someone onstage whom I was about to have a first date with. It didn't ruin the show. I just had to allow for occasional errant thoughts. Mostly about who this person in a cat suit really was. I'd say I was anxious but still committed. Oh, and did I mention Lon came with me?

The writer Raymond Chandler wrote, "The French have a phrase for it. The bastards have a phrase for everything, and they are always right." The personification of joie de vivre was sitting next to me . . . with purple hair.

"It's not purple, it's black tulip," Jillie Mack enthusiastically told me.

"Oh."

We were at the White Elephant restaurant on Curzon Street in Mayfair, having that cocktail. By *we,* I mean Jillie Mack and me and, yes, Lon. I know, but I found a certain comfort and safety in knowing that dinner would not be as much a *date* as a kind of *meeting.* The White Elephant was quite elegant and private. I'd heard it was a favorite hang-out for the Beatles. That has absolutely nothing to do with my story, I just thought you'd like to know. I was pretty sore from the day's work, so I explained, "I had this big fight scene with Warren Clarke . . . You know, one of the four guys in *A Clockwork Orange . . .*"

"I'm sorry, I don't know your work."

"Oh."

She explained that Kenn Wells, who played Skimbleshanks, had said to her at the interval, "Do you know who keeps looking at you? Tom Selleck."

"Who the fuck's that?"

She wasn't being sarcastic, just quite simply honest. And I quite simply wasn't offended. For someone who might have one dinner with someone and then end up being the picture on her Christmas card, that was music to my ears. She explained that she lived on the other side of the river in a place called Clapham, and she and her two roommates had gotten robbed. And their TV and VCR had been stolen. Then she added that the police had told her the robbers were working in the neighbor-hood and could come back.

"I was alone a lot of nights. So I would sleep with a tap shoe in one hand and a can of hair spray in the other."

Look, that's serious stuff. But the way she told the story, with such spirit and humor, it was somehow charming. And it was clear to me that this *person in a cat suit* was not one to wallow in being a victim. We had a great time. Jillie Mack ate like a horse, and all of us laughed a lot. My driver, Tommy Lee, had had a long day, so I told him I'd get a cab to take Jillie home. He said he didn't mind and dropped Lon off at 47 Park Street, where we were both staying, and drove us across the river to Clapham. Jillie asked if I'd like to come in.

"Okay."

I did, and she fixed me a cup of Nescafé instant coffee. We talked a lot, laughed a lot, and I asked her if she'd like to have dinner again, maybe without Lon.

Jillie Mack said yes.

Sambuca on Sloane Street in Chelsea had become one of my favorite London restaurants. By now, I knew the staff and was comfortable there, so it was the perfect place for dinner the very next night. We talked a lot about our work. Mostly about Jillie's. I was most interested in where this character-driven approach had come from.

"Most of it came from our choreographer, Gillian Lynne," Jillie said while never bothering to stop eating. "She would always say there is no such thing as the chorus, just individual characters. Actually, Gillie Lynne is my mentor. She calls me Little Chip, and I call her Big Chip."

Jillie told me she had worked with Gillie on *My Fair Lady*. It was in a smaller part, so the character didn't have a name. "So I gave her one. Violet Elizabeth."

———

Mayfair was a very exclusive part of London, and 47 Park Street was quite a place. My room was more like an apartment, and the room service was from the famous restaurant below, Le Gavroche. Bettye had scouted ahead, and her suggestion was perfect, as usual. Expensive but perfect. But I had decided I wasn't going to look at the right side of the menu this trip. What had Bettye said? "You have to celebrate your wins." I had a strong deal on this movie, and this time my per diem wasn't in Yugoslav dinars. I also had ten additional first-class round-trip plane tickets in my contract. My mom and dad, Bob and his wife, Laurie, and brother Dan came over during the shoot. I put them all up at 47 Park Street and was thrilled to be able to do it. It was so much fun being able to share my success with my family. I'm afraid Marti and her husband, Kevin, drew the short end of the stick: my sister was pregnant. Doug and Tessa came down from Wales and stayed there too. And someone else was now occupying my time: Jillie Mack. We both had jobs, and I was learning that Jillie shared my ethical obligation and reverence for the work. Neither of us was about to ignore the thing that brung us. But we still managed to see each other or at least talk to each other every day. I would end up seeing *Cats* eight and a half times (once I worked late and arrived at the interval). I became a regular, that guy sitting in seat *whatever,* watching the show, watching Jillie, who always stayed in character. No winks or smiles my way. The emotional and physical commitment was always there, and for me as an actor, each performance was inspiring, not to mention that now I had a dog in the hunt. Before or since, I don't think I've ever had that kind of balance between the work and a life outside the work. I'm not really sure why. But I was doing good work, maybe even better because of that balance. No doubt the civilized British filming day helped. I wasn't burning the candle at both ends. Jillie and I had work to do. But somehow I also had a life.

As with all good things, well . . . Jillie and I were standing at the loading gate, putting on brave faces. This was the life we had chosen. Jillie had four more months as Rumpleteazer, and I had my fourth season as Thomas Magnum. But we had some time around Christmas. A really good hug, a very long, good kiss, and we were both left in our own thoughts. *That person in the cat suit was one of a kind.* There would be two dozen red roses at the New London Theatre for Rumpleteazer every Friday night.

———

"There won't be a dry eye in the house."

Don was excited. He was talking about our fourth-season premiere. "I won't tell you what it's about. I want you to read it first. But Tom, I promise you there won't be a dry eye in the house."

So I read it. And I gotta say, Don had outdone himself. "Home from the Sea" was indeed deeply moving for the guy who had been walking in Thomas Magnum's shoes for the last three years. It helped me close the circle on who he was and where he came from. Just as in "Don't Eat the Snow in Hawaii," "Memories Are Forever," and "Did You See the Sunrise?," Magnum's past plays an active role in his present, and memory becomes his story. And this time, Don managed to tell that story in just a one-hour episode.

Magnum's closest friends knew he always went off to spend time alone on the Fourth of July. So they aren't surprised when he paddles his surfski out into the vast Pacific. When he is swamped by an irresponsible power boater, he loses his surfski. In heavy swells, he can't see twenty feet in front of him and decides the safest choice is to swim the two or three miles to shore, an easy swim for him. After an hour's swimming, he is much farther away from shore than when he started. He realizes he is caught in a strong current, the Molokai Express, next stop Japan. His only hope is to tread water until he is found—*if* he is found.

As the minutes turn into hours, Magnum, who is talking out loud to no one in particular and sharing his thoughts (in narration), remembers when he was six years old and his dad taught him to tread water in the same ocean, near San Diego. His dad challenged him to stay afloat for five minutes.

The story also follows Magnum's friends Rick, T.C., and, yes, Higgins, who slowly become concerned about him. They all sense in their own way the danger Magnum may be in. A sense created by the bonds between these men, the past dangers they have shared, and the affection they have for each other, even though it is usually expressed in constant bickering.

By dawn, they have a sense of where he might be and go looking for him: Rick in the King Kamehameha Club boat and T.C. in the Island Hoppers helicopter with Higgins, who jumps out with a life preserver. But after more than a day in the water, Thomas Magnum is still in delirious conversation with his father. He refuses to be rescued until he completes his father's challenge.

After he finishes his last thirty seconds, Higgins secures him, and Magnum cries out, "I made it, Dad. Why didn't you?"

In flashback, we see six-year-old Tommy sitting next to his mom as his father, a Navy pilot, is buried with full military honors. His dad was shot down over Korea on July 4, 1951. And now we know why he always celebrates the holiday alone with his thoughts.

"Home from the Sea" was an incredibly ambitious script. And Don was no less ambitious in how he wanted to make it.

"Tom, are you okay if we shoot in the actual Pacific Ocean?"

"Don, I'll do whatever it takes to make this as good as it should be."

That was all Don needed to hear.

He wasn't about to shoot the ocean scenes in a swimming pool, using only close-ups and stock footage of the ocean in between. That's what most television series would do, or at best rent time at one of the L.A. studio lots' water tanks. But there was no big studio water tank in Hawaii. And I kinda knew that was not where Don was going when he posed his question. He knew he had written something good. I knew he had written something good. And the studio knew the script was exceptional. Together, I think we knew we had the *juice* to do things in a different way. A less "TV" way. A far better way. It would be expensive and, I was sure, way over budget. But our success going into our fourth season had given us that juice, and if it hadn't, I'm pretty sure Don would have done it anyway. It was that stubborn side of Don that I most admired . . . most of the time.

Each morning, we would stage on the Makai Pier near the Robin Masters estate location in Waimānalo, the same pier where T.C.'s Island Hoppers set was. Don wasn't going to direct. That would be done ably by Harvey Laidman. Charles Johnson and his more than able production staff were ever vigilant. In an ironic way, the shooting day was like a military operation. The crew did their prep. Then the shooting team climbed aboard a big barge, and the towboat took us away from the pier and into the open ocean. When you move out of shallow water into the open ocean, the color of the water changes into a deep blue. That's where we anchored. The pier was by now completely out of sight. For safety reasons, our shooting team was reduced to what was essential. A couple of camera crews, sound, a few lights, an assistant director, and Harvey, our director. The towboat stayed nearby with our safety divers and John Nordlum, my always able stand-in, who was an experienced diver. John would spend even more hours in the water than I was going to while we set up the shots. I was asked if I wanted to use some kind of flotation device, and I said no, that actually treading water myself would help to create the sense of Thomas Magnum's problem. John, as always, told me what to expect and added that Archie Ahuna from special effects and Jack Aaron of Aaron's Dive Shop would be underwater with bang sticks to handle the problem of the hammerhead sharks in the area. I'm not sure knowing that was helpful, but John was always very thorough. So, into the vast Pacific I went.

Once in the water, I was bobbing up and down in heavy swells. At their peaks, I could see Waimānalo way off in the distance. In their valleys, all I could see were the ten-foot swells surrounding me and the front of that big barge holding the crew. I basically had two jobs: The first was to somehow keep the same distance from the barge, so I would be in camera focus. The barge would rise up at the peak of the swell and crash down in the valley before the next one. So it was kinda crucial that I made sure not to get sucked underneath the barge when it crashed down. That was the second job. From then on, I was on a mission. I so wanted to do justice to the faith that Don's fine work had placed in me. Whatever it took.

You always have to deal with technical distractions on a film set, and yes, these were big ones. But for me as an actor, it all helped *feed the machine,* so to speak. I didn't have to pretend I was in the middle of the Pacific Ocean. I *was* in the middle of the Pacific Ocean. And it wasn't that hard to feel alone. In many ways, I *was* on my own. So it wasn't that hard to have that long conversation with myself . . . or, rather, Thomas Magnum's self. Don's "Don't Eat the Snow in Hawaii," "Memories Are Forever," and "Did You See the Sunrise?" had indeed given me the sense of security that memory would always define Thomas Magnum's story. I think "Home from the Sea" may well be the best episode of television I have ever been privileged to be part of. When it aired on September 29, 1983, *there wasn't a dry eye in the house.*

———

I don't remember if I called Don or he called me when "Home from the Sea" aired. It doesn't really matter. Both Don and I were excited and very proud of the work we'd done. But then that was always the case with Don's shows.

I haven't meant to give the impression that we had a contentious relationship. I don't think we ever had harsh words or even raised our voices with each other. We had developed a friendship, and I feel we both knew we each owed the other a lot. Both of us had waited our turn or, rather, waited for our opportunity. And *Magnum* presented itself as just that. How I wish we could have seen each other every working day, sat in the same room, and celebrated that. Distance and time were the enemies this particular success confronted us with. In other words, the Pacific Ocean and the demands of twenty-two episodes each year. And there wasn't really time for "Don, I got a real problem with the next episode." Or "Don't worry, Tom, I'm rewriting it."

Also, a funny thing happens with the kind of success that had come to us. For the actor, the studio doesn't really want you to do anything else. But for the successful writer/showrunner, they want you to do as many projects as you are willing to create. Don had often spoken to me about his frustration of having to share the *created by* credit with Glen Larson. It would go something like "Everything in my script was new except for the character's last name and the car." Look, I get his frustration. But right or wrong, the Writers Guild had other ideas. Maybe that explains the spin-offs and *Tales of the Gold Monkey,* I don't know. I guess I never will.

———

Charles Johnson made a difference really from the moment he arrived. It was clear he had Don's respect, and he absolutely had mine. The very fact that he would just pick up and move to Hawaii for the entire season showed his commitment to the work we'd been doing. And he fully understood the problems that distance and time had created in a process that needed to speak with one voice. He had been an actor, so he understood that *Magnum* was less plot-driven than character-driven. I don't want to embarrass him, but he was a man of intelligence, grace, and patience, and his communication skills enabled us to straddle the Pacific Ocean . . . most of the time.

By his second season, Charles was instrumental in making structural changes. Chris Abbott-Fish came on as a writer. But there was another big difference. She would be based with us in Hawaii. The simple fact is that sometimes the problems in a script don't reveal themselves until the actors rehearse the scene. There is neither the time nor the money to call L.A. while the whole crew sits around having snacks. Chris could be on the set to work out the changes. And she would earn her billing as executive story consultant. Just as importantly, the writers would now follow their scripts to Hawaii. So if there indeed was an us-against-them dynamic, their presence would help defuse that. They could take pride in their work and be partners in its evolution. Also, a couple of weeks in Hawaii was a pretty good gig.

As always, my friend and agent Bettye McCartt had her fingerprints on making all this happen. And although I could have no way of knowing it at that time, Charles and Chris would become more indispensable to the future of *Magnum* than I could imagine.

———

Chris's first writing assignment was the dreaded Christmas episode. The dread was coming from me. It seemed like sooner or later, every TV series did one, and they very seldom worked. They were usually too sweet, too sentimental, not to mention too merry. But I don't think Chris saw it that way. She partnered with our very talented producer/writer Reuben Leder. Together, they wrote "Operation Silent Night."

T.C.'s helicopter, with Rick, Higgins, and Magnum on board, is forced to make an emergency landing on a small deserted island. They find out the island is deserted because it serves the U.S. Navy as a gunnery practice range. See? Not too merry or sweet. Instead, the characters constantly bicker and kid one another while desperately trying to fix the helicopter. I'm not sure the audience felt the characters were going to be stuck there and die when the Navy launched its barrage, but I mean, come on, it *was* a Christmas show. They get out, you guessed it, just in the nick of time.

Rick, Higgins, and Magnum say, "Merry Christmas."

T.C. says, "Happy Kwanzaa."

Then, high up in the star-filled Hawaiian sky, they all sing "Silent Night."

Yes, sweet and sentimental, but Chris and Reuben did their best to earn it. It was a good show.

———

If you're an actor, you haven't really lived until you've had Carol Burnett climb up on your shoulders and wrap her legs around your head . . . I'm not sure that came out right. Let me rephrase: wrap her legs around your head *for stability* as you are both getting soaked by the emergency sprinklers while she hysterically tries to turn a big valve on the ceiling to shut the water off. I hope that clears things up.

In only her second script assignment, Chris was tasked with writing an episode for Carol Burnett. No pressure, right? "Rembrandt's Girl" was the result, happily a very good one. At Higgins's insistence, a bank employee, Susan Johnson, hires Magnum to help her ex-con father stay out of trouble. While they are inspecting the bank vault, Susan tells her story, but Magnum isn't interested. Angry, she presses the emergency button on the keypad and locks them in the vault. After some bickering and apologies, she punches in the code to open the door. The keypad fizzles, sparks, and they're trapped inside. A confident Magnum fiddles with some wires and asks Susan to punch in the code. The door does not open . . . but the sprinklers come on. And there we were.

For the guy who used to sneak into *The Carol Burnett Show*'s stage and watch her rehearse, working with her was a big deal. I mean, I was about to do what was essentially a two-hander with one of America's great comic actresses. I was excited about it but also a little nervous. I guess I didn't want to disappoint her or our audience, or myself, for that matter. This was probably one of those times when I would have to tell myself, *You're enough, Tom.*

I know, Carol and I were friends now. But we hadn't really had time to keep in regular touch. When you're working mostly six-day weeks for nine months of the year most of the time, you only get to see each other at awards shows. The Emmys, Golden Globes, People's Choice, or Esme Chandlee's favorite, the Hollywood Women's Press Club. And even then you just have time for a hug-and-how-ya-doin' before something or someone interrupts you.

The day before we started shooting, Carol came to visit the set. When she arrived at the parking area, of course, that drew quite a lot of attention. My friend and motor home driver, Dave Muntz, told me later that he didn't want to bother her, but she walked right up to him, offered her hand, and said, "Hi, I'm Carol." That's just who Carol is. An actual, regular person. A complete person.

I was working with Larry and Roger at the set of the King Kamehameha Club beach bar, and when Carol walked up, it literally *stopped the show*. I gave her a big hug-and-how-ya-doin' and was interrupted by Roger and Larry, who, I've gotta say, seemed a little starstruck. Carol obviously knew the realities of production. After a few more hellos, she said, "I didn't mean to interrupt. See you at dinner, Tom."

Charles had arranged an early dinner at an out-of-the-way restaurant upstairs from the Diamond Head Market. Carol knew my friend Lon Bentley, who joined us with his wife, Manu, and someone else. Jillie Mack. Jillie had come over after *Cats* to stay with me through the holidays. Charles, Lon, and Manu already knew Jillie, and she and Carol really hit it off, as I kinda knew they would. And we had a great old time.

So, Susan climbs down off Magnum's shoulders and, in desperation, pounds her fists on the wall next to the keypad. The sprinklers stop. They are both by now soaking wet.

Magnum says, "Thank you."

Susan says, "I'm sorry that I got you all wet."

"Oh, that's okay. I'm sorry that I yelled at you."

"I'm sorry that I locked us in here . . . Your turn."

"I've run out."

From the moment we started rehearsing that morning, all my doubts just seemed to blow away. You take a really good script like Chris's, it still takes the actors to figure out what it's really about. The great director Elia Kazan talked about the audience not caring as much about the words as they care about the subtext. And that's where Carol was going with the work. She welcomed my collaboration, and that was all I needed. We just went to work, and what a joy it was.

Susan conveniently has a gift from her father. She calls it her backpacker's pal. It has everything from a Swiss Army knife to a transistor radio and even a bottle of wine. As the oxygen is running out and they've had the bottle of wine and their inhibitions are breaking down, the bickering turns to attraction. Magnum finds a station on the radio, and they dance to the song "Strangers in the Night" (my favorite part). Susan says, "You know, I have this theory. You can really tell when you might be compatible with each other by the way you dance together." Magnum, true to his character, does not reply but pulls her closer.

Obviously, I'm proud of "Rembrandt's Girl." Proud of the work. And proud that my friend Carol wanted to do it. And I love her dearly.

———

Actually, "Rembrandt's Girl" had a bonus feature: an uncredited appearance by Jillie Mack. Charles thought Jillie might enjoy being a part of Carol's episode. He ran it by me, and my response was "We'd be lucky to have her . . . but this can't come from me." I told Charles that he would have to call her and, if she was interested, set up an interview with Margaret Doversola, our casting director. Jillie is a fine actress and a professional, and I didn't want her to think she had to do us a favor or, worse, that we were doing *her* a favor. Also, word gets around quickly in a film crew, and I didn't want the perception to be "Oh, Tom put his girlfriend in the show." Once Jillie started to work in the scene with Roger, Larry, and John, I knew the perception would actually be "We were lucky to have her." Jillie has within her a quality that always seems to *win the crowd*.

Rick and T.C. think Magnum has left town, so they throw a big party in Robin Masters's guesthouse. Magnum's crowded living room is filled with loud music and dancing partygoers. Higgins has planned a meditation weekend and is disturbed by the noise, so he bangs on the guesthouse door. One of the dancers stands out (I wonder why) and climbs the stairs to the door. As Higgins bursts in, she mistakes him for the pizza delivery man and says in a Cockney accent, "Paradise Pizza?" There's a little more to it than that, and Jillie of course committed to it. Later, Higgins has warmed to her (as had John a long time ago, I might add). She comes into his office, gives him a kiss, and says, "See you, Johnny." And Higgins is charmed.

Christmas at my mom and dad's a few weeks later was just great. And there wasn't any of the customary there's-someone-I-want-you-to-meet pressure. Jillie had already met my family in London. My sister, Marti, and her husband, Kevin, the only ones who had missed the London trip, quickly came into the fold. Everybody's kids were there. And Maggie, my mom's twin sister, was staying with my dad and "Sissy," as she called my mom. Aunt Maggie was my godmother and favorite aunt. So the gang was all there, something my family was blessed with every holiday in those days. And Jillie quickly won the crowd.

Jillie had come over in late November and was going to stay until January, when she would have to go back to London to look for work. Look, I had fallen in love with a professional actress, and her commitment to her work was every bit as strong as my own. To my way of thinking, that was all to the good. She told me the story of how, as a fifteen-year-old living in the small town of Devizes in the county of Wiltshire, she forged her parents' signatures on a letter applying to the Bush Davies School to study ballet. When a big brown envelope came to their council house, she had to fess up. She told me that all Betty, her mom, said was "Well, I hope the writing was mature." Her dad, Peter, had to buy a used car to drive her to East Grinstead, Sussex, to audition. At fifteen, she was already behind most of the students auditioning. She was not accepted but was told to come back in six months. She worked hard, came back, auditioned again, and was accepted. Noreen Bush, who ran the ballet school, said to Jillie's dad, "She'll never be a ballet dancer, but she has something."

Back in Devizes, Jillie had to apply for a grant to be able to afford the school. The council had very few grants, but she interviewed and was awarded one. Bush Davies was where she would be for the next three years. Miss Bush was tough, but Jillie respected and revered her. The time came when Miss Bush would address Jillie and the rest of the class: "I tried to break Mack, but I couldn't." I think that was Miss Bush's way of showing that "Mack" had earned her respect. Maybe that's what Jillie had wanted most from Miss Bush. All Jillie said to me was "I loved Miss Bush."

CHAPTER SIXTEEN

Unfinished Business

was going up Lankershim Boulevard toward the Hollywood Hills and turned left just before the Hollywood Freeway. I stopped at the main gate of Universal Studios. The guard recognized me and told me where to park. As I drove onto the lot, immediately to my left was a monolithic square building that rose about twenty stories high. The building was all black. I don't know what all the big-time executives inside called it, but everybody else on the lot called it the Black Tower. I parked my car, and waiting for me at the entrance was my agent, Bettye McCartt.

On January 22, 1984, Don Bellisario launched his new series, *Airwolf*, on our network, CBS. That's when I knew for sure that "Home from the Sea" would be the last script Don would write for the rest of our season.

Yes, the scripts were getting better, and the writers were doing a good job. And Chris and Charles's collaboration, once they got to Hawaii, was a big plus. But the shows were staying safely on the lighter side. We needed a few shows that put more *muscle* in the mix. Shows where the stakes were higher. Those always came from Don. He alone had the keys to our ship. A ship that needed his rudder. Not some of the time but all of the time. Our audience, having invested in Thomas Magnum's history, deserved that.

I had a seven-year contract. I had every reason to think that the show was going to have at least that long a life. And that wasn't just pie in the sky. At the end of our third season, *Magnum* shattered all syndication sales records by selling for three and a half million an episode, a record that would last for over a decade. And that sale was for *all shows produced.* So Universal obviously wanted to make as many shows as possible. And while I was committed to be there every day, it appeared to me that Don was drifting away, coming and going when he felt the need and using the show as a launching pad for spin-offs. And that he wouldn't be there at the end.

As I have mentioned, I had many conversations with Don about how to confront all this . . . in my head. It was time to have the conversation in person.

———

I talked to Charles and told him the time had come. I had to go to the mainland and meet with Don. I knew Charles understood. But before I made any calls, my wise friend suggested we make a plan. The episode we were doing would finish at the end of the week. I could fly on the weekend, meet Monday morning and the rest of the day if needed, and fly back Tuesday. Then Charles told me the hard part. There wasn't even a half day's work without me in the next episode. The company would have to shut down shooting for those two days.

"That's the price, Tom."

"I gotta go, Charles."

"You're not scheduled to work Saturday. So if you work the four days when you come back, it'll only cost us a day."

"Charles, it's time. I have to go on record."

All Charles said was "I understand."

At her suggestion, Bettye set up a meeting for me, her, Don, and a Universal executive named Al Rush. She wisely told me the bosses may not even be aware of any dysfunction on the show and needed to be in the meeting. First thing Saturday morning, I was on a plane to L.A. While I could have used a nap, I instead spent the flight having a hundred different versions of the coming meeting in my head. The thing that kept haunting me was I had no idea what was being said about me. The image of a temperamental actor, throwing scripts against the wall or being offended because his favorite hot dogs flown in from Coney Island were arriving late and cold, was an easy sell to TV executives. I didn't think Don would ever try to make that sell. But there were executives who could conjure up that image all by themselves. Many had experienced or heard stories of actors driven mad by success. I had to find a way to show them and Don that this was a business meeting and not a venting session. That would be the most important card I could play.

Bettye didn't say much when I met her at the entrance to the Black Tower. As we walked through the lobby, she told me we would be meeting in Al Rush's office and that he was head of the entire MCA-Universal television group.

"Sounds like he's a big deal."

"He is a big deal, Tommy."

We got in the elevator, and up we went. It seemed to me that the floors were arranged in ascending order of importance, based on the power of the people in the offices. And we went pretty high up. But not to the top. As the elevator came to a halt, I could almost feel the presence of the big bosses, Lew Wasserman and Sidney Sheinberg, hovering over us from above. Al Rush's office was right off the elevator, and Don was already in the reception area. He stood up, said hello, and we shook hands. Yes, it was a little awkward, but there was no rancor in the exchange, and the three of us sat down in the waiting area. I gotta say, there wasn't a lot of small talk. I was grateful that we were quickly invited to go in. As we stood up, Don came over to me and said in his quiet, sincere way, "Tom, I'm not a writer." Yes, that's what he said. I think I know what he meant, that he didn't want to be *just* a writer. *Okay, so just say that!* But "I'm not a writer" was just a little too coy for me. Have you ever had something that really bothers you, and when you give it voice, you find yourself getting more and more pissed off? I couldn't afford to do that. So I just left it alone and went in.

This was not my first rodeo, even though this one was kind of the major league of rodeos. At this level, everyone knows ahead of the meeting what the meeting is going to be about. I was sure Bettye had talked to both Al Rush and Don. I was sure Don and Al Rush had talked. And Al Rush's goal was to keep the peace. He was, after all, dealing with a couple of valuable assets. My job was twofold: First, I wasn't looking for miracles, but I was hoping to get a commitment for at least three scripts each year from Don. And second, it was essential that I present my point of view as a reasonable professional actor and a partner in a highly successful show. Al Rush was gracious, respectful, and never patronizing. It was clear that he understood *the talent,* both actors and writers (sorry, Don). Bettye, as always, had confidence in me, so she gave me the floor. I won't bore you with what I said. Actually, I don't remember what I said. But I did it well. All that was left for me to do was play my card.

I told Al Rush that I was well aware of the financial impact of my coming to L.A. to meet. And that, in the spirit of cooperation, I would be giving back my salary for the episode to help with costs.

After a significant pause, Al Rush said, "That isn't necessary, Tom."

All I said was "I know. But I insist."

As with all meetings like this one, nothing was really settled. There were no real commitments, decisions, or mandates given. But I had said my piece, and the problem had been presented in the best way I knew how. It was worth the price. Mr. Rush gave me his card with his personal contacts and told me he would always be happy to take my calls.

Skip Brittenham called me when I got back to Hawaii and told me he'd heard the meeting went well.

Then he said, "They want to give you your salary back."

"Why?"

"They're afraid it's a ploy, some kind of trick so you can get out of the show."

"You're kidding me. Sorry, Skip. But I insist."

———

In Magnum's voice-over narration, he often begins with the phrase "I know what you're thinking." Well, I think I know what you're thinking: *What more could you want, Tom?* I get it, we were currently the sixth most watched show on television. And we were being taken seriously by our peers. To my surprise, I had been nominated for an Emmy in 1982 and in '83. What was even more unexpected was our nomination for Outstanding Drama Series in those two years. Shows that spent as much time as we did on the light side of life often aren't taken seriously. We were.

So the question is, rather, *What are you hoping for, and where are you going?* The simple answer is *to sustain the quality and grow.* We had been given a gift. Our audience didn't know what to expect each week. And they had accepted and embraced that. But if you're not mindful, that kind of acceptance can be fleeting. I've always felt that if an audience begins to think they're being taken for granted, sooner or later you're gonna lose them, at least some of them.

I can't really say I was surprised when Bettye told me I was nominated for an Emmy again in 1984. "Home from the Sea" was a formidable, strong entry. I was certainly grateful that it was noticed. We were also nominated again for Outstanding Drama Series. And there was a new, well-earned addition to that list: The Great Hildini was nominated for Outstanding Supporting Actor. If there was an omission—and there certainly was—it was Don not being nominated for writing. That would have been helpful and undeniably well deserved. At any rate, the show was clearly in the sweet spot.

Carol was nice enough to call and congratulate me on the nomination. I knew she was going to host, so I thanked her for the call and told her I would see her there. That's when I found out I *wouldn't* see her there. Carol told me she had the flu—or at least she thought she did. Now the doctors had told her it was a persistent virus, and she had been ordered to four weeks' bed rest. She assured me she was going to be fine.

And that's when she said it: "So, I was hoping you could take over for me and host the show."

"Oh."

I can't say that's exactly what Carol said. But whatever she said, it scared the hell out of me. "But I'm not funny." I didn't actually say that, but it *was* one of the many thoughts racing through my mind. All that was quickly overshadowed by the fact that my friend was hurting and needed help. "Of course I will, Carol. Don't worry, just get better." That's what came out and what should have come out.

Hosting a major awards show had never been on my bucket list and never would be. But here I was, at the Pasadena Civic Auditorium, for two days of rehearsals before the event on September 23, 1984. *Magnum* was in production. But my home network, CBS, was broadcasting the Emmys, so they made it work.

Buz Kohan, the head writer, was my constant companion. Buz was also a writer-producer on *The Carol Burnett Show;* I figured my friend Carol had been looking out for me and told him to stay close. She knew I would be nervous and need help, which I surely did. Hosting major awards shows was not in the actor's handbook, if there even was one. Major-awards-show hosts, not actors, host major awards shows. That my friend Carol could do both was also not in the actor's handbook. And telling myself, *Tom, you're enough*, wasn't going to help me. But here I was, and I wasn't going to screw this up for Carol.

Buz obviously knew his stuff. If I had a problem with the words, he would calmly help me find a solution. When I felt an introduction was too cute or too funny, he would help me find an alternative that was less cute or less funny but not boring. At a certain point, my mission became clear. Most of all, I did not want to ruin what should be a special evening for my peers. I told Buz that all awards shows go too long, and the best contribution I could make was to be brief, hopefully not boring, but brief. It wasn't my night. It was theirs.

We did endless run-throughs. And at one point, Steve Binder, our director, interrupted things. Steve was also a calming influence and very helpful. He told me that this was the point where my award came up.

I said something like "My award? Steve, have you seen the nominees?"

"Well, in the unlikely event that you do win, just know you will receive the award stage left and then have to cross to stage right for your next introduction."

"Got it. Thank you, Steve."

And we went on with the run-through.

———

"Have you thought about what you want to say for your opening remarks?"

". . . No, I haven't, Buz."

While maybe that question wasn't cause for panic for Buz, for this rookie it was. On a break, I sat in my little dressing room alone, thinking. The first thing I thought of was going out and saying, "Hi, I'm Carol Burnett." Actually, kind of funny. But immediately, my second thought was *Yeah, and where are you gonna go after that, Tom? What's the next joke?*

I opted for the brief, honest approach: to admit I was nervous and get on with the show. I have no idea why I thought of a line in one of my favorite movies, *The Magnificent Seven,* but I did. Steve McQueen had talked about a guy who suddenly jumped into a bed of cactus. When asked why he did it, he said, "It seemed like a good idea at the time." I stole Steve's line, and I would follow it with "Anyway, my mom said I'd do just fine."

I think I said a couple of other things, but those two are all that have stuck in my mind. Obviously, I knew I wasn't going to burst onto the scene as the new Richard Pryor, but so be it.

On the night of the show, I was sitting in my dressing room in my tuxedo, about to go on, reading my script one last time. Buz came in and told me we had to start thirty minutes late because the football game was going over. Our show was supposed to end at eleven-thirty EDT, and now all the important awards would be crammed into overtime.

"So, anything you can do to move it along would be great."

"Buz, you're preaching to the choir."

I wasn't crazy about sitting around for half an hour with my head full of errant thoughts. But so what.

When I came out, boy, it was so different from rehearsals. When we did run-throughs, a lot of the empty seats had cardboard cutouts with the names of the people who would be sitting there. Now those people were *actually sitting there,* staring back at me. I think the first person I made eye contact with was my friend Steve Cannell. (After the show, Steve relentlessly kidded me about the cactus line.) The only other thing I remember was that they played sentimental background music over my brief speech. They had never done that in rehearsal, and it made my remarks even more corny. At least I was well rehearsed, and from then on, the teleprompter was my new best friend.

After each introduction, I would go backstage to a spot in the wings where the stage manager was planted. My script was there, and I would review my next introduction. When the time came, I introduced the cast of the sitcom *Alice:* Linda Lavin, Beth Howland, Celia Weston, and Vic Tayback. They would present the award for Outstanding Lead Actor in a Drama Series. I retreated to my spot backstage. I had company this time. Larry, Roger, and John were there. After the winner in my category was announced, I was to go back out and introduce my costars, and we would all present the next award. It was kind of an unusual, special thing, being with them backstage. But all of a sudden, the nominees were announced.

William Daniels for *St. Elsewhere.*

Ed Flanders for *St. Elsewhere.*

John Forsythe for *Dynasty.*

Daniel J. Travanti for *Hill Street Blues*.

Tom Selleck for *Magnum, P.I.*

And the winner is . . . *Tom Selleck.*

I was absolutely stunned. I want to be completely honest here. You tell stories on talk shows, in interviews, and, yes, in books, and it's easy to fall prey to exaggeration, hype, and false modesty. All bullshit aside, I really hadn't even entertained the possibility. And no, I hadn't planned a speech just in case. I'd heard that William Holden had just simply said "Thank you." I admired that, but still . . .

The boys were genuinely thrilled. They all spoke at once. There was a group hug as they pushed me out on the stage. I wish I'd taken in the audience as I crossed the stage, but I don't think I did. Linda Lavin handed me the Emmy. Again, I wish I had a clear vision of *that* moment. I was in the process of starting to move from stunned to thrilled. Then it was suddenly just me standing there with my Emmy in hand. I put the Emmy on the podium and stood there for a moment, then said, "Ah . . . I didn't have a speech for this. There's something I always wanted the nerve to say . . . and I haven't done it already. And that's just 'Thank you.' . . . That's all."

A part of me was still in host mode. I grabbed my Emmy and ran across the stage to my host podium. I put down my Emmy and looked out at the applauding audience for the first time. When I did, the applause grew louder and stayed that way for quite a bit longer than I expected. That was really nice. Then I actually ad-libbed something, "We really had a cute, clever thing planned when I lost," and I got a warm laugh. "I'd just like to share this with three of my close friends. Mr. John Hillerman. Mr. Roger E. Mosley. Mr. Larry Manetti."

The boys came out, all smiles. John shook my hand, and then came a group hug from Roger and Larry. Roger smiled and said, "I guess when we get back to the islands, it'll be separate canoes from here on in." That got a big laugh. Larry chimed in with "Way to go, Big Guy. Thomas, we're happy for you." "Congratulations, Tom, and certainly well deserved," John said, and then moved right into the introduction, which I'm sure made Buz happy. I stood behind my three friends, holding my Emmy, shaking my head in disbelief, trying to grasp what had just happened.

What had just happened was a big deal, something I'd never thought was in the cards for me. I'd felt my lot would always be the guy sitting near the stage in an aisle seat, a remote cameraman uncomfortably close, and me pretending he wasn't there. Then applauding and smiling, again pretending I was happy someone else had won. It didn't happen that way this time. And I wasn't sitting in an aisle seat. It happened in a much different way, an unusual way. But that in no way trivialized the accomplishment. I won an Emmy.

CHAPTER SEVENTEEN

Always Expect the Unexpected

C harles said to me, "Tom, you gotta read this." It was a very long article about the show. It was written by University of Texas professor Horace Newcomb, one of the nation's leading television scholars.

"Okay, I'll read it after work."

"No, read it now, Tom."

The article was titled "*Magnum,* the Champagne of TV?"

In a typical television series, the professor wrote, "Each episode stands by itself. Characters and situations develop only slightly, if at all." But *Magnum* was different. "Its creators have established and refined a new television form that stands between the traditional self-contained episodic forms and the open-ended serials. Call it the 'cumulative narrative.' One episode's events can greatly affect later events, but they're seldom directly tied together. Each week's program is distinct, yet each is grafted onto the body of the series, its characters' pasts."

Magnum was all about memory and storytelling, according to Newcomb. He singled out the show's voice-over narration, which he said provided "a central perspective and permit[ted] Magnum's ongoing moral dialogue with himself." And all of it, the professor said, was true to the post-Vietnam world that Americans found themselves living in.

"Magnum hates Navy bureaucrats, official policy, and public posturing. His motivation for being a detective, like that of many fictional detectives before him, seems to relate to the disillusionment, the anger, and the violence of war. Because his war is the war of our own most recent past, it is quite possible to say that in being about memory and history, *Magnum* is about Vietnam."

Thank you, Don.

"All this explains why *Magnum, P.I.* is, for me, the best show on television. It repeatedly explores some of commercial television's most powerful recurring themes—the gauzy relations between memory and history, private and public, personal and social. Its narratives capture the terrible and delicate sense of random causality that all of us have felt. The unexpected flows naturally. The most formulaic characters behave in unexpected ways. . . .

"Always, because a dense and textured world has been established, I find myself learning more about the characters than one script itself tells me. *Magnum* revels in familiarity, but surprises me with new perspectives. It never forgets that its premise is popular entertainment, but neither does it condescend by assuming its audience will not notice and be delighted by small shifts in perspective.

"This suggests moral complexity, and that is what I most appreciate. Even those things that offend me in *Magnum* may, in time, be questioned by the program. They may even change. Having seen this series, I see detective shows differently. I see television differently. And because the show examines, in a television way, the world I have personally experienced, I see the world differently. *Magnum* is a show that does not forget. And it refuses me the luxury of forgetting the past that brought me here."

What can I say? Actually, I didn't have to say anything. I read the article alone in my motor home. Then I read it a second time. Horace Newcomb was now my hero. He *got* it. He had articulated all that our show could be and, at its best, was.

———

The news was promising. We were opening season five with a two-part episode written by Don. What good news! Don hadn't told me what it was about, just that it was a story he'd always wanted to do. It had been a year since "Home from the Sea," and we hadn't really done any shows that supported my new favorite term, our *cumulative narrative*. So when I got the script and saw the title, "Echoes of the Mind," I was sure that's where Don was going. Actually, that wasn't where Don was going at all. "Echoes of the Mind" was a story about twins, a good twin and an evil twin. Maybe you can guess the rest. I sure could. Don may have always wanted to do a story like this, but a whole lot of TV shows and movies had done stories like this.

I had a real conversation with myself before I wrote about this. I don't want to beat up the episode or Don for trying something; writing is hard. But I mean, where did this idea come from?

I had a lot of problems with that script and still do. I felt the audience would be ahead of the characters. There was just too much in the stories that got in the way of their suspension of disbelief. Actually, Magnum had to suspend his own disbelief. The only way he could do that was to act stupid at times and be totally smitten with the rather unstable good twin. And that went completely against the cumulative narrative we had established. I just didn't think the guy who had found out the wife he dearly loved did not die in Vietnam—but was still alive and over there—could then suddenly fall in love. What did Horace Newcomb say? "*Magnum* is a show that does not forget." On top of all that, the script was as serious as a heart attack. It never found the humor in tragedy or the tragedy in humor, and Higgins's story was equally serious. I'll stop now.

I don't think I'd ever given Don notes on one of his scripts. It wasn't like that was a Don rule; for me, it was out of respect for his writing. Whatever problems I had, the actor's job, once the die is cast—and it certainly was—is to commit. So, commit I did. We had a good director, the actor Georg Stanford Brown. And in the lead, we had a talented young actress. Her name was Sharon Stone. Sharon committed to the part, or parts, completely. It was a complicated, difficult role, and she saw the opportunity and made the most of it. She was a joy to work with, not to mention easy on the eyes. That made my job a whole lot easier.

After "Echoes of the Mind" Parts 1 and 2 aired, I would always get the same question. Maybe not right away, but over time, as Sharon's star rose. The question was "What's it like to take a shower with Sharon Stone?"

When Diane, the good twin, is threatened by two vicious Rottweilers, Magnum steps in to protect her and is chewed up pretty good by the beasts. No, I have no idea where the Rottweilers came from or why they were there. *Sorry* . . . I said I wasn't going to pick apart the script. I will continue the story without comment. Diane is clearly in danger, so Magnum stays at her place that night. He is in the shower nursing his wounds when Deirdre, the bad twin, appears, lets down her hair, and joins Magnum in the shower. Thomas is surprised, but he is not the least bit dead. So when she grabs him he responds and plants a passionate kiss. After much kissing and embracing, that is the end of Part 1.

The simple answer to that question is "I don't know. I've never taken a shower with Sharon Stone. If I did, I'd remember. And if I had, I wouldn't be telling you about it." The question should really be "What's it like to film a shower scene with the actress Sharon Stone?" Sorry if I've ruined it for you. But if you believe the scene—and it *is* pretty good— then the answer is that it's more of a technical achievement than what the original question implies.

If the behavior was real, nothing else was. There was no bathroom, just a shower stall and two walls. No ceiling, lots of lights, and about forty people watching. The fact is, on television and in most movies, love scenes are really about what you can't show. The shower stall conveniently had kind of smoky glass from the floor to just above where Sharon's breasts would be.

We would be doing our best to *stay in the moment,* and Georg would say "Cut" and explain that they'd seen a glimpse of Sharon's flesh-colored top. We would start over, hopefully, as if we were doing it for the first time. On the close-ups, the most important parts were the kiss and passionate embrace. Georg would say "Cut," and, being an actor, would gently say things like "Sharon, can you slant your head a little more away from Tom, and Tom, you need to slant your head a little more toward us. We need to see both your faces." I guess the point is, if you are going to *kiss for the first time,* you are going to have to kiss for the first time many, many times. If you think the scene works in spite of all that—and I think it did—all I can say is "Thank you."

———

On September 20, 1984, *The Cosby Show* premiered on NBC. It placed first in the ratings and was the most popular premiere for NBC in almost a decade. Great news for a good show. But it wasn't great news for us. It was slotted against *Magnum* on Thursday night at eight o'clock. NBC's gifted president of programming, Brandon Tartikoff, had smartly scheduled the *Cosby Show* premiere the week before our premiere of "Echoes of the Mind, Part 1." Brandon made sure that Bill Cosby's show was promoted all over television. Bill Cosby was on all the talk shows and took quite a few shots at our show, characterizing it as Hawaiian shirts, a Ferrari, and a couple of dogs. I didn't appreciate that, but this was the big leagues, and we were all big boys. All these happenings brought to mind one of my cautionary thoughts: Always expect the unexpected.

While our first episode may not have been our strongest choice to open the season, there may have been nothing that could have slowed the *Cosby* juggernaut. I don't think there has been any season premiere even close to it since, well, the *Magnum* premiere. The *Cosby Show* premiere had 21.6 million viewers, placing it ahead of runner-up *60 Minutes* for the week. There was no way our premiere could come close to that, and things only got worse. *Cosby* in its rookie year ended up the third-most-watched show after *Dynasty* and *Dallas*. *Magnum* had dropped from sixth the year before to fifteenth. In our sixth season, *Cosby* had reached number one. It drew half the people watching TV in our Thursday-night time slot. *Magnum* had now fallen to forty-eighth.

All that news was pretty hard to swallow. We had gotten used to success, the great ratings, the recognition. I'm not saying we were taking it for granted, but maybe we weren't reminding ourselves often enough that success needs to be constantly nurtured. That it can be fleeting. I mean, you never know.

We all knew we were far from done. *Magnum* was too valuable to Universal and CBS to simply give it up. There was nothing wrong with our show. There was just a whole lot right with *The Cosby Show*, and every minute you look at the scoreboard is time away from looking down the field. Our job had to be to stay the course, keep laying bricks.

In an interview, Charles said, "Our ratings weren't anything to crow about, but we didn't end up being the outcast. Your ego got a little bruised, but it wasn't desperation time."

I was concerned that the media might latch on to the idea of making the competition into a feud between me and Bill Cosby. So I wrote a letter to Bill congratulating him on *The Cosby Show*'s well-earned success. And the next time I was in New York, I surprised Bill and the cast when they were rehearsing an episode. Bill loved that and took me to dinner that night. No, that didn't make me a magnificent human being, only a human being who was well aware of the concept of enlightened self-interest.

Obviously, we needed Don more than ever, both as a writer and as our showrunner. But I have to say, I don't think he was really the present force we needed to depend on. And the saddest part that came out of this challenging time was that Don Bellisario never wrote another script for *Magnum*.

—

Charles, Chris, and I and our writing staff kept laying bricks. And no, I don't mean deadweight bricks. I mean bricks that moved us toward rebuilding our house. We did a lot of good shows that first year against *Cosby.* Funny shows. Shows that serviced the cumulative narrative.

Shows that you couldn't put in a box. And unlike most of television, that was our sweet spot.

When it came to Jillie working on the show, I always felt my role was to be Switzerland. But writer Jay Huguely really liked her cameo in the Carol Burnett episode. So he wrote "Professor Jonathan Higgins." Jillie had earned the right to be offered the part, and that's what Charles, Chris, and Jay did. Obviously, it was a new version of the Audrey Hepburn and Rex Harrison classic *My Fair Lady*. In Jay's version, Jillie played a new character (Sally Ponting), a punk rocker who was Higgins's distant cousin and in need of a makeover. John and Jillie had shown a chemistry in Carol's show, and now the two of them made the most of it. And I no longer had to act as Switzerland. Jillie was terrific.

At the end of the year, an article came out titled "CBS Beefs Up Magnum's Beefcake Part." In it, Harvey Shepherd, the head of programming at CBS, was quoted as saying, "*Cosby* is too strong." Harvey went on to say, "To give *Magnum* a shot against *Cosby* and *Family Ties,* the detective drama will be revamped, and Tom Selleck's beefcake role . . . will be beefed up. Selleck, who has deferred to John Hillerman in some episodes, 'will be alive in every show.' Shepherd promises 'he will no longer be a bookcase for Higgins.'"

Harvey passed away in 2019, and he was under a lot of pressure when this article was published, so I don't want to beat him up. But if we were in the same room back then, I would have told him it was a stupid piece. Why say something that isn't going to happen? *And it was not going to happen.* It just meant that we were going to be asked the wrong questions when we were in the media trenches. Charles was quoted in response: "The producers have continued to make the show they wanted to make and remain proud of their work, even if fewer people are seeing it."

—

That time when Jillie did her cameo in the Carol Burnett episode was during her first trip to Hawaii. We had a great time at the Outrigger when I wasn't working. She would come by the set near the end of the day to hang out with everybody, then we'd go to dinner. That left her with a lot of time on her hands. So, after my driver Dave Muntz got me settled at the stage or on a location, he'd take a studio car, pick up Jillie at Black Point, and the two of them would go to the roller-skating rink. Dave was a good friend and knew how to roller-skate. Jillie didn't. But she wanted to get good at it so she could audition for Andrew Lloyd Webber's *Starlight Express,* his West End musical on roller skates. Jillie was never a jogger, but she took it up. If I was playing volleyball in the afternoon, she would jog up Diamond Head Road, all the way around the volcano, and back to the Outrigger.

My point is, Jillie was not going to just relax on the beach and get a tan. As I have mentioned, I had fallen in love with a professional actress whose commitment to the work was every bit as strong as my own. If Jillie wasn't working, she was working toward the next job. That meant ballet and jazz classes, not to mention singing lessons, to stay ready. Frankly, at her advanced level of skill, she wasn't going to find those in Hawaii. I think I've also mentioned that I thought our mutual reverence for the work was all to the good. The demands of an hour network series have come all too often with a price. The cost was in many cases the relationship. We weren't going to let that happen.

Around the time Jillie did "Professor Jonathan Higgins," she decided to move to L.A. (No, not Hawaii.) Bettye knew Jillie well by now and called me. "Tommy, this is gonna be harder on Jillie than I think she realizes. I'd like to call her and invite her to stay with me for a while, till she gets her feet on the ground." What a gracious gesture! Bettye was looking out for us. She knew Jillie wasn't going to be happy in a hotel. And L.A. wasn't London. How was she going to get around? She would have to learn to drive. Someone had to help her get to interviews and classes. Where did she want to live? So many things on her plate. It wasn't like Bettye had a mansion. She had a nice three-bedroom house. I could never ask a friend to do all that, but Bettye offered and followed through. Jillie ended up staying with Bettye for almost a year. Such a good friend.

All this gave Jillie the time to find the best ballet and jazz classes and a talented singing coach. Having acted in musical comedy, she wanted to expand her talent in drama. That Jillie ended up with Sal Dano meant she was in great hands. And most importantly, regular trips to Hawaii were now very much in the mix.

———

For season six in September 1985, we premiered with another two-parter, "Déjà Vu." It was shot in and around London. Chris wrote another good script. It had drama, suspense, and humor, and needless to say, it was very expensive. That signaled the support we still had from Universal and CBS. It's hard to say whether the idea of moving the show out of its "universe" was compelling to an audience. In a vacuum, it probably was, but *The Cosby Show* was filling that vacuum. So we'll never know.

I have no idea whether the studio meant the trip to England as validation for five years of good work. Whether they did or not, our creative team took it that way. The inner circle now consisted of Larry, John, Roger, Charles, Chris, and me. We had a three-day sequence at Leeds Castle in Kent, and the six of us stayed there. We were, to say the least, treated in grand fashion. What a time we had!

Of course, we didn't forget about the work. John got to play one of his now-anticipated dual roles. This time, he got to play Higgins's own father. But most of my memories center around a lot of other stuff. Jillie and I got to spend time with her mom and dad and her sister, Carol, in Devizes. I got to be reunited with my friend and driver Tommy Lee and visit my *Lassiter* hangouts Sambuca and Johnny Gold's legendary disco, Tramp. All in all, it was a great gig.

Cosby had surged to the number one show on television. It would be wrong to say we were depressed or even frustrated. Every day, we were committed to making the show that had so rewarded us, as well as we knew how.

It's funny the things you think about. I remembered being at the Golden Globes in 1983. I had just arrived at my table in the *big-time section* in front of the stage. A very polite young man came up to me and said, "You don't know who I am, and you probably never will. My show is up against *Magnum,* and you're killing us." I don't remember how I replied. Then he said, "So for the record, my show is *Family Ties,* and my name is Michael J. Fox." And he shook my hand. *How 'bout that?*

Gary David Goldberg's *Family Ties* was now the number two show on television. And not just because of its lead-in. *Cosby* was a half-hour show, and it provided a window in the second half hour for *Family Ties* to excel. But the show earned that spot. And it earned Michael J. Fox an Emmy for Outstanding Supporting Actor in a Comedy Series. And, for the next three years, Outstanding Lead Actor in a Comedy Series. Well done, Michael. You never know.

———

Ever since *Cosby* had premiered, Charles, Chris, all our writers, and I had come to realize that the future of *Magnum* was in *our* hands. I had learned that Don was going to do what Don wanted to do, and that was pretty much *Airwolf.* His latest show was not performing well in the ratings and was way over budget. His occasional presence on *Magnum* was, honestly, more disruptive to the process than helpful.

For our seventh show that season, Chris wrote "Going Home." Charles by now had a hand in every show we did, as did I. But I had no notes on this one. It was terrific.

After thirteen years away, Thomas Magnum returns to his home turf of Tidewater, Virginia, for the funeral of his grandfather. It was a complicated story, complicated the way families are. As in all good scripts, the complications made the story easy to understand. And that story reveals another part of Magnum's history. He had a younger brother, Joey, who suddenly left home so he could be just like his big brother. Thomas Magnum had never come to grips with Joey's death.

We had a great cast: Gwen Verdon (as my mom), Joe Regalbuto (from *Lassiter*), David Huddleston, Julie Cobb, and Brandon Call. We did a very good job creating Tidewater in Hawaii. But there was no substitute for the Wall. So Charles; Chris; our director, Harry Harris; and I made the ten-hour trip to Washington, D.C. When "Going Home" aired on October 31, 1985, the final scene has Magnum walking in the Vietnam Memorial. Joe Cocker is singing "I Shall Be Released" in the background when Magnum finds Joey's name on the wall. Thomas Magnum reaches out his hand and touches it. At that moment, well . . . I'd heard the phrase once before: *There wasn't a dry eye in the house.*

———

When we first got to the Vietnam Memorial, there was a lot of time while the crew set up. And I had another mission to fulfill. I had heard over the years that a close friend from USC had died in Vietnam. I had no idea whether it was true or one of those stories that get around. Like Thomas Magnum, I had never been to the Wall. I went into the memorial, down the walk, looking at the names beside me. A walk all Americans should try to make. I stopped short when I saw it. 2LT Ronald M. Montapert. I can't even try to describe the emotions, the memories, that flashed through my mind. Ron was my Sigma Chi fraternity brother. He was one of the seven of us who went through our fraternity's Hell Week initiation together. Ron was a self-described surfer dude whose favorite word was *radical.* He was gung ho about everything in life. He was a foot soldier like I was, and his Army Reserve unit was activated about the same time as my National Guard unit. On April 15, 1969, in Kiên Giang Province, he stepped on an anti-personnel mine, and we lost him. Ron was twenty-five years old. He was a good guy.

There is a poem I have always remembered:

If you are able,
save them a place
inside you
and save one backward glance
when you are leaving
for the places they can
no longer go.
Be not ashamed to say
you loved them,
though you may
or may not have always.
Take what they have left
and what they have taught you
with their dying
and keep it with your own.
And in that time
when men decide and feel safe
to call the war insane,
take one moment to embrace
those gentle heroes
you left behind.

MAJOR MICHAEL DAVIS O'DONNELL
DAK TO, VIETNAM
JANUARY 1, 1970

—

I had never regretted missing out on cotillion. My friends who went hated it. My big brother, Bob, had gone because some of his friends went, and he hated it. But when Esme called, I wondered all of a sudden if I should have gutted it out. I could always tell when she was bringing good news.

"You have been invited to a state dinner at the White House on Saturday, November 9, 1985, for Princess Diana and Prince Charles."

"Okay."

"You don't seem excited, dolly. I hope you know it's the hottest ticket in town."

"Okay."

"It's Princess Di's own guest list, and there are only three actors on it. You, Clint Eastwood, and John Travolta."

"Well, I guess I'm flattered, Esme. But I'm just trying to figure out how I could possibly get there."

"Don't worry. I'll see that it happens, dolly."

So there we were, in the receiving line at the White House, Jillie in her brand-new Oscar de la Renta black-and-white ball gown and me in tow. Jillie, being a Brit and with her experience in *Cats,* had been my tutor on proper behavior when meeting members of the royal family. It's not that I wasn't excited, but I was a little anxious. Jillie curtsied, the princess offered her hand, and I gently responded. We exchanged pleasantries, and I moved on. What was she like? I mean, it was only a moment, but she was charming and gracious and very beautiful. Prince Charles was very nice and well schooled in the art of making you feel like you were important to him in your moment together, a skill most of us could use a little more of. Jillie and I knew the Reagans, so while it was still "Mr. President," it was a little less formal than with the Brits. Dinner in the State Dining Room was an elegant affair in a beautifully decorated setting. It wasn't crowded. There were only nine tables. I was sitting at a table between Nancy's close friends Betsy Bloomingdale and Princess Yasmin Khan. There was a lot of hardware (silverware) in front of us, and yes, I knew to use the utensils from the outside in. *Thanks, Mom and Dad.*

At Jillie's table, she was sitting between Neil Diamond and William F. Buckley's wife, Pat. Pat was always a lot of fun, and they were all having a great time. After dinner, everybody moved to the East Room for music and dancing. President Reagan and Princess Diana danced, and Charles danced with Nancy. Then John Travolta and the princess started dancing. Clint Eastwood and I knew each other pretty well. We exchanged a look, knowing what might be coming. We kind of slipped away from all the dancers and moved to a spot slightly around the corner. By now John and Princess Di were dancing to an up-tempo number and rocking out. Everybody else stopped dancing and formed a circle around them, clapping their hands. Clint and I stood our ground.

I was having a very good conversation with Clint when I heard "Sorry to interrupt." A woman with a very clipped British accent was speaking very rapidly. "Mr. Travolta and the princess are dancing for a second time together. We can't have that. We don't want to start rumors, do we?"

Clint and I said nothing.

"Mr. Selleck, you must step in and replace him."

"I'M NOT CUTTING IN ON JOHN TRAVOLTA!" was my reply, probably in too loud a voice.

She was not happy.

"Very well. The next dance, come with me."

As she pulled me away, all I got from Clint was a wry smile. Thank goodness it was a slow number. However, not being schooled in ballroom dancing, all I knew was kind of a box step and a dip. Well, I was not going to dip the Princess of Wales. When we started, I apologized for my dancing. Princess Diana was lovely, and there was a very shy quality about her in spite of her being well schooled in the art of conversation. I gotta say she seemed to be having the time of her life. I was relieved she talked most of the time. Let's just say it was not my finest hour as a conversationalist.

While I danced with the princess, Jillie was dancing with Prince Charles and was smart enough just to have a good time. He said to Jillie, "Thank you. I was so happy you rescued me. All of Nancy's friends kept stepping on my toes." The prince asked Jillie for a second dance. Clint took over for me, and I got to dance with my friend Nancy. She was relaxed, and I was relaxed. They were playing a song from the 1940s. I wish I could remember what it was, because Nancy was quietly singing along. What a nice way to end the evening.

CHAPTER EIGHTEEN

Rebuilding Our House

G oing Home" broke new ground in a lot of ways. It was the first show that Larry, John, and Roger weren't in. That wasn't a good thing, just a necessary thing to tell that story. Joe Cocker's "I Shall Be Released" was what we call a *needle drop.* It means we paid to use the actual recording. And it inspired us to add that element to the show from time to time. But most important, this resurrection of the cumulative narrative came out of the minds of Chris, Charles, and me. We didn't have Don when we needed him most. But I think we knew we were capable and equipped to do our show on our own.

I'm going from memory here, so I'm not sure whether my idea brought about "Going Home" or "Going Home" brought about my idea. I'm pretty sure it was the latter. My idea was simply that we had already lost Don, so why not make it official? *Magnum* needed a changing of the guard, so to speak.

When you make a difficult decision, the easiest path is to choose to be offended, nurse that grievance into a rage, and lash out. I wasn't going to do that. There is an expression in baseball when you are not hitting: You have a *hole in your swing.* We had a hole in our swing, a hole that could be fatal. I was long past being offended or angry. I just knew it was time. I talked to Charles and Chris about what I was going to do; I wanted them to stay out of it for the sake of their careers. I talked to Bettye and Skip and told them what I had to do: The studio *must* move Don upstairs and out of *Magnum.* I got the impression that my two friends had expected something like this for quite a while.

Quite simply, I was the only person with the juice to do it. The guy I was looking at in the mirror every day was now going to be the executive producer. The only thing I asked was that the studio *not* put my new job title in the credits of the show. For me, that would have looked a little self-congratulatory. I never could have made the decision without the irreplaceable collaboration of Charles Johnson and Chris Abbott-Fish. But I could already feel the weight of responsibility that decision put on my shoulders. However, it was necessary. So no regrets.

When our last show of the season aired in early April 1986, we had already been renewed for season seven. That was the good news. The bad news was we had lost a third of our audience. But the *promising* news came from head of programming Harvey Shepherd, who announced that CBS was moving *Magnum* to Saturdays for the summer reruns. "We're elated," Charles said in the announcement. "We've been under the hammer of the *Cosby* phenomenon for two years. Under the circumstances, we've done pretty well, but what can you do against an immovable force?" Harvey's quote was a lot less enthusiastic and a lot more cynical: "We have to try something else. By moving it, we may get another season or two out of it." That *something else* was Saturday nights at ten o'clock for the summer. The not so good news was that our lead-in was, somewhat ironically, *Airwolf.* Don's show had finished sixty-fifth for the season. On April 15, Harvey Shepherd announced his resignation, citing the overwhelming pressure of the job; yes, I felt bad for Harvey. Then we got some great news when CBS announced their fall schedule. *Magnum* would be moved to Wednesdays at nine p.m. The not so good news was that we were up against *Dynasty,* which had tied *The Golden Girls* for seventh place. Welcome to the roller coaster of network television! And like I said, every minute you look at the scoreboard is time away from looking down the field.

—

Our seventh season was like an overripe jar of strawberry preserves that's been sitting on the shelf too long and suddenly bursts open. Forgive me—that's a line I've always remembered from our first season's show "Adelaide." But it kinda fits. Charles had set up a retreat in Sonoma in the California wine country with me, Chris, and all our writing staff well before we started shooting. This was pretty much unheard of in "the old days." But we still had some juice. It freed up a whole lot of suppressed creative energy and promoted a sense of risk-taking in our ideas of where we were going to take our show for the seventh season. And, of course, we needed to think about how we would end *Magnum* if this was the last season. I don't mean by being canceled. The studio and the new regime at CBS had no intention of doing that. But it was the end of my seven-year contract, and while I had no idea what I was going to decide, I had some thinking to do.

—

We started shooting in mid-July. Charles was by now co–executive producer, and Chris was supervising producer. They both would work with the writers developing the early drafts of the scripts while I was acting my little brain out. Then my professional life got a lot more complicated. When we were shooting at the studio, my workday would be: Rehearse a scene, go down to Charles's office and give notes on the next script to him and Chris, go back and shoot the scene, come back and give any notes on the rough cut of the previous show, go back and rehearse the next scene, and then . . . you get the idea, no downtime. A nap at lunch. Be careful what you wish for. All the added responsibility was a lot more work for the three of us, and while it was harder, it was better.

For my money, the 1986–87 season was by far our best. You may say that because I was now a big-time (albeit uncredited) executive producer, I could be biased. You could say that, but it just ain't so. And I would in no way want to diminish all the exceptional episodes we'd done in our first six years. It was simply that we had quite a few more of them in our seventh season. In many ways, we had fixed the hole in our swing. We now had a *process* that worked at a time that we needed it the most.

Starting on October 29, our sixth, seventh, and eighth shows aired three weeks in a row. They challenged our audience with three very different episodes told in three very different styles. For our creative team, they validated how much we felt we were in our groove.

"Death and Taxes" was a dark story about a serial killer murdering prostitutes. He dresses like Magnum and kills to please him. The episode has a terrific investigative montage with the help of the Genesis song "Mama."

"Little Girl Who" is a deep dive into our cumulative narrative. Magnum's former wife, Michelle (Marta DuBois), and her husband, Vietnamese General Hue (Soon-Tek Oh), have both been undercover operatives for U.S. Naval Intelligence. When they are discovered and are in danger of being assassinated, Michelle leaves her five-year-old daughter, Lily, with Magnum to keep her safe. Lily speaks only Vietnamese and French. Because of Lily's age and with sheer hope on Magnum's part, he believes Lily is actually his daughter.

In "Paper War," a feud breaks out between Higgins and Magnum. Magnum blows up Higgins's prized model of the Bridge on the River Kwai. Higgins decapitates Magnum's cherished rubber chicken. Somehow they end up trapped in an elevator, in a building that is going to be demolished by blowing it up. This is where Magnum confronts Higgins with his theory that Higgins is really Robin Masters.

While there are at least seven other exceptional episodes on my closely held secret list, I am not submitting a résumé here. Let's just say it was a very good year.

———

Sometime in November, something startling happened. Something that wouldn't even fit in the Always Expect the Unexpected category but was more in the Who Woulda Thought category. I was sitting with Charles in his office, and Larry called.

Larry didn't mess around. He just said, "T, Frank wants to do our show."

"What are you talking about, Lar?"

"Frank wants to do our show."

"Larry, if this Frank is a pal, you know we don't hire pals."

"Frank Sinatra wants to do our show."

". . . Oh."

"But he wants to be asked, T. So you have to call him."

"Oh."

Charles asked Chris to come in.

I said, "Look, I don't know if this is real, but Larry says Frank wants to do the show."

"Frank?"

"Frank Sinatra."

"Oh."

We were in the middle of production, and most scripts were already in development. The news was a serious complication. Chris said, "Well . . . we gotta at least try." I could tell she was excited. So I called Frank Sinatra while Charles and Chris watched. Speakerphones were less than adequate in those days. There was some small talk. Then I just blurted it out: "Larry says you want to do our show." I knew as soon as it came out that it didn't sound like a request at all.

"It's nice of you to ask. I'd love to do your show."

I nodded to Chris and Charles. "Well, we'd love to have you."

"Say no more."

Actually, I did have to say more. But before I could figure out what to say, he said, "Tell you what. I'm not gonna charge you anything. Just pay my expenses."

"Thanks, Frank . . . Look, we want to write a special script for this. Any idea what you want to do?"

"Oh, I don't care. Just make sure I get to beat somebody up."

And that was about it.

———

Actually, the phone call would have been a lot harder if I hadn't gotten to know him a little bit. Frank and his wife, Barbara, had invited Larry and me to be their guests at a concert he did in Hawaii at Blaisdell Arena. Afterward, he hosted a small dinner at Canlis, the then-famous restaurant in the middle of Waikiki. Tom Dreesen, a comedian who often opened for Frank, was there. Danny and Natalie Stein, his good friends, were there, along with Larry, Jillie, and me. Frank loved Jillie, and he loved her name. He said, "Jillie Mack, Jilly Rizzo is my good friend. And 'Mack the Knife' is a favorite song of mine." After a while, he took his coat off and put it on the back of his chair. His shirt was absolutely soaking wet from the concert.

Frank produced the '85 Reagan inaugural gala. He asked me to be one of the cohosts. That was a great night. My favorite moment was when he sang "One for My Baby," accompanied by Mikhail Baryshnikov dancing. Frank threw a small party afterward at the Madison Hotel for his cast. Jillie and I had a great time at a table with Elizabeth Taylor, Robert Wagner and Jill St. John, and Don Rickles and his wife, Barbara. Baryshnikov came over for a while with Twyla Tharp, the great choreographer. Off and on, as Frank was cruising around the room, he would come over and sit with us. I remember, late in the evening, I got up knowing I had the first flight out in the morning to go back to work across the continent and the Pacific. Frank, cocktail in hand, said, "Where you goin', Selleck? Sit down."

———

Chris wrote a really good script for Frank called "Laura." She wrote it on a serious deadline, as Frank had only a small window of availability. In "Laura," Frank would play retired NYPD Sergeant Michael Doheny, who comes to Hawaii in search of two killers who raped and murdered his young granddaughter, Laura. Frank was happy with Chris's script, so we were good to go.

Charles came out to the location where we were shooting with some unanticipated news. Frank was in the hospital with a serious case of colitis. News like this always brought two questions: Most importantly, "Is he going to be okay?" Charles told me that Frank was expected to make a full recovery. Great news, but in our business, that prompted the second question, one you always felt a little guilty about asking but had to: "What are we gonna do?" We were already in prep for "Laura," and no other script was ready to replace it. Episodic television shows don't often have that luxury. And we weren't about to recast Frank Sinatra with another "Frank Sinatra." Charles is a very thorough man, and he told me that Frank had insisted they speak. From his hospital bed, Frank said, "Don't worry. I said I'll be there. I'll be there."

Okay, it wasn't exactly full speed ahead but, rather, kinda *keep moving forward.*

———

Late afternoon on the day before we were to start shooting, Frank Sinatra arrived in Honolulu and checked into the Colony Surf Hotel. I was working on my last day of a very good show called "Forty," about Thomas Magnum turning forty, so I couldn't be there to greet Frank. Chris and Charles handled that ably. When we wrapped "Forty," it was already dark, but Charles and Chris were waiting for me. We had planned a celebratory dinner with our cast, including actor Joe Santos, who was also guesting. That wasn't going to happen. No meet-and-greet. No read-throughs. No meet the director. All that had evaporated in the name of necessity.

"So . . . how's Frank doing?"

Charles said, "He's pretty worn out."

We exchanged one of those this-is-the-life-we've-chosen looks. Charles added, "Frank said, 'See you in the morning.'"

"Well, see you in the morning."

———

Deluxe motor homes were not plentiful in the islands. I asked Charles to give mine to Frank and to have Dave Muntz (my driver), Pualani (my indispensable assistant), and Lon Bentley (my makeup man) take care of him.

Frank arrived early that first day of shooting. We had done our homework, so Charles, Chris, Dave, Pua, Lon, and I had arrived earlier.

Lon was waiting when Frank and Barbara got to the motor home. Lon wanted to work with Frank on the look Frank had in mind for the show. Frank had been wearing a small hairpiece during his concerts but said he didn't want to wear one for this character. Lon told him he could subtly fortify his hairline. Lon worked on it, and Frank was happy. Lon told me later that Barbara liked it so much, she wanted Frank to use that look for his concerts. Then Frank was off to our costume department to make his wardrobe decisions. Normally, all this would have been done during prep. Now it was squeezed in on his first day of work.

When Frank walked onto our soundstage, there were a lot more people waiting, kinda like when Carol Burnett had arrived. He got a big, prolonged round of applause and graciously accepted it. I guess if you're Frank Sinatra, you are used to it, but I'm not sure anybody would be used to it given the week he had endured.

Our first scene was in a jail holding cell. Doheny is sitting on the lower bunk, reading the paper. Magnum sits next to him, and Rick is sitting on the top bunk. Frank was having a lot of trouble with his lines. While it was costing us time, I understood and, in a way, took a certain comfort that even Frank Sinatra could have problems on his first day. Especially considering the first day he'd had. It kind of reassured me that we were all part of the same tribe of actors.

After quite a few attempts, Alan Levi, our director, found an excuse to take a break. Larry was sitting in his chair, and Alan came over and said, "Larry, this isn't working. He's just not Frank."

"Alan, it's his first day, and he's nervous and pretending he isn't."

Larry reached into the pocket of his chair, pulled out his script, and ripped out a page. "Here, paste this in the newspaper he's reading. Nobody's gonna see it but Frank." It was something we had all done at one time or another. It reassured Frank, and we were off to the races.

When we finished a long day's work, the crew applauded. Charles, Chris, and I took Frank aside and thanked him for a good day's work. Frank said, "I know I promised you seven days, but you only have six. I gotta get back to L.A."

We told Frank to get some rest and that we would give him as late a work call as we could. It was dark by now, and Charles, Chris, Alan, and I went down to Charles's office. The first thing Charles said was that David Mayreis, my costumer, had told him that, during the wardrobe session, they'd learned that in order to get out of the hospital, Frank had gotten a temporary colostomy and he didn't want anybody to know. He was in quite a bit of discomfort and wanted to get back to L.A. to get hooked back up. Look, if Frank was still alive, I wouldn't be telling you this. But at the time, we were looking at a real profile in courage.

———

Frank always wanted to appear the tough guy. Obviously, he *was* a tough guy. He was also fiercely loyal to his friends and had a heart of gold.

When we started work the next day, nothing was said by the handful of us who knew his actual situation. Frank didn't want it known, so we made sure that was the way it was going to be. Frank was in good spirits after a night's rest and ready to go. That was a good thing, because there were a whole lot of places we had to go, and we had one less day to get to them. I was pretty sure Charles was thinking what I was thinking, that Frank had two foot chases and two fight scenes . . . I stopped right there. I was wearing too many hats. The only hat that fit at this moment was my actor hat. If you're going to work with Frank Sinatra, you'd better clear your head of errant thoughts and stay in the moment, because that sure as hell is where he's going to be. Frank's work always had a spontaneous, volatile, improvisational quality because often he was in fact improvising, volatile, and spontaneous. *So, Tom, forget about the production, the schedule, and the clock. Commit to the work you were trained to do with the enormous talent that is looking back at you.*

All of this reminded me of what my friend Brian G. Hutton, the director of *High Road*, had told me about Frank and Faye Dunaway and their vastly different work rhythms. Now that Frank was pretty much up to speed, I would get to experience it in person. We did a scene in Doheny's hotel room. It was a complicated one. And when Frank finished, he had that look he got when he thought he'd nailed something. The sound mixer went over to Alan Levi, our director, and whispered something in his ear. Alan came over and said, "Frank, we're going to have to do a pickup in the middle of the scene. You said 'Mag-*nin*.'"

"No, I didn't. I'll bet you a thousand dollars I said 'Magnum.' Next!"

And Frank just walked away. On his way to his chair, he said, not in an angry way, not in a mean way, just in a Frank way, "Who you got on sound, Johnnie Ray?"

Johnnie Ray was a popular singer who was known to be hard of hearing. Look, I'm sure Frank knew and liked Johnnie Ray and vice versa. Come on: I mean, he referred to me as the Moose, and I loved it.

He wasn't having fun at Johnnie Ray's expense, but he might have been poking fun at the sound department. It was just one of those ways Frank made a point. And no, we didn't do the second take.

Frank was right about the spontaneity of a first take. It's hard to match. But film work is about matching. Most of the time you do a scene many times—for close-ups, different angles, stuff like that. Frank had the patience of a saloon singer. That was part of his talent as an actor. But there were times that could catch him up, catch *us* up, and I couldn't let that happen. I wasn't going to produce a show that didn't showcase him in the best possible way.

As I walked down to my temp dressing room (formerly known as my office), I put my producer hat back on. Dave was there hanging out with Pua. I asked her to see if Alan, Charles, and Chris could come down while the crew was lighting the next setup. The only thing I knew for certain now was that working with Frank Sinatra would always be an adventure. When they came down, we went into my office, which was now cluttered with clothing racks and a makeup table. I explained that when I was acting with Frank, I had to just be an actor, so we were probably going to need a lot of these clandestine, how-we-doin' meetings. Charles pointed out that we couldn't and shouldn't try to change the way Frank worked. "That's pretty much baked in by now," he said. "We're just going to have to be honest with him about what we need when something can be better."

"I agree, Charles. But I can't help with that when I'm working with him. I just can't."

No disagreement there either.

We put our heads together and asked Alan if he could design his setups so when we shot the master (the wide shot), our second camera shot Frank's close-up at the same time.

Alan answered, "I can some of the time but not all the time."

Pua stuck her head in. "They're ready for you."

It wasn't a solution but at least a way forward.

So, let Frank be Frank. And the adventure continued.

———

Larry wasn't on camera that day, but he was there to keep Frank company, as he had promised. Larry idolized Frank, so it was kind of a labor of love. Frank was waiting for Larry when the company broke for lunch. He was standing next to his limo. "So, let's go to lunch, Larry." When we would break for lunch, the crew had forty-five minutes from when the last person in line got their food. Larry accidentally forgot to tell Frank that. Frank Sinatra had never had a forty-five-minute lunch in his entire film career. They climbed into the limo, and off they went.

"Take me to that Italian place you and the Moose go to all the time."

Sergio's was in a small hotel on a side street in Waikiki. Larry and Frank walked through the quiet lobby (everybody was at the beach). The restaurant door was locked. Sergio's didn't serve lunch. Larry went to talk to the hotel desk. The guy told him, "He's in there, just bang on the door."

When the door opened, all a stunned Sergio could muster was *"Mamma mia!"* Frank was very gracious, introduced himself, and politely asked if Sergio could make them some calamari. Sergio was somewhere between overjoyed and ecstatic. And in they went.

Sergio brought over not only some calamari but also his specialty— fried baby artichokes with marinara sauce. The three of them had a great old time until they heard "Hey, they're looking for you." Gabe Aio was a *very* big local guy who was assigned as Frank's bodyguard. Gabe was not happy.

When they drove up, everybody was waiting for them but started pretending they weren't. Larry sneaked a look over to me out of the corner of his eye. I was not happy.

———

With his compressed schedule, Frank had a full load of work every day. This day, we also had *TV Guide* at the studio to shoot a cover and do interviews with Frank and me. Then we moved to a location where the company had already set up a bar for the big fight scene. We had a very good stuntman ready to double Frank, but Frank insisted on doing the whole fight himself. We were concerned but couldn't show it. And if Frank insists on something, it's going to happen.

Bob Minor, our stunt coordinator, had put together a group of stuntmen to be the antagonists in the fight. Bob kinda had pick of the litter. Everyone wanted to work with Frank Sinatra. Rehearsing a fight scene is a lot like rehearsing a dance. And Frank knew his stuff. Larry and I knew our stuff as well. The three of us did a big master shot, and the fight worked as planned. Then we shot Frank's coverage, and he did it perfectly. It was great to see this old pro in action. Every punch landed. And most importantly, Frank seemed no worse for wear.

There was a Polaroid camera back then that, when you took a picture, pushed out the photo but retained it so you could watch it develop. Someone from camera came over to Alan and said something that completely drained the smile from his face. Alan kinda sheepishly went over to Frank. "We're going to have to do your close-up again, Frank. Someone took a flash picture during the take." A flash picture is a definite no-no when shooting on film. Frank was not happy. We were not happy. We looked around the room until our eyes landed on . . . Larry. He was holding his Polaroid camera with a photo sticking out of it. "I didn't do it, I didn't do it" was Larry's defense as the picture developed of Frank throwing a perfect punch.

———

It must have been a Friday night. I'm pretty sure, because we were going to shoot all night. If you're night-shooting, the only way you can turn a crew around for the day's work on Monday is to shoot Friday. After five straight days, Frank was pretty worn down. He didn't say it, but we could see it. Frank was cranky. Actually, we were all pretty worn down, if you want to know the truth.

We were shooting on Hotel Street, a pretty rough part of Honolulu. Doheny is looking for the killer, Magnum is looking for Doheny, Rick is looking for Doheny, and so is Lieutenant Page (Joe Santos). Each of those stories had to be told in separate setups. Since it wasn't a controlled set, we all couldn't hang out in our chairs together, for security reasons. Frank had to stay in the motor home while the rest of us did our stuff. What Charles, Chris, and I didn't know was that Barbara and Danny and Natalie Stein had gone to dinner at Sergio's. This was not a promising confluence of events. I'm not saying Frank needed a babysitter, but he *did* like company. Put it this way: If Larry had known Frank was by himself, he would have joined him.

It was well past midnight when Frank asked Dave to come into the motor home. "Get me some of those round cheese-puff balls. You've gotta love 'em, because they're like eating air."

Dave said, "I'll see what I can do, Mr. Sinatra."

"And I need a bottle of Jack."

"Oh."

"Thanks, pal."

Dave knew I didn't have any hard liquor in my motor home, just a couple of longneck Coors Lights. Off Dave went. He eventually found some round cheese-puff balls at an ABC store (the islands' equivalent of a 7-Eleven). But all they had was beer. It was getting late. So Dave went to a bar on Hotel Street.

"Can you sell me a bottle of Jack Daniel's?"

"Can't do that, brah. It's illegal."

"See, I got a problem here. We're shooting an episode of *Magnum* down the street, and Frank Sinatra wants a bottle of Jack Daniel's."

"For real?"

"For real."

The bartender reached behind the bar and held up a bottle of Jack. "It's on da house, brah."

I gotta say something here. Frank always wanted to be the tough guy, the guy who could drink everybody else under the table. But I would watch him when I was with him socially, and while he always had a cocktail in his hand and his waiter was always quick to bring him a new one, he had nowhere near finished the one he had. I don't think I ever saw Frank drunk. Even if he did in fact have a couple that evening, his work was on the money all night long.

There was one pretty long sequence where Doheny is questioning, not to mention bullying, the Hotel Street locals about the killer. Frank did a great job of improvising the sequence. And right in the middle of it, Lon walked into the shot. Alan said, *"Cut!"* Doheny by that time has a gauze bandage wrapped around his right hand from punching his fist into a mirror. The bandage had slipped, so Lon needed to adjust it, and since the scene was improvised, he didn't realize it wasn't over. Alan said, "Frank, we're going to have to do it again." Frank didn't say anything. Over five days of working together, Frank had developed a loyalty to Lon and didn't want to embarrass him any more than he already had. Frank took a very deep breath. "Okay, Alan. Let's do it."

Then we moved to the roof for the scene where Doheny confronts the killer. Or, as Frank would call it, "the scene where I get to beat somebody up." The actor who played the killer deserves mention. Kevyn Major Howard had just come off a fine performance in Stanley Kubrick's *Full Metal Jacket.* For an actor, this part was pretty one-dimensional. He certainly didn't need to do it. But Kevyn was enthusiastic about it because, you guessed it, everyone wanted to work with Frank Sinatra.

In the scene, Doheny confronts and closes in on the bad guy. The scene involved what we call a tracking-dolly shot. After a long setup, it was about four in the morning, and we were finally ready. Frank was more than ready. In the middle of the shot, something went wrong, and Alan yelled, "We gotta cut. We have to start over, Frank." A frustrated Frank Sinatra went to one of his old standbys, saying to no one in particular, "Who you got on camera, Stevie Wonder?"

Our director put together what was a very complicated Hotel Street sequence. He did a terrific job. When the show aired, that sequence was maybe ten minutes long and supported by a needle drop of Phil Collins's Genesis song "Tonight, Tonight, Tonight." And, of course, included a fine performance from Mr. Sinatra.

———

After what was left of the weekend, Frank had one final scene to do—in terms of Doheny's story, maybe his most important scene. Doheny, having returned to New York, visits his granddaughter Laura's grave. He kneels at her gravesite, takes off his hat, crosses himself, and touches her name. He takes a lei out of the box he is carrying and drapes it over Laura's headstone. His face wears the gravity of his loss. "We got him, honey. We got him."

It was a simple performance. By that, I don't mean an easy performance. Just simple in the sense of a few words carrying so much meaning.

On the scoreboard, "Laura" was our highest-rated show in two years. I might add that Universal was shocked when they got the bill for Frank's expenses. I don't know the exact number, but it was in the six figures. Someone at the studio said to me, "I thought he said he would give us a deal." My only reply was "He *did* give you a deal."

We had no way of knowing at the time, but it was his last acting role. And Frank couldn't have come to a more welcoming place. All of us, the staff, cast, and crew, were in his corner. Not that we had to pull him through it. Frank Sinatra pulled his weight. He delivered the same complex mix of cockiness, emotional honesty, and vulnerability that he brought as a singer, and that's a hefty load. And what seemed like a very long week was just a moment in time, and suddenly, it was over.

———

Over the next years, I would try to keep in touch with Frank, something that our business can make hard to do. I wouldn't see him most of the time, but still many times. I've always remembered being with him a couple of years later. Not because something monumental happened but because something ordinary happened. Larry and I were sitting at a big table across from Frank and Barbara at a famous old restaurant in Chicago called the Italian Village. And Frank was bored. You could tell when Frank was bored because . . . you could just tell. Frank looked at me and Larry and gave us a surreptitious nod and a glance to the hallway. Well, we all ended up inside a small waiters' cloakroom. He took out a pack of cigarettes and offered us one. I wasn't really a smoker, but . . . *so what?* Larry had a book of matches, so we lit up. I have no idea what we talked about, but I know what I was thinking. I wasn't a fellow actor or an acquaintance anymore. We were just three friends sneaking a cigarette and bullshitting in a closet. At some point, the owner stuck his head in and said, "Barbara's getting suspicious." Frank killed the cigarette with his fingers, put the butt in the pocket of a freshly starched waiter's coat, said, "See ya at the table," and was gone.

Time passed, as it has a habit of doing. In 1994, Frank asked me to his last concert at Radio City Music Hall. He even requested that I escort Barbara. Frank hosted a party at the 21 Club after the concert. I was sitting next to him on his right. He was quiet. As always, he'd given his all that night. He was hunched forward in his chair, leaning on his elbows, looking down at the table, just thinking. This guy came up from behind and slapped him on the shoulder. Frank kept looking down, but it was clear to me he didn't appreciate the gesture. And the guy said, "Francis, you were in fine voice tonight." Frank did not look up. "Yeah? Compared to what?" I had a pretty good idea what my friend was thinking.

On May 14, 1998, we lost Frank Sinatra. Jillie and I went to the service at the Church of the Good Shepherd in Beverly Hills. It didn't really seem like a funeral, just all his friends getting together to say goodbye. There were a lot of laughs and a lot of love. Gregory Peck, Robert Wagner, Kirk Douglas, Sidney Poitier, and Tony Bennett all spoke. Nancy Reagan and ex-wives Mia Farrow and Nancy Sinatra were there, along with Sophia Loren, Debbie Reynolds, Jack Nicholson, Don Rickles, Joey Bishop, Dionne Warwick, Paul Anka, Vic Damone, Liza Minnelli, and so many others. There was a moment in the service when everything stopped. We all sat in the quiet for some time, alone with our thoughts. And then the church was filled with Frank singing. He was singing, "Put your dreams away for another day, and I will take their place in your heart."

We were all the better for having known him. We were lucky to have him. My friend was one of a kind.

CHAPTER NINETEEN

The Elephant in the Room

Back when we had our retreat in Sonoma, Bettye came up for dinner one night with me and Charles and Chris. When we got back to the hotel, Bettye and I started a conversation that lasted well into the night. That conversation would continue over the next couple of months. It revolved around one question.

"Tommy, is this season going to be your last?"

"I just don't know, Bettye. I'm not tired *of* it, but I am tired *from* it."

I had taken on a lot the last year, and that had taken its toll in what I would call brain damage. But I knew how to push my limits, and so I had. I knew myself well enough to know that I would do the same this season. Also, it was nice, and important, to go to the Emmys, the Golden Globes, presidential inaugurations, and state dinners for Princess Di. But those events always seemed to happen when we were in production, so each one amounted to a kind of commando operation. Finish work, get right on a plane for five or ten hours, go to the event, get right back on a plane, and get back to an added workload to make up for the work our company had lost.

"Bettye . . . I think this is it. I love this show. But I guess it's time, while I'm still in one piece."

"I understand, Tom."

I felt I owed it to Universal to let them know, and Bettye agreed that I should. I called Bob Harris, the president of Universal Television.

Bob was a good guy, and we had talked many times. He told me he was sorry to hear it.

"I want to ask one favor, Tom. Please don't announce it. I've been here before, and things may change for you. I mean, you never know."

"I guess I owe you that much, Bob."

Bob was really just doing his job. For the studio, it was a no-brainer. The longer I chose to do the show, the more money they could put in the bank. They owned *Magnum,* and their record-breaking syndication sale was for *all shows produced.*

For CBS, we were the strongest show they could put up against *Cosby,* and with our new time slot, our TV boss at CBS, Kim LeMasters, couldn't have been more supportive and committed.

So *Magnum* was there for me for pretty much however long I wanted to do it. But I had never started a season feeling like I was running on fumes. Even if it was self-serving on his part, what Bob had said was good advice. You never know. Because, to be honest, I wasn't sure if I was thinking right. I mean, there are fumes, and then there are *fumes.* And either way, I wasn't going to have much of a private life for this season.

It worked for a while. With each new episode, the quality of the work sustained me. But as time passed, the limbo for everybody connected with the show created an elephant in the room. Nobody knew where they stood. For the crew, this wasn't the mainland, where they could just move on to another job. *Magnum* was *it.* John, Larry, and Roger were also entitled to be able to plan their futures. And while Charles and Chris knew a little of what I was struggling with, they were very much in limbo. The plain fact was we were a family. I knew most everybody by their first names. And I knew I would be the one causing the divorce. I started getting the feeling that my family, when I was out of earshot, was saying, *How's Tom doing? You think he's happy?*—things like that. Clearly, the elephant had grown very large, and I was more freighted down by the decision than by the work.

I think it was around when we finished the Sinatra show that I asked Charles if we could postpone the start of shooting that day. I told him I wanted to make an announcement. He gathered everybody in the parking lot in front of the stage. Maybe that was a little dramatic. But what the hell? I'd earned a little drama.

I came out of my motor home and faced my family. They were pretty quiet. I'm not much on big speeches.

"Hey . . . relax. We're coming back."

It was a good day.

———

I think it was early December when Bettye called.

"Jeffrey Katzenberg, the chairman of Walt Disney Studios, wants to meet with you."

"Wow! That's great, Bettye. When?"

"Right away."

"Bettye, I can't do it until Christmas break."

"He wants to come to *you*."

"Oh . . . okay."

"He has a project he wants you to do."

"You mean audition for?"

"No. He only wants you."

"Oh."

Bettye explained the project was a remake of a French comedy called *Trois Hommes et un Couffin* (*Three Men and a Cradle*).

"There's a videotape of it coming to you on the next plane. Please watch it, Tommy."

I did watch it, and it was very good. Even with subtitles. I don't think we had dinner. All I remember was sitting at a conference table with Bettye and a very prepared, very convincing Jeffrey Katzenberg. It would be hard to imagine that he was faking his enthusiasm for his idea.

He had brought along the director of the French film, Coline Serreau. She was very polite and very serious. Jeffrey explained that Coline would also direct the remake. I complimented her on her film, and she said, "Merci." Obviously, Jeffrey was leading the charge.

Unaccustomed as I was to having the head of a studio pitch a movie to me, I went with the flow. I had kinda figured out which bachelor he wanted me to play, and I was right. I asked if he was thinking about anyone for the other two leads. He said he wanted Ted Danson and Steve Guttenberg. Jeffrey seemed to know exactly what he wanted. And he said it with a certainty that made me think he would make that happen.

"I'd like to think about it, Jeffrey."

Jeffrey said that he would be in touch. And that was about it. And they all got on the next plane back to the mainland.

———

Now that I was a "big-time executive producer" (albeit uncredited), I was going to have a chance to test a theory I had developed over the years. As a doer and a watcher, I had a sense that in series television, jeopardy to the main character doesn't really work. Oh, it can be useful in a given moment, but its dramatic effect dissipates quickly. Sooner rather than later, Joe Six-Pack is bound to say, "He's not gonna die, Mabel. It's a series." So when I read a script that depended too heavily on whether Magnum would live or die, my note to our writers was to make the jeopardy momentary. And to make the other characters compelling enough to carry the weight of the jeopardy.

At our preseason retreat in Sonoma, I found that I was contradicting myself. I felt strongly that life-threatening jeopardy to Thomas Magnum could work, but only in one instance. In a final episode. And the more impossible it appeared to be that he could survive, the stronger the episode would be.

We did not know then whether our last show that season would in fact be our last. But I felt, either way, it ought to look like it was. If it was our last, then I felt the most courageous choice was that Thomas Magnum dies. But if it wasn't, we sure as hell better have a way back to our eighth season.

In the almost-*Raiders* era, Steven Spielberg and I had a chance to share some thoughts. There were two not-necessarily-famous films that we both loved: One was Lewis Milestone's *A Walk in the Sun,* a World War II movie that I have to think influenced him in making his classic *Saving Private Ryan.* The other movie was *A Guy Named Joe,* the Spencer Tracy/Irene Dunne/Van Johnson film that Steven remade into *Always* with Richard Dreyfuss, Holly Hunter, and my friend Brad Johnson. I would be lying if I didn't admit that *A Guy Named Joe* provided a template to build what could be our final episode. I felt that a similar story could be built around our cumulative narrative.

We called it "Limbo," I wonder why. It might have had something to do with our state of mind during that seventh season. The story begins with a life-threatening firefight where Thomas Magnum ends up shot and motionless. In the next scene, he walks up the beach to the King Kamehameha Club beach bar. It is totally deserted except for a new incarnation of his friend Mac. Magnum is in a coma and having an out-of-body experience. Look, this is my nickel, and as I have mentioned before, when I describe a plot, I find I don't want to see it. So I'll just say that, while no one can see Magnum, he says his goodbyes with a very big assist from John Denver's "Looking for Space." At the end, Magnum walks off in the clouds. His daughter, Lily, is looking his way. Can she see him? Magnum keeps walking. We hear Higgins's voice: "Magnum, I demand you come back immediately." Magnum stops, turns, and looks back. Did he hear Higgins? We see the hint of a wry smile as Magnum turns away and walks off into the clouds. No, this is not a trick to get you to buy a DVD or stream it, although you could do a lot worse with your money. I was so proud of it that, for the first time, I took my producer credit.

—

We were on our stage that day, shooting scenes from "Limbo." Our director, Jackie Cooper (yes, the former actor), had the crew lighting our next setup. I was sitting in my chair, working on my lines, when Pua came in and hurried over to me.

"Tom, I have Jeffrey Katzenberg on the phone. What should I tell him?"

"I'll come right down."

Jeffrey had stayed in touch like he'd said he would. Now *Three Men and a Baby* was set to go. So a call from him wasn't unusual. But I knew Pua pretty well, and something in her tone told me this call *was* unusual.

Jeffrey told me right out they were replacing Coline Serreau as director. It was a little late for that; the movie was already in prep. Honestly, I wasn't surprised; I kinda knew that the idea of a director remaking their own film had to be full of traps and pitfalls. Obviously, Jeffrey had seen them coming.

He didn't say much except that Coline had envisioned a much more serious version of her original, and she'd wanted the three bachelors' apartment to be like a dark womb. I didn't have any say in the matter, but if asked, I would have freely said, "That's not a good idea." Or as my little brother, Dan, would say, "D.D.I.I." (Don't do it, idiot.)

I gotta say, there was something very sustaining about having the chairman of Walt Disney Studios so involved in what was now *our* movie. It was pretty clear that this project was something he wouldn't walk away from. It was *his* baby.

Jeffrey told me he had already hired a new director, and he said it in the same positive, enthused way that compelled you to listen. "I've hired Leonard Nimoy to direct."

I think I just said, "Okay."

I've been pitched many times, and more than a few times I've been sold a bill of goods. This wasn't that. Sure, Jeffrey had his own agenda.

We all do. But he had been honest with me, something that was hard to come by in my chosen business. And in doing so, he had shown me respect. I wanted to be in business with this man. I wanted to work for his studio. I'd bet my career on it. Which, of course, I was.

———

It didn't take long to figure out that Jeffrey had made a wonderful choice with Leonard Nimoy. When I arrived in Toronto, he was welcoming, great fun, and so prepared, so ready. For the curious, there wasn't any trace of Spock to be seen. That he had created such a memorable character was a tribute to his ability and talent as an actor. Good acting most often involves characters trying to cover up their emotions. Like real people do. Leonard's Spock wasn't supposed to show any. But his skill as an actor somehow left room for the audience to suspect that underneath Spock's mask, he was struggling to control them. Spock, after all, was half human. So I think I can speak for Ted and Steve when I say we were grateful to have this highly skilled actor who spoke our language directing us. We wouldn't be dealing with a "traffic cop" telling us what to do, where to go, and how to say our words.

I had come up to Toronto soon after we finished "Limbo," a little too soon for me, but so what? I was gettin' paid. A lot of preparation had already taken place. Most importantly, filling out the leads. No, not Ted and Steve. They had been on board for some time. I'm talking about the fourth occupier of the title. Yes, the baby. Casting out of Toronto, where we would shoot most of the movie, they auditioned a thousand babies. Or should I say a thousand sets of identical-twin babies? They called back five hundred. By *they*, I mean Leonard and producer Robert Cort. Eventually, they narrowed it down to ten. Leonard and Robert were very smart, looking not only at appearance but also at temperament and reactions. The ten sets were narrowed down to five sets of finalists. Four-month-old Lisa and Michelle Blair were finally chosen to play Baby Mary. In a later interview, their mother, Geriann, would say, "I was just looking for something to do. I thought it was something to fill the day, and it turned into something way different."

When you are working in a scene with a baby, the easiest, cheapest way is to use a doll, hiding the face, and show the baby in a few close-ups. Leonard was talking about a whole different ball game. His vision was to have the baby in every scene from start to finish. Leonard pretty much charted Lisa and Michelle's body clocks: when they slept, when they were alert, when they were hungry, when they might want to go potty, stuff like that. Fact was, they were the real stars of this film, and the schedule had to be planned around their wants and whims. First and foremost, all this had to be governed by their well-being.

I think we had about a week to prepare before we were to start shooting. That start date was cast in stone. Jeffrey wanted *Three Men* for Disney's Christmas release. They had built an elaborate set on a sound-stage just outside of Toronto for the three bachelors' apartment. Leonard and Robert were very proud when they showed it to Steve, Ted, and me. Inside, it was like a real apartment, except there was no ceiling. It was full of open air and light and in no way resembled a womb. The three of us spent a lot of time there, getting comfortable with the floor plan, checking out our bedrooms, actor stuff.

It had been clear to me when Ted did our show in 1981 that he knew his stuff. "Bad guys" are hard to play. The script can give things away. Or the actor can fall into the trap of proving he's the bad guy. Ted didn't let any of that happen. He brought a certain *simpatico* to his character. I knew he was headed in the right direction. And in September 1982, the whole country found out where—to Sam Malone in *Cheers*. I would see Ted at awards shows and events. We got to share a moment from time to time. Like in 1984, when I was hosting the Emmys and Ted was nominated in two categories. What a ride my friend was on.

I didn't know Steve, but I knew his work. Of course, in comedy, but also in drama, like *The Boys from Brazil* and *Diner*.

Ted and Steve had success in both drama and comedy. Actually, the only one who hadn't proved his chops in comedy was me. The three of us had a few dinners together. Steve was a great guy, easy to get to know. I did remind Ted that the last time we'd worked together, he'd been attacking me with a grappling hook on the deck of a cabin cruiser. We had a laugh, and Steve wanted details. All this stuff was so important for actors, and I think we were all grateful that we had a director who knew just that.

The first few days involved shooting a very clever, I thought, credit sequence and a birthday-party sequence for my character, Peter Mitchell. It helped us establish our characters before *the problem* arrived. Then we were down to the nitty-gritty.

We found that Leonard's plan was going to be exactly as advertised. Except for one thing: We rehearsed with a doll. We would block the scene for camera and get our dialogue down cold. Then they would light the scene. Only then would the star arrive. Either Michelle or Lisa, depending on who was in the right mood. Working on film is as much (or more) about reactions as it is about dialogue. You can invent reactions to your heart's content in a rehearsal with a doll, but now you're in a room with a real, live person. The most important person in the room, I might add. The entire focus of your attention shifts, and you are in a completely different scene. Accidents happen, good, welcome accidents, and you react to them without thinking or planning. All this speaks to Leonard's insight and, if you will allow me, the genius of his approach. One scene that comes to mind demonstrates that and something else, something hard to figure out. In the scene, I am sweetly reading aloud from a boxing magazine as a lullaby to put Mary to sleep. It is a graphic passage about a prizefight. I explain to Steve's character that it isn't what you say but how you say it. Steve's character leaves, Mary listens (Lisa or Michelle, I don't know) and gets sleepy, and I put her in her basket and lie back next to her, thinking. Anyway, that's what the script said. But I gotta say, you would have thought she'd read the script. I know, babies don't have words. At least I don't think they do. I'm not a scientist, I'm just an actor. But we did the whole scene in one take. And I think it was . . . magical.

———

Jeffrey called. He told me the picture was finished. I had been bugging him to let me see it. He told me it was terrific. I had long ago learned to expect a certain amount of hype. After all, I would have to go on the road to promote it. But Jeffrey continued, telling me that the movie had the longest sustained laugh he had ever experienced. "It just keeps building for about ten minutes. Look, I don't want you to see it in a screening room. We have an *audience* screening coming up. I'll sneak you in the back and watch it with you." The scene was when Steve and I tried to diaper our new arrival, and yes, it was funny. Really funny. And yes, *Three Men and a Baby* was indeed terrific.

Jeffrey called. It was the week of November 25, 1987. "We were through the roof, number one for the week."

Jeffrey called. And he called me every Saturday morning after that for . . . well, for a long time. *Three Men and a Baby* was number one Thanksgiving weekend, Christmas weekend, New Year's weekend, and every weekend in between and beyond.

I had gotten to know Jeffrey Katzenberg pretty well. And it was really neat to see how proud this big-time studio head was of realizing his vision. He had reason to be. *Three Men and a Baby* was the first Disney film ever to make over a hundred million dollars domestic. One hundred and sixty-eight million, to be exact. Number one for 1987. It made two hundred and forty million worldwide, and all that on an eleven-million budget. Well done, Jeffrey. But enough of the scorecard.

When I was home for Thanksgiving, my son, Kevin, came over to our apartment on Wilshire Boulevard in Westwood. We took a walk down Wilshire to Westwood Village, turned left on Westwood Boulevard, and walked down the block across the street from the Crest Theatre. Our side of the street was deserted, but across the way, there was a line of people as far as we could see. Kevin gave me a hug. Jillie gave me a hug. I gave them a group hug. How did I feel? I don't know. Feelings are hard to describe. But I guess it was a little like sitting in the back of the movie theater watching all the people having a good time.

I need to digress here because . . . well, because it's important. When we finished shooting in Toronto, I took stock of what we had done. I had worked with a terrific director who'd put together a great cast. I'd worked with the best producer I had ever worked with, Robert Cort. And the whole endeavor had been shepherded by the head of the studio. I liked where this was going. But I didn't hang around to celebrate. It was important to get back to L.A.

Jillie and I were getting married.

———

How do you come to terms with fame? You can't go to school for it. But you have to find a way to handle it or it will eat you alive. No, I'm not knocking celebrities who have found a way to feed off of fame. Good for them. But that's never been me. And it wasn't Jillie.

The expression *it goes with the territory* is something I've always had little patience with. Just whose territory is that? Someone who's never been there? Everyone needs a private place where they can go where no one can see them, see what's inside them. And with success, or perceived success, the sphere of entitlement for that which is private grows. Fame and celebrity may squeeze that private place into a smaller box, but what's left needs to be fought for, every inch, every day.

"If I tell you something, you have to keep it a secret, because I said I wouldn't tell anybody. So don't say a word. Jillie and Tom are getting married."

That conversation never happened, because Jillie and I didn't tell anybody.

After the season wrapped with "Limbo," we made our decision. We wanted our marriage to be *ours,* not the public's. We wanted to keep our memories in our own little box.

Jillie didn't come up to Toronto. The last time we'd been in Canada, she'd come back early and gotten seriously hassled by U.S. immigration, even though she had a visa. We didn't need that problem under our promising circumstances. We talked every day and formulated a plan for when I got back to L.A. We wouldn't have much time before I started the eighth season.

My big brother, Bob, was point man in our secret mission. He was up at Lake Tahoe with his wife, Laurie; daughter, Michelle; son, Robbie; and young twins, Jennifer and Jessica. The whole Selleck family had many summers up there in Tahoe City, so that was where we were headed. Bob went down to Reno, Nevada, to check on the rest.

My mom and dad; my brother Dan; my son, Kevin; and Jillie and I got on a plane for the hour-and-a-half trip to Reno. My sister, Marti, and her husband, Kevin, couldn't come. Marti was pregnant again, with their third son, Gavin. Poor Marti always seemed to miss the fun.

We had only three days, so we all just had carry-on luggage. But Jillie did have a very long garment bag with a you-know-what in it. We hoped it didn't arouse any suspicion and that no one would take a peek inside. Thank goodness that didn't happen.

Bob was waiting at the airport in Reno with two SUVs. We drove right to the Washoe County clerk's office. That's when Jillie realized she didn't have a ring for me. Since it was Reno, across the street was one of those last-stop-before-you-get-married stores. I stayed in the car, and Jillie and my dad went inside to pick out a ring. The store carried garters, artificial flower bouquets, small bags of rice and confetti, and, yes, a small selection of rings. My dad tried them on, figuring if one fit him, it would at least be close. This odd couple got a few judgmental looks from the saleswoman, but they persevered.

Back to the county clerk's office, and Bob and Dan went in with Jillie. It wasn't crowded, there was no line: good news. The three of them went up to the counter.

Bob said, "Does the man she is going to marry have to be here?"

The clerk said, "Well, yes, absolutely. Which one of you is him?"

Dan piped up, "Will you excuse us for a minute?" Bob and Dan left while Jillie kept filling out the forms. When they got to my car, I rolled down the window.

Bob said, "Tom, they say you have to be there."

My mom looked over at Laurie and Kevin. "Oh, dear."

I walked inside with Bob and Dan, wearing my brilliant disguise: a baseball hat and sunglasses. At the counter, I took off my sunglasses. "Hi, I'm Tom." I shook the woman's hand. Her mouth dropped just slightly. I signed the form and said, "Uh, maybe you could help us here . . ."

Jillie took over. "Please, we need to keep this quiet. We don't want to share this with the press. Is there anything you could do to help us?"

"Well, births, deaths, and marriages don't usually come out till the end of the month, but—"

Bob spoke up. "I don't know, maybe you might keep putting it at the bottom of the pile."

"I can't promise anything . . . but let me see what I can do."

She was very nice and at least *seemed* to understand. I think we all said "thank you" at the same time and got out of there as quickly as we could, lest we be noticed.

Then we were on the move with commando-like precision. Bob guided our little caravan for the hour drive up to Tahoe. When we arrived at Incline Village, we stopped at one of those small strip malls. The chapel was upstairs. There, we were greeted by the Reverend David and his wife. Jillie immediately went into a small side room with her long garment bag. My dad was going to walk her down the aisle, so he stood by the door in case she needed help.

I feel awful that I can't remember the name of Reverend David's wife, because they were both such kind, nice people. But my mind was, after all, racing a little bit. They were clearly excited but very respectful.

As you would expect, the chapel was small but very nice and very tidy. The aisle was covered in green Astroturf with seven or eight neatly arranged white plastic lawn chairs on either side. The wedding platform was raised a step, with a floor covered in the same green Astroturf. The platform was backed by white latticework, bordered by some very nice artificial green shrubbery. You could tell they had made a real effort to be sure the place was just perfect.

The reverend's wife was doing most of the talking, and clearly, she was a fan of the show.

"I have a little surprise for you, you being in the entertainment business. I've got some wedding music from the sixth year of *Dynasty*." She was so proud of that, I didn't have the heart to mention that *Dynasty* was our competition on Wednesday nights.

By now, my dad, my mom, and Laurie were in the room with Jillie. Reverend David showed us where our places would be on the platform. Bob was my best man. Next to him were Dan and then Kevin. On Jillie's side would be my mom and Laurie. Then Reverend David said, "I'll just sign the license and we'll be ready to go."

We all looked at each other.

Bob said, "All I've got is the ring."

Dan said, "I think Dad or Jillie has it."

Kevin said, "I'll go get it."

On his way back, we heard it. A tremendous amount of noise and chattering inside the room. I recognized Jillie's voice. It was the loudest. We couldn't understand what they were saying, but it didn't sound good. My dad came out and walked over to us. "We don't have it."

In our haste to get out of the county clerk's office, *we had forgotten the license.* None of us knew what to say. We were stuck. It was Reverend David who spoke first.

"I'm going to do the ceremony anyway. And I know you planned a wedding dinner. I'll drive down to Reno, pick up the license, sign it, and drop it by for you at the restaurant. Don't worry. Enjoy your special time."

Such a grand gesture. Taken, and with our gratitude.

So Jillie and I got married. Well . . . what did you expect? The memory was for us alone. Just because I'm writing a book doesn't make it any less important to us now. We did take some wedding pictures after the ceremony. Polaroids. Eighteen, to be exact. They are well kept, safe in our little box of memories.

The family, kids and all, spent the next day the way we had done so many times in the past: on the dock of Tahoe Tavern Properties in Tahoe City. We flew home the day after and kinda waited for the other shoe to drop. But it didn't. Not for at least a month. That nice woman at the county clerk's office had done us a solid. So, thank you, wherever you are. In Celebrityland, keeping our secret for a month might be a record. On August 7, 1987, Jillie and I officially started our journey, and no one knew it. To this day, no regrets.

When the news did get out in early September, of course, there were some hurt feelings. Certainly on the part of Bettye and Esme and, yes, a lot of friends. What seemed to help them at least try to understand was when Jillie shared with them, "I didn't even tell my parents or my sister."

On September 20, Jillie and I were going to the Emmys. With the word now out, we knew the red carpet would be a bit of a challenge. That Sunday, our friend José Eber opened his salon in the morning to do Jillie's hair. Lon Bentley joined them to do her makeup. As good friends, it was just something they wanted to do. The three of them had a great time. Jillie looked very beautiful when she stepped out of the limo at the Pasadena Civic Auditorium. And happy. On the red carpet, our answers were polite but succinct. At least until near the end, when a reporter stuck a microphone in Jillie's face and said, "So, show America your ring."

Jillie simply replied, "No."

CHAPTER TWENTY

Do the Right Thing

Over that summer before our eighth season, I had to negotiate a whole new deal for *Magnum*. I had lived up to my seven-year contract, and as Skip told me, I was really in the catbird seat. The studio and the network wanted as many episodes as they could get.

Our seventh season had beaten me up pretty good. And it wasn't the workload. I'm talking about the decision I'd put on my shoulders and let sit there for way too long. Once I told our family that we were coming back, the workload seemed like a piece of cake.

I couldn't count the times I had worked with unprofessional, ungrateful actors and promised myself, *If I ever get my own show, I'm going to do this right.* That my obligation would be to not just play the lead but provide leadership. James Garner had taught me well. So there was just one final question to ask in that conversation with myself: *Why'd you come back, Tom?* And only one answer: *For the cast and crew.* Asked and answered. I honestly felt that bill had come due.

The most important thing for me when I was negotiating my new deal was that it had to be announced that the eighth season was *it.*

Skip said, "I can get you more money."

"I don't want more money."

"You deserve more money, Tom. You can have what you want *and* more money."

"I don't want more money."

I know, that was stupid. But I guess stupid is as stupid does. And yeah, it probably *was* stupid. I don't mean to say that it wasn't thought through, just that it was an emotional decision. How do you show gratitude for a job that changed your life? I didn't want anyone to think that last season was just a ploy to get more money. Actually, it really didn't matter what the studio thought, but it mattered a whole lot to me what *I* thought.

Under Charles's steady hand, the show had decreased our budget overages each year. By overages, I don't mean to imply that our budget had ever been realistic or adequate for the quality of the show the studio expected. But they had always insisted on the precedent of a seven-day schedule. I felt that an added day would ultimately be cheaper. So I asked for an eight-day schedule. In addition, if our crew delivered our biggest budget savings yet, I wanted them all to have a bonus. The studio said yes to the eight days. But they responded that they could not under any circumstances talk about crew bonuses, that it would set a dangerous precedent. They always invoked precedent when you had an original thought beyond their contractual boilerplate. Honestly, that pissed me off.

"Then *I* want a bonus."

Wanting to keep me "happy," Skip said, their response was "Sure, if that's what Tom needs." That *really* pissed me off. And I won't tell you the amount, but it was substantial.

Skip also said, "They're still trying to give you back the episode money you gave them. It's worrying them." I'd like to think I responded with something clever, like "No, that would be a dangerous *precedent* for me."

There was one thing I wanted for myself or, rather, for the future. That Charles, Chris, and I would have a production company at the studio with pilot commitments.

That was an easy yes. I had Skip and Bettye to fight for the rest. As Skip once said, "Our job is to beat them up for Tom." I was in good hands.

———

So, how did I spend my summer vacation? Well, I planned our eighth season, shot a movie, got married, started shooting *Magnum,* commuted to the Emmys, traveled back to Hawaii, laid more bricks. Let's just say I was busy.

On October 7, 1987, "Infinity and Jelly Doughnuts" premiered our season. I was about to get busier.

There was a lot of pressure from the network to have as many episodes in the can as possible, so we'd be ready for November sweeps. Sweeps happened four times a year: November, February, May, and July. Those ratings were the most important, not only for the network but to their advertisers.

In addition to promoting *Magnum,* I had interviews and a publicity junket in L.A. for *Three Men and a Baby,* while also making time for Johnny Carson and the other talk shows and for the three of us to do a special for *Oprah.*

I was channeling my basketball coach Bob Boyd's mantra: "You have to play through fatigue." And one of mine: "It's never going to say in the credits that 'he would have been better if he wasn't so burned out.'" I had long ago embraced the idea as one of the few constants in a fickle business where perception is often more important than reality. No excuses.

I guess it was when we were shooting our sixth episode. "The Love that Lies" featured Kathy Lloyd, who played one of Magnum's best friends, Carol, and guests Celeste Holm and Eileen Brennan. All three were giving exceptional performances, and I loved being along for the ride. So that wasn't it. But what I couldn't escape was a sense of something I couldn't shake off.

When we made the deal, I said I would do my best to give the network twenty-two episodes. But I couldn't promise more than thirteen. We had very strong shows coming up. My friend Carol Burnett graced us with an encore. "Unfinished Business" was a deep dive into our cumulative narrative, where Magnum is told that both his wife, Michelle, and his daughter, Lily, have been assassinated. "Legend of the Lost Art" was an homage to and a spoof of *Raiders*. They all earned my full commitment. As they should have.

The thing I couldn't shake off was, no matter how much fatigue I played through, the tank was on reserve. It was hard to come to grips with that, but there was no escape from the reality. I wasn't throwing in the towel by any means. But better to keep my promise of thirteen than chalk up nine more and risk being out of gas for the end of the game. Our last show needed to be our best, a home run in the bottom of the ninth. We called it "Resolutions."

—

On January 13, 1988, Carol's encore, "A Girl Named Sue," aired to our highest ratings for the season. Well, what did you expect? By now, the number of episodes we had left was quantifiable. It was not that we had a blackboard and checked them off as we finished each one; honestly, I don't think anybody wanted to talk about the end or was even prepared to confront it. But I would bet that if you asked anyone in our crew on any given day at any given moment how many shows we had left, they could tell you in a heartbeat. I have said about the work that you have to allow for *errant thoughts*. Believe me, I had them, and they would creep in without warning.

On February 17, we aired "Transitions," episode number eleven. The plan had always been to do our series finale as a two-hour movie. CBS decided—wisely, I think—to hold "Resolutions" back until May sweeps. That would give them time to promote it as the event it had earned the right to be. So for a change, we had the breathing room to concentrate on Chris and Stephen A. Miller's fine script and our prep for our finale. Maybe for the first time since I started the series, I had the breathing room to recharge my batteries and concentrate on just one single thing. Actually, there *was* one other thing. Maybe you remember the bonus I asked for. By this time, there was no question we would make our budget target. After we closed the deal, I simply chose not to consider the bonus *my* money. Now it was time to execute my plan.

I called Skip and Bettye and told them to tell Universal—not ask them, *tell* them—to issue thousand-dollar checks to every regular member of our *Magnum* company in both Hawaii and L.A. And that since it was coming out of *my* bonus money, there was no *precedent* involved. Skip and Bettye both knew me so well that they could hear the resolve and the glee (yes, glee) in my voice.

I knew I was holding some pretty strong cards. And the studio wanted to keep me "happy." We did, after all, have a big movie to shoot. I don't know, maybe you can tell by now that I didn't have any patience with the idea that my happiness should be part of a business negotiation. Happiness comes from within. And negotiating a contract ought to be about both parties, at least hopefully, trying to do the right thing.

When the checks came out, I got a picture from our L.A. crew standing on a bleacher with big smiles on their faces. In front of them was a very big oversize check for a thousand dollars. The caption below read, "Thanks, Tom. What a 'grand' gesture." *That* made me happy.

———

Charles, Chris, and I were able to treat our script for "Resolutions" as a perpetual work in progress over the course of the season. We were anxious and excited to start shooting. We had a great story, not an excuse to be sentimental wrapped around a story. "Resolutions" was really the step-by-step journey of a man with a whole lot on his mind. And any resolution for him would come at the end of that journey. We had resolved from the very beginning that we wouldn't try to answer every question our cumulative narrative had created, nor should we try. It wouldn't be in the spirit of our show. We wanted our audience to answer some of those questions on their own, in their own way. There were what you could call resolutions for our three main characters, Rick, T.C., and

Higgins. But I prefer to think of them as big changes in their lives. The story did have to resolve the question of whether Magnum's slim hope that his daughter, Lily, could still be alive was true. And our story had to have life-threatening jeopardy to Magnum. Which it did, though "Resolutions" wasn't completely built around that question.

Holding the show till May sweeps also gave us more time to promote the finale. And go figure, we got an unexpected lift from one of the tabloids (no names). I'm not saying that was their intent, but still . . . There was a rumor that someone had sent them a copy of our last scene in "Resolutions." Attached to the scene was a note: "Tom Selleck is an asshole! Here's the last scene in their season finale. And Magnum dies. Selleck can kiss my ass!!!" The note was unsigned. I guess someone must have written a counterfeit scene because Magnum doesn't die at the end. And I couldn't possibly imagine someone doing such a thing.

True to their nature, the tabloid knew it was too good a story to pass up. They accidentally forgot to do any checking to verify it. And they published the story. You know what? It created an enormous appetite and curiosity to see our show. So I owe them my *qualified* thanks.

I think I know what you're thinking: How could I possibly know about the note? Well . . . I just do. So don't ask. Let's leave it at that. Oh . . . all right. Can't tell a lie. I not only *knew* about the note, I wrote it.

———

The story in "Resolutions" was broad in scope. Magnum's journey started at the Naval Academy, went to Tidewater, and then went home to Hawaii. The plot, while crystal clear to the viewer, would be hopelessly confusing if *I* tried to describe it. So I won't. And all I can say to you is "You're welcome."

When we were shooting at the Naval Academy in Annapolis, our extras were midshipmen. Being trained for something much more demanding, they handled it with ease. Nobody looked at the camera, and they weren't particularly interested in the civilians among them. That was their mission.

When we broke for lunch, things changed. A group of midshipmen came over to me with a large chair, hoisted me into it, and carried me into a big dining hall with a full house of midshipmen cheering at the top of their lungs. I was put down at a table of honor. As a veteran, as an actor, and merely as a person, I was deeply touched.

Things calmed down a little when they served lunch. About then, someone with a slightly older, more seasoned look about him came up to me. He was wearing the Budweiser, the badge of the Navy SEALs. He was simple and direct in what he said: "I became a SEAL because of Thomas Magnum. Thank you." He shook my hand and walked away.

That was a good day.

At the end of "Resolutions," there is a big wedding. Rick's wedding. He is marrying Cleo, a reformed hooker played by series regular Phyllis Davis. The wedding guests include just about every series regular since the show's beginning. T.C. is best man, next to him Higgins, and next to him is supposed to be Magnum, who is missing. With the introduction to the wedding march, Thomas Magnum bursts in. He has a haircut, a Navy haircut. And he is dressed in Navy whites. He hurries down the aisle and takes his place next to Higgins. Then the flower girl comes in, with that smile. It is Magnum's daughter, Lily. That's all I'm gonna tell you. Oh, I don't know, maybe you might want to watch it. For that matter, watch the whole eighth season. Or maybe all 163 episodes. We couldn't be more proud of them.

I was very confident our audience would enjoy "Resolutions." I worried about only one thing. That they might not watch the credits. After our usual credits would be when we said goodbye. So . . . we cut back from the credits and see them rolling on the TV set in Magnum's guesthouse. Magnum, wearing his Navy whites, is holding Lily's hand, and they are walking away down the beach. Magnum gets up off the couch, moves to the TV, reaches down, and shuts it off. He then turns around and looks into the camera. Thomas Magnum is now wearing his Navy day uniform. He picks up a remote control, says to us, "Good night," clicks the remote, and our screen goes to black.

———

The scorecard. I'm not crazy about scorecards, although I like this one. But I promise I will be brief and not dwell. We were the number one show for the week of our final episode. And to this day, *Magnum*'s is the fifth-highest-rated season finale in television history. We had 50.7 million viewers. And, oh yeah, *Cosby* is only sixth. We finally beat *The Cosby Show.*

All through the shooting of "Resolutions," I had been planning to give the cast and crew a wrap party. Hopefully one they wouldn't forget. Actually, I should say *we* planned one. I couldn't have done it without Dave Muntz and Pua. With their help, I chartered the *Ali'i Kai,* a great big catamaran that specialized in sunset dinner cruises off Waikiki. It had a huge dance floor, so we booked a terrific band. I wanted a couple of surprises, so Dave and Pua managed to quietly get everyone's sizes. There was going to be a custom crew jacket with each person's name embroidered on it. Also, I had joked with crew members many times about giving out gold Rolexes. So we made up a T-shirt with a picture of a gold Rolex Submariner on it. And we hired a fireworks company for our own private show.

The crew and actors, including our regulars, were invited to bring their families. My entire family came over. Jillie's, sad to say, was far away in England. Of course, Bettye came. So did Esme. It was a great night. I had my moments but, surprisingly, no tears, just a whole lot of conversations to be remembered and cherished. And the fireworks, coming at the end of the evening, provided us with what we seemed to need, a private moment to be alone with our thoughts. So, after eight years and nine months of every year going to work with a family, we all said goodbye, each in our own way. How did it feel? Well . . . there was no script for this one. I guess it depends on which moment of each day you ask me.

Not long after, Charles called to say that Universal's Kerry McCluggage had told him the Smithsonian Institution contacted him to request three items for their archives at the National Museum of American History: Magnum's Detroit Tigers hat, his red Hawaiian shirt, and his Cross of Lorraine team ring. I thought that was pretty neat. Who knows, maybe they'd put my stuff between Archie Bunker's chair and Mary Tyler Moore's beret.

When we got to the Smithsonian's National Museum of American History, of course there were pictures. Then Roger Kennedy, the museum's director, spoke. I wish I could have written down his speech. But what he said was that *Magnum* was the first to portray Vietnam veterans in a positive way at a time when the nation was still dealing with the wounds of the Vietnam War and its impact on American popular culture. Until that moment, I hadn't realized the real gravity of why the Smithsonian was honoring *Magnum*. They *got* it, just like Professor Horace Newcomb *got* it. It was vindication for me of a hard-fought victory over the objections of the studio and the network. Honestly . . . my next thought was: *I wish Don was here.* That battle had been fought by the two of us in the days when we spoke with one voice. I don't know, maybe he wasn't asked. Maybe he didn't want to come. I just don't know. But here's what I do know: The concept for *Magnum* was *his* idea, not Glen Larson's . . . and not mine. All I can say is "Well done, Don."

———

I had to like where things seemed to be going. There was talk of a sequel to *Three Men,* I had found a script for a western called *Quigley Down Under* by John Hill, Disney was talking about a four-picture deal, Warner Bros. was interested in a relationship, and Charles and Chris and I were forming a production company. All to the good.

But you never know. It could all be pie in the sky. I guess the other way of looking at it was that I might just be sugarcoating the fact that I was currently unemployed. And me being me, I had my cautionary thoughts—nothing is certain till it's certain, and always expect the unexpected. They had served me well in the life I had chosen. So I kept them in my hip pocket and delivered myself to the uncertainty of the future.

Don't know where I'm goin', but there's no use bein' late.

Of Milestone and Memory

I love my work. I love the craft of acting. How fortunate that the somewhat aimless path I was on was altered simply by serendipity. How fortunate that one single accidental opportunity would open my eyes to the possible.

The sun is up, and so am I. I have things on my mind. Coffee, my *Wall Street Journal* and *New York Post,* and I'm out of the house. Which is where I want to be, out on our ranch. The ranch that *Magnum* afforded us the opportunity to be a part of for the last thirty-five years.

Jillie will be up soon with our three Cavalier King Charles spaniels, and Monte, our four-year-old English setter. Coffee in hand, she will soon be checking on her personal free-range sanctuary for birds, squirrels, deer, and ducks. We are already missing our daughter, Hannah. She left yesterday for Lisbon, Portugal. Hannah is an accomplished equestrian show jumper now and will be riding for the United States team in the Nations Cup in Spain and Portugal. Before she packed it, she proudly modeled her new red U.S. team riding coat. On rare occasions, there is a moment in time that can be shared equally. For your child who fell in love with riding when she was four years old and, through hard work and overcoming adversity, reaches a justified moment of genuine gratitude and celebration. And for her proud parents . . . well, just pride.

I ride my ATV down the cobblestone driveway under the canopy of hundred-year-old oak trees and across the old bridge (1926) over the streambed that in winter delivers water to the valley downgrade. I don't go out the front gate but turn right toward the access road. The dirt road is an easement with my neighbor. Go figure, the easement was originally signed between William Holden and Dean Martin, who previously owned our ranch.

Just up the road on the right is our old three-horse barn. When Hannah was eight years old, my friend Wilford Brimley gave her a blue roan mare in foal. Hannah named her Misty Twilight. Jillie, Hannah, and I spent many a late night comforting Misty through five babies and comforted each other after the loss of a beautiful stillborn foal. The fact is, it's almost impossible to be anywhere on our sixty-three acres without memories slipping in. But today, the higher I get up the road, the more my mind focuses on what has most occupied my thoughts. Getting back to work on *Blue Bloods.*

The ATV keeps climbing, stopping at the highest point on the property. Hannah named this spot Fire Peak after the devastating fire of '93. I check on our best well to make sure it is functioning normally. We've had a blessedly wet year, and our water storage tanks are full, and the well's backup generator is in good working order. Satisfied, I walk up a small slope to a wooden platform at the very top of Fire Peak. I climb the stairs and sit on the bench with my coffee. I look out across the valley to the unspoiled mountain that is part of the Santa Monica Mountains Preserve, and I catch myself taking a deep breath. That always seems to happen when I'm up here. But today I look inward.

For over five months, our industry has been shut down by a Writers Guild and Screen Actors Guild strike. The writers have settled, but the actors haven't yet. This, of course, reminds me of the long SAG strike that prevented us from starting our first season of *Magnum.* My opinion has always been that the results couldn't justify the loss of income for so many in our industry. Today the industry is at a similar crossroads. There are estimates that the Hollywood-related workforce has already lost five billion dollars in income and forty-five thousand jobs. But both sides are still arguing. It's time for both of them to put on their grown-up pants, stop the arguing and the name-calling, and actually negotiate and settle this thing. I am optimistic that will happen; at least I hope so. I miss my family.

That's what we've become on *Blue Bloods,* a family. Not just a bunch of actors playing family members, but a bunch of actors who have become a family themselves. And time has graced us all with the opportunity to embrace that. With gratitude, *Blue Bloods* will be starting its fourteenth season. And the show is still *bringing it.* It continues to be one of the top three scripted shows in all of broadcast television. And it's remained the number one show on Friday nights since its premiere in 2010.

Way back when Kevin and I went off the top of the parking structure of the Outrigger in my Jeep, I remember thinking on the way down, *I can't be that lucky twice.* In a much different way, in the early days of *Blue Bloods,* that little voice in my head was saying the same thing: *I can't be that lucky twice.* Turns out we sure have been. The simple fact is that *Magnum* did 163 episodes. *Blue Bloods* has already moved well past 250.

These are just numbers. And, naturally, good fortune plays a role. Yet luck is unpredictable. But talent tends to take advantage of it, so the talented tend to have more luck, with again a nod to my friend George Will. Then again, it's not just talent. It takes consistent hard work and, most importantly, starting with a damn good idea.

I guess I first met Leonard Goldberg on the set of *Charlie's Angels.* I was playing Jaclyn Smith's boyfriend. I was excited about it because the part was supposed to recur. They were thinking about giving the Angels more of a personal life. Well, they changed their minds, and the one show was *it.* As actors do, I, of course, thought I just wasn't good enough. When I went for a meeting with Leonard for a series called *Reagan's Law,* I kidded him about it. "So, why'd you fire me, Leonard?"

He laughed and quickly moved on to the subject at hand. "What did you think of the script, Tom?"

"I liked it, Leonard. I think I'd go crazy doing a procedural. But your script is more character-driven."

I went on to tell him that I particularly liked the family-dinner scene with this Reagan family. "But it's about eight pages long, and I'm sure the network will want to cut it down, and that will ruin it."

"I'm not about to let them do that, Tom. It's meant to be the centerpiece, not only of the pilot but in every episode."

Leonard told me that he had always remembered a Norman Rockwell painting called *Freedom from Want*. It depicts a family all sitting at a table for Thanksgiving dinner. And he thought, *What if that family was all in law enforcement?* Basically, an Irish family of New York cops. Well, it starts with a good idea, and this was a damn good idea.

"Who else do you have for the show?"

"I want Donnie Wahlberg for your oldest son and Len Cariou for your father. I'm sure they'll be interested—if they know you are. And honestly, I don't want to do the pilot without you as Frank. CBS feels the same way."

"It's nice of you to say that . . . Okay, Leonard, you get those two guys, then we'll talk some more."

The pilot for *Reagan's Law* was going to be shot mostly in Toronto for budget reasons. We would then move to New York for exterior shots. Pilot schedules are almost always compressed. The networks want them in the can as quickly as possible so they can test them and do whatever else they do to decide which pilots they want to put on the schedule. So I remember having only a few days' prep in Toronto. No time to really work on my character. No time to sit down with the cast for a table read, and that would have been pointless anyway, because the Reagan family wasn't all cast yet. By then, I had met Donnie and Len. When I got up there, I met Amy Carlson, who was playing Donnie's wife, and also real-life brothers Andrew and Tony Terraciano, who would play Donnie's boys. But we didn't have an Erin, and we didn't have a Jamie. I think I met Bridget Moynahan the night before we were to start shooting and Will Estes the morning we were to start shooting.

Life isn't fair, and neither are film schedules. The first scene, the only scene we were shooting on our first day, was the family-dinner scene, the centerpiece of the whole pilot.

So this newly introduced group of actors (a group of strangers, if you will) is about to play an important, complicated scene about people who've known each other for their entire lives.

Looking back now, I think I know why Leonard didn't seem concerned about the difficult task at hand. He knew there are no excuses in our business. It's never going to say in the credits, "We had a very tough first day or the show would have been better." And if it did, the audience couldn't care less. This group of actors knew that too. Leonard already had a well-earned reputation for finding exceptional talent and putting them in the right vehicle. I think, or at least I *like* to think, that he knew he had the right people, the right pieces in place to do the job. Or maybe he was as nervous as we all were. Either way, this gifted ensemble of actors did their job. And the family dinner turned out to be, in fact, the centerpiece of the episode.

I finish my coffee and find myself with a little smile on my face, so I allow myself one more memory on Fire Peak before I move on.

When the show was ready for broadcast, we officially became *Blue Bloods* . . . thank goodness. I never thought *Reagan's Law* was a good idea, and I was reminded of what it was like having to live with the *P.I.* tacked onto *Magnum*. That's why I'd made it my personal mission never to refer to it that way.

When we started production and the scripts started coming in, I was reminded again of the early days of *Magnum*. There was a problem, and I was certain it was coming from the network. Just as the network wanted to move away from Vietnam on *Magnum*, there was now an effort to move to a more predictably procedural *Blue Bloods*. That little voice in my head was saying, *I don't really need to be that kind of lucky again*. Well, there's no education in the second kick of a mule. It was now or never. I called my agent, Bettye McCartt.

"Something's going on, Bettye."

"I've seen the scripts. I understand, Tommy."

Time may have cost my dear friend, at eighty, a couple of steps. But her advice, as always, was spot-on. It was all I needed to hear.

I told our production people that we needed to shut down early, that I had production meetings with the network. I asked Bridget, Will, and Donnie if they could meet me in my dressing room. The simple version is I asked if they were happy with the *spirit* of our pilot. They were. Had they noticed a change in the scripts we were getting? They had. And did they prefer the character-driven approach we started with? They did. Knowing we were united meant the world to me. I told them I didn't want them to risk their personal capital with CBS on a new series. And that I was the old guy here, and I had my own personal capital with this network, and I was prepared to risk it to have the series we wanted.

"Just, please, sit tight and let me see what I can do."

I, of course, knew Leonard would know about it by now, but I didn't call him first. I immediately called the head of CBS Entertainment, Nina Tassler. Nina seemed surprisingly sympathetic and, I gotta say, earned my trust during the conversation. She told me she wasn't interested in *Blue Bloods* being a procedural.

Leonard came to my dressing room. I wasn't really sure where Leonard stood on this. But we had a heart-to-heart, and I got the sense that he felt he was being pushed out, that CBS had added a new producer. At the end of our conversation, all Leonard said was "Let me weigh in on this and see what I can do." At the end of a long day, Leonard came to me and said that the new regime would be gone. A tacit admission that my suspicions were, in fact, the reality.

He added, "Of course, we already have some scripts in development. You'll have to be patient."

"No, Leonard, you mean *our whole cast* will have to be patient."

Whew! That's a lot to absorb, and that's the short version. Maybe the longest day of my professional life. And serendipity played no part in this. This came from experience and knowledge that developed out of hard knocks and disappointments and the willingness to take a risk or else be stuck in a show that would never be what it could and should be.

Leonard called me about a week later. "Tom, I had a meeting with a writer today, Kevin Wade, I think you may know him."

"Are you kidding? I not only *know* Kevin, I worked with him on a film I did."

I told Leonard that Kevin came in to rewrite a troubled script of *Mr. Baseball* back in '92 and that "he literally turned a lemon into lemonade."

Kevin Wade was an accomplished playwright and wrote screenplays for films like *Meet Joe Black* and *Working Girl,* which got him nominations for a Golden Globe and a Writers Guild award.

Leonard said that he'd told Kevin they were having trouble writing for the police commissioner in a cop show. He said Kevin's reply was that the police commissioner was not a cop. He was more like a CEO. But in this case, his employees were people who put their lives on the line every day.

Hallelujah! Somebody gets it!

"Leonard, if Kevin Wade is interested in writing for us, you gotta close the deal."

A couple of days later, Kevin came down to the set. I was in the middle of a scene, so Kevin introduced himself to Siobhan O'Connor, our best writer, who had written this episode. At the end of the setup I was doing, Kevin and I had a chance for a welcome reunion.

With our writers freed of network constraints and Kevin on board, *Blue Bloods* was off to the races.

We lost Leonard in 2019. I lost a friend, and the loss of our boss was felt not just by us but by the entire industry. And as he would want, he left us a show that was strong and vibrant and still growing. Our best writers had remained loyal, and with Kevin as our showrunner, the quality of our shows was not only consistent but expanding. And with the addition of Vanessa Ray and so many irreplaceable characters, our family of actors had grown into the finest ensemble I had ever had the privilege to work with. We were more than prepared to deliver ourselves to the uncertainty of the future.

As I move back down the road, I finish my mental inventory of what has been one of my greatest sources of pride: the five hundred plus (I lost count after that) native, carbon-eating oak trees. Over the time I'd been steward of this land, I had put them in the ground myself. My "family" now has mature adults, teenagers, and youngsters. With the luck of a wet year, most are thriving, and the sick ones are recovering. This is a good day.

I make one last stop, the old hunting lodge next to our barn. It was built around 1910, and I had spent time and affection restoring it. I settle into my favorite chair with my mug of fresh coffee. There are family pictures on a side table, and hanging on the wall above them is my treasured 1876 Winchester Centennial Model rifle. A portrait of director John Ford hangs on the old stone wall next to the fireplace. On the mantel is a bronze by the artist Harry Jackson called *Safe and Sound*. It presents a cowboy riding into the face of a blizzard with a rescued motherless calf draped in front of the rider's saddle. In many ways, sitting here, I am out of time, and that's fine with me. Sometimes you think there's something you want, and when you get it, you find out you were wrong. I wasn't wrong about that feeling I first got on *The Sacketts*. I had fallen in love with the life and the land.

I cast my mind back over a half century of work. Over thirty years since *Magnum,* over fifty years since my earliest acting jobs. A lot of miles from the USC basketball court to . . . to where, I'm not sure. It's been a long, bumpy road. A lot of singles, doubles, quite a few home runs, and a whole lot of strikeouts. A lot of miles, some pretty good ones too. And the best thing is, when I look down the road, I can't see the end.

I have talked about the stories that have made up my life. There are stories I know like the back of my own hand. There are stories I have told that, in the telling, changed shape or acquired meaning. Stories I have never told anyone. And all have helped me to understand myself, but also to remember all the people who were part of my life and what I learned from them. I am the steward of those stories, the same way I am a steward of my land. It is a trust. One last sip of coffee and it's back to work. There are chores to be done.

—Tom Selleck, September 2023

The end of the last day.

Acknowledgments

Couldn't have done it without 'em:

Annett Wolf

Dave Muntz

Pualani McGinness

Lon Bentley

Charles Floyd Johnson

Dan Selleck

Marti and Kevin Ketchum

John Daykin

Bernie Budnik

Steve Burkow

Nina Nisenholtz

Kevin Wade

Warner Loughlin

Tony Makris

Jane von Mehren

Carrie Thornton

And, of course, Ellis Henican

About the Author

TOM SELLECK is an award-winning actor, writer, and producer, best known for his iconic role as Thomas Magnum in the original *Magnum, P.I.* television series. Among the many unforgettable roles he has played are private eye Lance White in *The Rockford Files,* Peter Mitchell in *Three Men and a Baby,* Matthew Quigley in *Quigley Down Under,* and Peter Malloy in *In & Out.* He was beloved as Dr. Richard Burke, Monica's older boyfriend in *Friends,* and has won a whole new generation of fans with his portrayal of NYPD Commissioner Frank Reagan in the highly successful crime drama *Blue Bloods.*